B STEIN
Morris, Roy, Jr., author.
Gertrude Stein has arrived :
the homecoming of a literary
legend

W9-BWO-390

Gertrude Stein Has Arrived

▼ ▼ ▼

Gertrude Stein Has Arrived
The Homecoming of a Literary Legend

ROY MORRIS JR.

Johns Hopkins University Press
Baltimore

Fountaindale Public Library
Bolingbrook, IL
(630) 759-2102

© 2019 Roy Morris Jr.
All rights reserved. Published 2019
Printed in the United States of America on acid-free paper
2 4 6 8 9 7 5 3 1

Johns Hopkins University Press
2715 North Charles Street
Baltimore, Maryland 21218-4363
www.press.jhu.edu

Library of Congress Cataloging-in-Publication Data

Names: Morris, Roy, Jr., author.
Title: Gertrude Stein has arrived : the homecoming of a literary
  legend / Roy Morris Jr.
Description: Baltimore : Johns Hopkins University Press, [2019] |
  Includes bibliographical references and index.
Identifiers: LCCN 2018055372 | ISBN 9781421431536 (hardcover :
  alk. paper) | ISBN 142143153X (hardcover : alk. paper) | ISBN
  9781421431543 (electronic) | ISBN 1421431548 (electronic)
Subjects: LCSH: Stein, Gertrude, 1874–1946. | Authors, American—
  20th century—Biography.
Classification: LCC PS3537.T323 Z757 2019 | DDC 818/.5209—
  dc23
LC record available at https://lccn.loc.gov/2018055372

A catalog record for this book is available from the British Library.

*Special discounts are available for bulk purchases of this book. For
more information, please contact Special Sales at 410-516-6936 or
specialsales@press.jhu.edu.*

Johns Hopkins University Press uses environmentally friendly book
materials, including recycled text paper that is composed of at least
30 percent post-consumer waste, whenever possible.

In memory of Barry Parker
Good man, good friend, good heart

CONTENTS

Gertrude Stein posing in front of a United Air Lines plane. Courtesy of the Beinecke Rare Book & Manuscript Library, Digital Collections. *frontispiece*

Dust jacket for the original edition of *The Autobiography of Alice B. Toklas*. The photograph was taken by Man Ray a decade earlier, in 1923. Courtesy of the New York Public Library Digital Collections. 2

A youthful Alice B. Toklas and Gertrude Stein in Venice, with pigeons, circa 1908. Courtesy of the Beinecke Rare Book & Manuscript Library, Digital Collections. 10

Gertrude and Alice in their famous Paris salon at 27 rue de Fleurus, 1922. Courtesy of the Beinecke Rare Book & Manuscript Library, Digital Collections. 40

Gertrude Stein's *Four Saints in Three Acts* in electric lights over the 44th Street Theatre, photographed by Carl Van Vechten, March 1, 1934. Courtesy of the Beinecke Rare Book & Manuscript Library, Digital Collections. 70

Gertrude being interviewed on NBC Radio in New York City by William Lundell, photographed by Rayhee Jackson, 1934. Courtesy of the Beinecke Rare Book & Manuscript Library, Digital Collections. 96

Charles Barney Goodspeed, Mrs. Charles (Bobsy) Goodspeed, Gertrude Stein, Fanny Butcher, Richard Drummond Bokum, Alice Roullier, Alice B. Toklas, and Thornton Wilder, at a party at the Goodspeed

AUTHOR'S NOTE

Gertrude Stein, of course, wrote *The Autobiography of Alice B. Toklas*. But in the interest of smooth narrative flow, I have chosen to quote some of the words from the book as Alice's own whenever it seems logical, in context, that she said them, or something like them. Gertrude, I think, would have approved. It was, after all, her idea in the first place.

Gertrude Stein Has Arrived

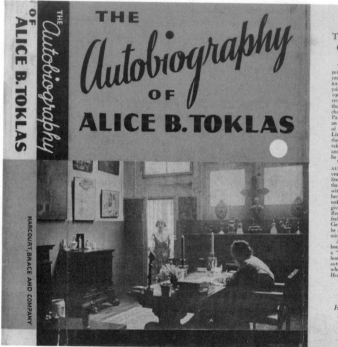

THE
Autobiography
OF
ALICE B. TOKLAS

HARCOURT, BRACE AND COMPANY

THE
Autobiography
OF
ALICE B. TOKLAS

THE AUTOBIOGRAPHY OF ALICE B. TOKLAS

Two significant publications recall the period that is covered by this book: two years ago, LINCOLN STEFFENS' AUTOBIOGRAPHY set forth a profound personal analysis of economic and political trends since 1900; a year ago Mary Austin's EARTH HORIZON pictured the American scene in the same period. During these years of change, Gertrude Stein's salon, her life in Paris, and her writings have been exerting an incomparable influence on the growth of the new art, music and literature. As Lincoln Steffens himself puts it, "she gave the young men and women all they would take. Ernest Hemingway sat at her feet and took 'not much,' she said, but it was all he could use and he wished it were more."

Written with monolithic simplicity, THE AUTOBIOGRAPHY OF ALICE B. TOKLAS reveals the essential honesty of Gertrude Stein's life—a life that has been devoted to the great revolution in the arts that came with the twentieth century. She is seen in her Paris *atelier*, advising the young and unknown Picasso, talking with Matisse, giving encouragement to Cocteau, John Reed, scores of others. Many readers will feel that here they become acquainted with Gertrude Stein for the first time, and will be able to understand the immensity of her mind and personality.

Alice B. Toklas, the "I" of the book, has been friend, secretary, editor, gardener, and a "good vet for dogs" in Gertrude Stein's home ever since they met in 1907. The autobiography covers Gertrude Stein's whole life from her Radcliffe and Johns Hopkins days to the present.

Illustrated from photographs

Harcourt, Brace and Company
383 MADISON AVENUE, NEW YORK

Introduction

I N THE SUMMER OF 1933, AFTER NEARLY THREE DECADES OF
writing and publishing everything from three-word poems
to one-thousand-page novels, American author Gertrude Stein
finally achieved overnight success. The surprising vehicle for her
literary stardom was an uncharacteristically lucid and readable
book, one that until the last sentence of the last paragraph of
the last page she had pretended was written by someone else.
That book was *The Autobiography of Alice B. Toklas*. Supposedly the reminiscences of her life partner, elfin, austere Alice
Babette Toklas of San Francisco, California, it was actually the
reminiscences of portly, genial Gertrude Stein of Allegheny,
Pennsylvania. Gertrude compared it, in her modest way, to the
Battle of Waterloo, quoting Victor Hugo's famous comment that
the fate of Europe would have changed completely had it not
rained on the night before Napoleon's epic defeat. "Of course
it is not so," she wrote, "if you win you do not lose and if you
lose you do not win." Still, Hugo had a point, and if the weather
had not been so lovely in France the previous autumn, *The Autobiography of Alice B. Toklas* might never have been written,
Gertrude conceded, at least "probably not then."[1]

As it was, the book Gertrude ghosted for Alice in October
and November 1932 at their country home in Bilignin, France,
near the Swiss border, would make both women famous, if not
necessarily rich. Published in America by Harcourt, Brace on August 31, 1933, the first printing of the *Autobiography* sold out its
initial fifty-four hundred copies nine days before it was officially

released. It was chosen as a main selection by the Literary Guild and was serialized in four consecutive issues of *Atlantic Monthly*, the only book to be so honored by that august publication. Readers waited at newsstands for the next issue of the magazine to arrive the way an earlier generation of Americans had waited at seaports for the next installment of Charles Dickens's *The Old Curiosity Shop*. (Little Alice, unlike Little Nell, remained stubbornly alive.) The unexpected success of the book, whose putative author disliked, among other things, the inclusion of her middle initial in the title, would place the real author's name before the American public in a way that three decades' worth of novels, stories, essays, poems, and plays had not. It would also bring Gertrude and Alice back to their native country for the first time in thirty years. "You'd better come over and take the tribute due you," their friend Carl Van Vechten advised them in September 1933, and fellow author Sherwood Anderson agreed. "Why don't you and Alice come to America as a great adventure next summer," he suggested, "Ford around [travel by automobile], come see us and others?" It would give them the opportunity, he said, to have "one big taste of America again."[2]

Despite the blatant appeal to their appetites, Gertrude and Alice ignored Anderson's advice for several months. "I am a person of no initiative," Gertrude observed later, "and I usually stay where I am. Why not as long as there are plenty of people about." Foreshadowing one of her most famous quotes, she added, "After all I am American all right. Being there does not make me more there." Following the French translation of the *Autobiography* in early 1934, the two women found themselves having too much fun to even consider leaving their well-known Paris apartment at 27 rue de Fleurus, near the Luxembourg Gardens. "Everybody invited me to meet somebody, and I went," Gertrude wrote. "I always will go anywhere once and I rather liked doing what I had never done before, going everywhere. It was pleasant being a lion, and meeting the people who make it pleasant to you to be a lion. So we went on accepting invitations and going to see the people, and we had engagements a week ahead for every day and sometimes twice a day." After three decades of hosting one of the most glittering artistic salons in Paris, they now found themselves on the receiving end of the social scale. They liked it.[3]

Eventually, the public clamor proved impossible to resist, and Gertrude agreed to undertake a lengthy speaking tour of America, commencing in October 1934. Alice, of course, would come along. "I used to say that I would not go to America until I was a real lion a real celebrity," Gertrude wrote in her characteristically unpunctuated style, "at that time of course I did not really think I was going to be one. But now we were coming and I was going to be one." In a way, she was being modest. The couple's much anticipated homecoming would last for nearly seven months and become a media sensation, garnering them a level of attention typically accorded, one biographer noted, "only to gangsters, baseball players and movie stars." Their travels would take them completely across the United States, from New York to California, from New Hampshire to Texas—thirty-seven cities in twenty-three states. The trip would be great fun, not merely for Gertrude and Alice but for thousands of literally depressed Americans who would find some much-needed diversion in the unpredictable antics of a pair of eccentric, accessible, uninhibited women who were apt at any given time to say or do anything. The headline crawl on the New York Times Building in Times Square—"Gertrude Stein Has Arrived...Gertrude Stein Has Arrived...Gertrude Stein Has Arrived"—was both literally and figuratively true.[4]

It had been, all things considered, a long time coming. Prior to *The Autobiography of Alice B. Toklas*, Gertrude Stein was known primarily to American readers for her dense, often indecipherable prose and for being an amusing, frequently quoted avatar of the modernist movement in painting and literature. Her face was well known, her writing not so much. "It always did bother me," she complained, "that the American public were more interested in me than in my work." The *Autobiography* changed that equation, or rather, it combined the public's interest in her and her work by making both the writing and the author a good deal more accessible. In any case, Gertrude was largely to blame for her own neglect. After publishing the comparatively traditional *Three Stories* in 1909, she had turned away from conventional forms of narrative fiction and begun experimenting with complex mixtures of rhythm, repetition, syntax, and sound to challenge readers on a subconscious level. Like most extreme stylists, she was easy to imitate, if not emulate, and reporters on her American tour had a great deal of fun aping her prose. Gertrude gave back as good as she got. When someone asked her, "Why don't you write the way you talk?" she retorted, "Why don't you read the way I write?" It was an open question then and remains, to a certain extent, an open question today.[5]

Her subsequent travels with Alice across the United States in the fall and winter of 1934–35 form the crux of this book. In those six-plus months the pair seemingly went everywhere and saw everyone, from a private tea with First Lady Eleanor Roosevelt at the White House to a celebrity-packed dinner party with Charlie Chaplin in Beverly Hills, from a midnight ride-along in the back of a homicide detective's squad car in Chicago to a meeting of the Raven Society in Edgar Allan Poe's old room at the University of Virginia. They toured Civil War battlefields in Richmond, ate Oysters Rockefeller at Antoine's Restaurant in New Orleans, enjoyed fifty-yard-line seats at the Yale-Dartmouth football game in New Haven, and paid a brief valedictory visit to sadly faded Scott and Zelda Fitzgerald in Baltimore. Toward the end of the trip they revisited Gertrude's childhood home in Oakland, California, about which she would famously say, "There is no there there."[6]

Throughout the tour Gertrude demonstrated strong appeal with American college students, who proved particularly receptive to her unconventional ideas about literature, painting, and life in general. She had a simple explanation for why students liked her. "You see why they talk to me is that I am like them," she told the president of the University of Chicago. "I do not know the answer, I do not even know whether there is a question let alone having an answer for the question." Eternally youthful herself, Gertrude did not talk down to students; she talked straight to them. They, in turn, listened attentively to what she had to say. "I just went to see what she looked like," said one rapt undergraduate, "and then she took the door of my mind right off its hinges and now it's wide open." She even took the time to expound on her most famous, if frequently misquoted, line: "Rose is a rose is a rose is a rose." "Now listen," she told a writing seminar at the University of Chicago. "You all have seen hundreds of poems about roses and you know in your bones that the rose is not there. I'm no fool; but I think that in that line the rose is red for the first time in English poetry for a hundred years." No one disagreed. Not until Timothy Leary's psychedelic caravan in the 1960s would another speaker rival Gertrude Stein's reception on American campuses.[7]

The runaway success of the *Autobiography* took both Gertrude and Alice by surprise. Before the book came out, Gertrude asked her partner if she thought it would be a best seller. Not sentimental enough, said the distinctly unsentimental Alice, who soon would have cause to revise her prediction. Proof of the book's popularity came regularly in cities and towns across the country, where the visiting couple was greeted like everyone's favorite maiden aunts. They fully returned the compliment, rediscovering along the way their own American identities after thirty years abroad. "I never knew it was so beautiful," Gertrude said of their homeland. "I was like a bachelor who goes along fine for twenty-five years and then decides to get married." There was no marriage on the tour, but Gertrude and Alice did enjoy something of a delayed second honeymoon on their epic jaunt across America. Every honeymoon must start somewhere, and theirs started four thousand miles away, in the French foothills of the Swiss Alps, where the two women could be found innocently at work—or in Gertrude's case, what passed for work—in the autumn of 1932, when a rose was still a rose and there was still there.[8]

ONE

A Bell within Me Rang

THE WEATHER IN SOUTHEASTERN FRANCE WAS UNUSU-
ally warm and dry in the autumn of 1932, and devoted gardener Alice Toklas was loath to let a day go by without working
in the terraced gardens of the home she shared with her longtime
companion, Gertrude Stein, at Bilignin, near the Swiss border.
The Louis XVI–era manor house she and Gertrude had rented
three years earlier featured two large vegetable gardens, one
located on the same level as the flower garden at the front of the
house, the other farther away on a slope behind the buildings.
If she wasn't in one, Alice could usually be found in the other.

With her swirling gypsy dresses and dangly earrings, tiny,
black-haired, dark-complexioned Alice was entirely too slight
and exotic looking to be mistaken for a local, but she gardened
with as much enthusiasm—indeed ferocity—as any native-born
Frenchwoman. Upon her arrival in 1929, she had been horrified
by the neglected state of the gardens. Pale, lumpy remnants from
a miserly crop of potatoes lay scattered in clumps amid the weeds.
Poking through them, Alice disturbed a nest of snakes—probably
harmless grass snakes, although venomous European adders and
aspic vipers are also found in the region. It took a delegation
of neighbors six full days to safely dislodge all the snakes and
clear the grounds.

Beneath the weeds Alice also uncovered a small flash of color,
a handful of ripe strawberries. Her course was set. For the next
fourteen years she would oversee the gardens at Bilignin, from
the first April plantings to the last October reapings. She would

grow, in their seasons, a formidable array of herbs and vegetables—radishes, lettuce, beans, peas, beets, pumpkins, squash, corn, and potatoes—and she would uncomplainingly spend an hour each morning gathering fresh strawberries for Gertrude's breakfast. It was, in all respects, a labor of love. "There is nothing that is comparable to it, as satisfactory or as thrilling, as gathering the vegetables one has grown," Alice would write many years later in a best-selling cookbook that now is remembered mainly for its recipe for marijuana brownies (p. 259). "The first gathering of the gardens in May of salads, radishes and herbs made me feel like a mother about her baby—how could anything so beautiful be mine."[1]

Neither Alice nor Gertrude was anyone's mother, nor were they likely to become ones in the future, but the point was well taken. The division of labor at Bilignin was set from the start. The gardens and household were Alice's domain. Gertrude, from her second-floor balcony, oversaw things from above, sedately monitoring the comings and goings of the partner she called by a welter of affectionate pet names: Gay, Kitten, Pussy, Baby, Queenie, Lobster, Cake, Daisy, Ada, Baby Precious, Mama Woojums, Wife, and She. (Gertrude in turn was called, somewhat less endearingly perhaps, King, Husband, Hubby, Fatty, Mount Fatty, Fatuski, Mr. Cuddle-Wuddle, Baby Woojums, and He.) Gertrude's only job was being a genius. It was hard work. "It takes a lot of time to be a genius," she said. "You have to sit around so much, doing nothing, really doing nothing."[2]

Gertrude had no doubts about her genius, but at age fifty-eight she was beginning to have considerable doubts about her ability to reach a wider, or at any rate more than infinitesimal, reading audience. Her often impenetrable experimental writings, all concerned in one way or another with the passage of time and the quest for identity and self-expression, were more admired in the abstract than read in the flesh. And though Gertrude numbered among her friends and acquaintances such creative luminaries as Ernest Hemingway, Ezra Pound, T. S. Eliot, F. Scott Fitzgerald, Sherwood Anderson, Pablo Picasso, Henri Matisse, Georges Braque, and Juan Gris, by late middle age she had barely scratched the surface of popular success. Whether or not she admitted it to herself, she was a good deal more famous for whom she knew than for what she wrote.

That was about to change. After years of entreaties by well-meaning friends that she write an account of her life in Paris during the first three decades of the century, Gertrude was ready to begin—or rather, she was ready for Alice to begin. Brushing aside Alice's myriad other duties as gardener, housekeeper, cook, typist, editor, publisher, manager, accountant, nursemaid, lover, debater, and friend, Gertrude thought it would be amusing for Alice to write the Paris book. She helpfully supplied a selection of titles: *My Life with the Great, Wives of Geniuses I Have Sat With, My Twenty-Five Years with Gertrude Stein.* For years she had been teasing Alice about writing an autobiography. "Just think what a lot of money you would make," Gertrude joked. Alice was not tempted. "I am a pretty good housekeeper and a pretty good gardener and a pretty good needlewoman and a pretty good secretary and a pretty good editor and a pretty good vet for dogs," she observed, "and I have to do them all at once." She couldn't imagine adding "pretty good author" to that list. Why didn't Gertrude write the book herself? She was, after all, the writer in the family.[3]

Ultimately, Gertrude agreed. In a burst of productivity that mirrored Alice's tireless gardening, she wrote the *Autobiography of Alice B. Toklas* in six short weeks in October and November 1932. It was unlike anything she had written before: clearer, more concise, and on the surface at least more impersonal. After declaring, "I am going to write it as simply as Defoe did the autobiography of Robinson Crusoe," Gertrude proceeded to do just that. Of course, *Robinson Crusoe* was a work of fiction—some would say the same about *The Autobiography of Alice B. Toklas*—but Gertrude seldom bothered with technicalities. Commencing with a brief overview of Alice's early life in San Francisco, the book brought an initially reluctant Alice to Paris, where she met Gertrude in September 1907 and attended her first dinner party at 27 rue de Fleurus (Pablo Picasso and Henri Matisse were there). It flashed back to sketch Gertrude's life before Alice arrived, particularly her ground-floor involvement with the rise of cubism. There were chapters on their life in Paris before World War I, the war itself, and the golden decade of the 1920s, when the brilliant young writers of the Lost Generation descended on Paris and, according to the book at least, learned much at the feet of Gertrude Stein. "We were constantly seeing people," Alice recalled, and many of the people they were seeing were, or were about to become, famous in their own right.[4]

Like many of the beloved paperback mysteries that Gertrude consumed at the rate of one per day, the *Autobiography* ended with a twist. In a bit of literary legerdemain so swift that it could almost be overlooked by the reader, she gave Alice the last lines of the book: "About six weeks ago Gertrude Stein said, it does not look to me as if you were ever going to write that autobiography. You know what I am going to do. I am going to write it for you....And she has and this is it." But despite the book's deflecting title and eleventh-hour role reversal, there was no real mystery about the author. *The Autobiography of Alice B. Toklas*, in fact, was *The Autobiography of Gertrude Stein*, as channeled through the dry distinctive voice of Alice Toklas, an inspired bit of literary ventriloquism that enabled Gertrude to present herself and her opinions modestly and indirectly in the third person. Alice, of course, was no one's dummy, and though the book was actually written by Gertrude, friends could clearly hear Alice coming through the pages. A large part of being a writer, Gertrude had said, was the ability to listen, and it was clear that she had been listening closely to Alice all those years—at least in those rare instances when she was not talking herself.[5]

Whoever was doing the talking, the book packed a considerable punch. Lively, fast-paced, and often quite funny, the *Autobiography* was a warmly personal, if highly selective, record of the expatriate life that Gertrude and Alice had been sharing in Paris for the past three decades. It would provide the template for celebrity tell-alls (or tell-somes) well into the twenty-first century, and subsequent generations of literary tricksters, from Jorge Luis Borges and Vladimir Nabokov to Thomas Pynchon, John Fowles, Don DeLillo, and Donald Barthelme, would learn to play with narrative voice, reader perspective, and unreliable authority in part, at least, from Gertrude Stein. Along the way, the book would settle old scores, start new feuds, and roil the waters of literary remembrance for generations to come. Artists as well remembered as Pablo Picasso and Ernest Hemingway or as long forgotten as Harry Phelan Gibb and Marie Laurencin would play their parts—parts written for them by Gertrude Stein—and a whole cast of colorful supporting characters would make their entrances and exits from the stage. The role of Gertrude Stein would be played by Alice Toklas.

▼ ▼ ▼

To a great extent their roles were the same role anyway, and had been for many years. At the time the *Autobiography* was written, they had been living together for exactly a quarter of a century. They met in Paris, which was where everyone who was anyone met in the first two decades of the twentieth century.

Gertrude, who was three years older, got there first, joining her brother Leo in London in 1902 and relocating to Paris one year later. The youngest of five children—three boys and two girls—of a wealthy Jewish stockbroker and his wife, she was born in Allegheny, Pennsylvania, a suburb of Pittsburgh, on February 3, 1874. Fittingly perhaps, given her celebrated expatriate life, Gertrude lived abroad until she was five. The rest of her childhood was spent in Oakland, California, a place for which she nourished little affection. The *Autobiography* dispensed with Gertrude's childhood in a few crisp pages: she came from "a very respectable middle class family." Her mother, Amelia Keyser Stein, was "a gentle pleasant little woman with a quick temper," and her father, Daniel Stein, was a humorless businessman whose professional dealings took them to Europe and ultimately to Oakland. There Gertrude passed her formative years, like many teenagers, "in an agony of adolescence."[6]

Orphaned by the age of seventeen, Gertrude moved to Baltimore to live with her mother's sister, Fanny Bachrach, and "a whole group of lively little aunts who had to know everything." The next year she matriculated to Radcliffe College, then called Harvard Annex, where she studied under famed philosophers George Santayana and William James. Graduating from Radcliffe in 1898, Gertrude returned to Baltimore and enrolled in Johns Hopkins University School of Medicine. Johns Hopkins recently had become one of the nation's first medical schools to accept women students, thanks to the vision of local railroad heiress Mary Elizabeth Garrett, whose $300,000 donation to the school stipulated that women be admitted and judged on the same basis as men. James had recommended that Gertrude apply, advising her that "a medical education opens all doors."[7]

She and Leo set up housekeeping at 215 East Biddle Street, within easy walking distance of the campus, and Gertrude commenced her medical studies. She did well the first two years, passing classes in anatomy, histology, pathology, bacteriology, physiology, chemistry, pharmacology, and toxicology. As a woman she faced the additional hurdle of endemic sexism from male professors and classmates. The female students, dismissively called "hen medics" or "damned coeds" by their male peers, were expected to do all the cleaning up after lab experiments and were charged with making and colorizing anatomical models of the brain, a job considered beneath the dignity of the men. It was, however, "an excellent occupation for women and Chinamen," their German-born anatomy instructor airily allowed.[8]

Gertrude initially intended to specialize in nervous disorders in women but soon found that she could abide neither childbirths (the school required a set number of bedside attendances) nor visits to the local hospital for insane women. "I did not like anything abnormal or frightening," she confessed. Nor was she particularly fond of her fellow students—or vice versa. Classmate Dorothy Reed Mendenhall would recall, "As a thinker, she was tops but she could do nothing with her hands, was very untidy and careless in her technique and very irritating in her attitude of intellectual superiority, which was marked even in her youth." Another classmate, H. D. Bloombergh, also had a dim view of Gertrude's performance. "I can truthfully say that she never impressed me as a brilliant woman," he said. "The rumor went the rounds early that she had been a favorite pupil of James at Harvard...we had our doubts." Florence Sabin, who would graduate near the top of their class and become one of the first women to serve an internship at Johns Hopkins Hospital, found Gertrude's work ethic sorely lacking. "Gertrude did not seem to care a rap," she judged. Gertrude, for her part, dismissed the studious Sabin as a typical sort of college girl, "pedestrian, dogged, faithful, and without much imagination."[9]

Gertrude looked outside the classroom for friends. Sisters Claribel and Etta Cone, whom she had known since first coming to Baltimore in 1892, were two of her closest. Like Gertrude, they had lost their father at an early age, but the family's controlling interest in a number of southern textile mills had left them comfortably fixed for life. Claribel, the elder, was ten years older than Gertrude and had a medical degree of her own from the Women's Medical College of Baltimore. Realizing, like Gertrude, that she did not enjoy physical contact with patients, Claribel concentrated instead on lab work. Her younger sister, Etta, concentrated on more prosaic matters, keeping house, preparing meals, and sorting through their steadily growing collection of paintings, fabrics, prints, sculpture, furniture, boxes, jewelry, and furnishings. They hosted regular Saturday night salons at their elegant home on Eutaw Place, during which Claribel held forth regally while Etta bustled about quietly in the background. In their interpersonal relationship, their collecting efforts, and their bifurcated hostessing style, the Cones provided Gertrude with a useful working model for how to manage her own life.

Increasingly Gertrude lost interest in her studies, largely because she had discovered a more captivating interest: a tall, lovely young woman named Mary Bookstaver, called May, who was a central figure in Gertrude's circle of Bryn Mawr–educated Baltimore friends. These friends met regularly at the shared apartment of Mabel Haynes and Grace Lounsbery, where they discussed women's suffrage, contraception, and other modish facets of the New Woman. Educated like them at an Ivy League school, Gertrude moved comfortably into the fold, although Lounsbery, a relative of the Adams political dynasty, found her "not at all well brought up, coming from a pretty rough sort of background." Small, athletic, and boyish looking, Lounsbery did not appeal to Gertrude either, but May Bookstaver was another matter. The romantically inexperienced Gertrude fell hard for her, apparently not realizing that May was already involved with Mabel Haynes.[10]

In her autobiographical first novel, *Q.E.D.*, written two years after the events described, Gertrude recounted the sinuous course of their romance. May Bookstaver, called Helen in the book, was "the American version of the handsome English girl...determined, a trifle brutal, and entirely impersonal, a woman of passions but not of emotions, capable of long-sustained action, incapable of regrets." Mabel Haynes, renamed Mabel Neathe, was immoral, passionate, and jealously possessive. The ensuing love triangle ended in a deadlock—Gertrude's word—in both fiction and real life. May and Mabel ultimately found husbands (May's had been one of Teddy Roosevelt's Rough Riders), and Gertrude, severely depressed, lost all remaining interest in medical school. She failed her four senior-level classes and was primly "not recommended" for a degree by the seven-man faculty committee. When a female classmate, Marion Walker, pleaded with her to "remember the cause of women," Gertrude responded tersely, "You don't know what it is to be bored." She left Baltimore—and America—a few months later, in the fall of 1903. She would not return for thirty-one years.[11]

▼ ▼ ▼

ALICE TOKLAS, LIKE GERTRUDE STEIN, WAS A DAUGHTER OF comparative wealth and privilege who had lost her mother at a young age. A true native of San Francisco—her maternal grandfather was an original Forty-Niner—Alice was one of two children born to former Polish army officer Ferdinand Toklas and his wife, Emma. Moderately talented as a pianist, she studied music at the University of Washington for a year before moving back to San Francisco to keep house for her widowed father and her younger brother, Clarence, who was then an undergraduate at Berkeley. "I led a pleasant life," Alice recounted in the *Autobiography*. "I had many friends, much amusement[,] many interests, my life was reasonably full and I enjoyed it, but I was not very ardent in it." The San Francisco earthquake of April 18, 1906, literally shook up her comfortable world, rattling her out of bed that cataclysmic morning to witness a great fire raging mere blocks away. "Do get up," Alice implored her father, who remarkably seems to have slept through the trembler. "The city is on fire." "That will give us a black eye in the East," Mr. Toklas sighed.[12]

While Alice gathered up the family silver and buried it in the backyard to hide it from looters, her father went downtown to see whether the vaults at his bank were still standing. (They were.) He returned home with a cache of four hundred cigarettes he had recovered from the rubble, which he handed to Alice—a lifelong smoker—explaining that "with these, one might not only exist but be able to be hospitable." Equally resourceful, Alice laid out a picnic lunch on the rubble-strewn sidewalk in front of their still-standing house at 922 O'Farrell Street. In the days following the earthquake she carried on as though nothing untoward had happened, taking bouquets of carnations to her neighbors, exchanging social calls with her friends, and even finding time to attend a performance of Racine's *Phedre* by Sarah Bernhardt across the bay in Berkeley. It would take more than an earthquake to stop Alice Toklas.[13]

But though she didn't know it at the time, the earthquake would completely change Alice's life. Gertrude Stein's eldest brother, Michael, and his wife, Sarah, then living in Paris, had returned to San Francisco to check on the damage to a string of apartment buildings they owned on Lyon Street. The Steins brought with them a trio of paintings by their current favorite, Henri Matisse, including a striking new portrait of Matisse's wife, Amelie, with a green stripe running down the center of her face. Michael, as Sarah reported happily to Gertrude, "sprang" the paintings on the city's unsuspecting artists' community, of which Alice was a member in good standing. Introduced to the Steins by her next-door neighbor Harriet Levy, who had met them a year earlier in Italy, Alice made a sufficiently favorable impression on the couple to be invited to return to Paris with them. She declined, preferring to remain close to her father and brother for a while longer and also wanting, perhaps, to avoid a weeklong ocean voyage with Sarah Stein, whom she considered—as did many—a bit overbearing.

The following year Alice changed her mind, motivated in part by an outbreak of bubonic plague in post-earthquake San Francisco and in part by glowing letters about life on the Left Bank from her childhood friend Annette Rosenshine, who at Alice's prompting had accompanied the Steins back to Paris in her place. After a parting shrug from her chronically laid-back father, Alice said goodbye to San Francisco and the United States, sailing to Europe with Harriet Levy in the late summer of 1907. They arrived in Paris on September 8, and with almost literary timing Alice Toklas met Gertrude Stein that very day.

Like most great accidents of fate, it was not planned in advance. Alice and Harriet's first item of business after checking into the Hotel Magellan on the Boulevard Saint-Michel was to pay a courtesy call on the Steins at their apartment at 58 rue Madame. Gertrude happened to be there at the time, tanned a deep golden brown after a summer in Tuscany, wearing a large round coral brooch, talking very little but laughing a good deal. Alice was immediately taken by her voice, "unlike anyone else's voice—deep, full, velvety, like a great contralto's, like two voices." It was love at first sound. According to Alice—actually, according to Gertrude writing as Alice—bells went off in Alice's head when she first encountered her future lover. "Only three times in my life have I met a genius," Alice says in the *Autobiography*, "and each time a bell within me rang and I was not mistaken." The three geniuses cited were Gertrude Stein, Pablo Picasso, and English philosopher Alfred North Whitehead. Gertrude, as always, came first.[14]

At the time they met, public recognition of Gertrude's genius was far from universal. She had only one published book to her credit, *Q.E.D.*, and in fact was much better known as an art collector than a writer. Almost accidentally, she and her brother had embarked on what she would describe in the *Autobiography* as an ascent into "the heart of an art movement of which the outside world at the time knew nothing." Going to art dealer Ambroise Vollard's gallery on the rue Lafitte one afternoon in the fall of 1904, they had purchased a few small paintings by soon-to-be-deceased Paul Cezanne. Then, at the famous salon show introducing the Fauves, the revolutionary "wild beasts" of French painting, they came across Matisse's scandalous and much-derided portrait of his wife, *Woman with a Hat*. Leo would remember that the painting initially struck him as "the nastiest smear of paint I had ever seen," but Gertrude convinced him to buy it for 500 francs, about $100. It was money well spent.[15]

With those initial purchases Gertrude and Leo took their place at the front, or just a little behind the front, of the ongoing artistic revolution that Gertrude dubbed "the heroic age of cubism." They quietly amassed one of the most impressive private collections of paintings in Paris, if not indeed the entire world. Soon they owned works by a virtual checklist of great French painters: Matisse, Cezanne, Degas, Gauguin, Manet, Renoir, Toulouse-Lautrec, Delacroix, and a young up-and-coming Spaniard whom Gertrude described on first meeting as "a good-looking bootblack with big pools of eyes"—Pablo Picasso. Leo had discovered Picasso's work in the picture gallery of an ex–circus clown named Clovis Sagot on the rue Lafitte, a few doors down from Vollard's gallery. Leo and Gertrude argued initially over the merits of Picasso's provocative painting of a nude, barely pubescent young girl holding a bouquet of red flowers. Gertrude disliked the painting, which she found "rather appalling in the drawing of the legs and feet." Sagot suggested helpfully that "if you do not like the legs and feet it is very easy to guillotine her and only take the head." In the end, Leo settled for the whole painting.[16]

The Steins began hosting regular Saturday night dinners for their artist friends at the rue de Fleurus. Matisse and Picasso met at one such dinner. They were, said Gertrude, "enthusiastic about each other, but did not like each other very well." At her suggestion they exchanged paintings, each choosing the least interesting work of the other so that he could use it as an example of his rival's alleged weakness as a painter. One of the rare women painters of the fauvist movement, Marie Laurencin, the girlfriend of Guillaume Apollinaire, had also begun coming around. Gertrude bought the first painting Marie ever sold, a group portrait of Marie, Apollinaire, Picasso, and his mistress at the time, Fernande Olivier. With a mistress's natural aversion to potential rivals, Fernande disliked Marie on sight, describing her as having "the face of a goat. She looked like a rather vicious little girl, or a little girl who wants people to think she's vicious." Actually, judging from her photographs, Marie was attractive enough in a somewhat avid, wide-eyed way. She mostly looked surprised, which was not an unreasonable reaction for a young artist of the time.[17]

▼ ▼ ▼

BEFORE LEAVING THE STEINS' APARTMENT THAT FIRST AF-
ternoon in Paris, Alice accepted an invitation from Gertrude
to come see her the next day at the rue de Fleurus. They could
go for a walk in the nearby Luxembourg Gardens. The visit
started badly. Alice was half an hour late, and although she had
sent Gertrude a pneumatic telegram advising her of the delay,
she was met at the door by a clearly incensed hostess who was
in no mood for excuses. "She was very different," Alice recalled
in her 1963 memoir, *What Is Remembered*. "She had not her
smiling countenance of the day before. She was now a vengeful
goddess and I was afraid." Stomping around the living room,
Gertrude raged at the smaller, younger woman for some time—"I
am not accustomed to wait," she said—then suddenly relented.
"She stood in front of me," Alice recalled, "and said, Now you
understand. It is over. It is not too late to go for a walk. You can
look at the pictures while I change my clothes."[18]

Alice did as she was told: she looked at the pictures. There
was a lot to see. In a place of honor on Gertrude's wall was
Picasso's severely vertical *Young Girl with a Basket of Flowers*.
Even more eye-catching was another Picasso painting, this one a
portrait done mostly in browns of a strangely walleyed Gertrude.
Executed laboriously over the course of ninety separate sittings
in the fall and winter of 1905–6, the original results displeased
the painter, who one day impulsively smudged out Gertrude's
face and replaced it with new, cubist features: mismatched eyes,
an elongated nose, and a severe slash of a mouth that scarcely
resembled his subject's rosebud-shaped lips. Her brother disliked
the portrait, calling it "as a whole incoherent," but Gertrude
pronounced herself well satisfied. "For me," she wrote, "it is
I, and it is the only reproduction of me which is always I, for

me." When visitors complained to Picasso that Gertrude did not much look like his portrait of her, he simply shrugged and said, "She will."[19]

Alice did not venture an opinion about Picasso's portrait that afternoon. Instead, she and Gertrude went for their walk and stopped in at a patisserie off the Boulevard Saint-Michel for cakes and ices. All was forgiven. A few days later Alice met Picasso for the first time at one of Gertrude's Saturday night dinners. She would remember it as "one of the most important evenings of my life." Like most of Gertrude's soirees, the dinner was a mixture of the formal and the comic. The first arrivals were Alice and a high-strung American painter named Alfy Maurer—"hair, eyes, face, hands and feet all very much alive," Alice recalled. They were ushered through the apartment to the stand-alone studio in the adjoining courtyard, where they milled about in the rain while Gertrude fiddled in her purse for the key. Upon entering, Gertrude immediately made her way to the cast-iron stove in the corner, where she took her accustomed place of honor in a high-backed chair near the fire. While they waited for Picasso to arrive, Alice had the opportunity to look more closely at the paintings. She was still a bit unsettled by the strangeness of the works. "It is very difficult now that everybody is accustomed to everything to give some idea of the kind of uneasiness one felt when one first looked at these pictures on these walls," she said. "The pictures were so strange that one quite instinctively looked at anything rather than at them."[20]

Alice was rescued from her unease by the announcement of dinner by Gertrude's longtime cook, Helene, a stolid, good-natured Norman who ruled the kitchen with an iron hand and took pride in producing three meals a day on a budget of 8 francs. According to Alice, who would have known, Helene was an excellent cook, especially of soufflés, but she "had her opinions." She particularly disliked Henri Matisse, who had a habit of turning up unexpectedly at dinnertime and asking—rudely, in Helene's eyes—what was for dinner. She took subtle Gallic revenge by fixing him fried eggs instead of omelets, explaining to Alice that "it takes the same number of eggs and the same amount of butter but it shows less respect, and he will understand." They had just sat down to eat—"We won't wait at least Helene won't wait," Gertrude warned—when Picasso and Fernande dashed in. "I am very upset," said the painter, "you know very well Gertrude I am never late but Fernande had ordered a dress for the vernissage [advance showing] tomorrow and it didn't come." "Well here you are anyway," Gertrude said gracefully. "Since it's you Helene won't mind."[21]

Alice paid more attention that first night to Fernande than to Picasso. "Fernande was a tall beautiful woman with a wonderful big hat," she remembered. "Fernande had two subjects[,] hats and perfumes. This first day we talked hats." Gertrude interrupted their fashionfest to introduce Alice to "a medium sized man with a reddish beard and glasses." It was Matisse. He and Gertrude were discussing a previous showing she had hosted, at which she had "wickedly" placed each painter opposite his own picture. "I know Mademoiselle Gertrude, the world is a theatre for you," said Matisse, "and when you listen so carefully to me and so attentively and do not hear a word I say then I do say that you are very wicked." Alice, who had not been at the showing, had no idea what they were talking about. A bit later she found herself standing next to Picasso, who asked her, in all seriousness, if she thought he looked like Abraham Lincoln. "I had thought a good many things that evening," recalled Alice, "but I had not thought that. I did not know whether he meant it or not but I was sympathetic."[22]

▼ ▼ ▼

SLOWLY BUT SURELY ALICE WAS ABSORBED INTO THE STEIN household. Art collecting was only one aspect of Gertrude's life—a secondary one at that. Mainly she was a writer. At the time Alice arrived on the scene, Gertrude had just completed a book of short stories, *Three Lives*, that would garner respectable reviews when it appeared in print two years hence. (The central story, "Melanctha," about a young African American woman in love with a physician, is probably Gertrude's most anthologized work.) Now she was plugging away at what she considered her masterpiece, a long experimental novel entitled *The Making of Americans*. The book logged in at an elephantine one thousand pages, all of which had to be typed by someone else—Gertrude refused to type, as she said it made her nervous. Alice offered to do the typing for her, and Gertrude promptly bought a new Smith Premier typewriter to replace the "wretched little portable" she had been using. In December 1910, Alice moved into 27 rue de Fleurus, joining Gertrude, her new typewriter, and an increasingly dissatisfied Leo, who had to give up his studio for Alice to use as a bedroom.[23]

At the time Alice arrived on the scene, Leo was dealing with a number of emotionally charged personal issues, chief of which was his failure to succeed as an artist in his own right. His quarrels with and about Picasso intensified, to the point that the Spaniard once asked him point-blank, "Why don't you like my painting?" and on another occasion told him brutally, "You have no right to judge. I'm an artist and you are not." Leo had also commenced a long, tangled love affair with a notorious artist's model in the Latin Quarter, Nina Auzias, who by the age of twenty-six had already carried on numberless affairs with the artists she posed for. She was currently juggling three lovers while pursuing Leo with a ferocity that seemed literally to make her wild frizz of hair stand on end.[24]

Gertrude and Alice, involved in their own deepening affair, left Leo largely to his own devices. He, for his part, took only grudging notice of their new flatmate, whom he dismissively called "the little typist." Alice, he told Buffalo, New York, heiress Mabel Dodge, "was making herself indispensable. She did everything to save Gertrude a movement—all the housekeeping, the typing, seeing people who called, and getting rid of the undesirables, answering letters—really providing all the motor force of the ménage." It was a perfect example, Leo groused, of "how the weaker can enslave the stronger," like a clinging vine strangling a tall tree.[25]

Though ungenerously put, Leo's basic insight was sharp. Alice had indeed made herself indispensable to Gertrude, partly as a result of Gertrude's chaotic writing process. Gertrude liked to write late at night, after the distractions of the day had ended. She wrote by hand, four or five lines of large, faint, scrambled letters per page in the blue French student's notebook she invariably used. She would drop the pages on the floor and Alice would tiptoe in and retrieve them the next morning while Gertrude slept. When the author arose—never before noon—she would read over the typescript of what she called, without apparent irony, "the daily miracle" and would be routinely surprised and delighted by what she had written the night before. In no time Alice became so proficient at reading Gertrude's handwriting that she could puzzle out words the author herself could neither read nor remember. For Alice it was heavenly, "like living history. I hoped it would go on forever."[26]

While Gertrude wrote and Alice typed, an increasingly distracted Leo withdrew from the scene. First, he stopped leading the discussions at their Saturday night salons, then he stopped contributing to the discussions, then he stopped listening to Gertrude lead the discussions, and finally he stopped attending the discussions altogether. "I would rather harbor three devils in my insides, than talk about art," the notoriously dyspeptic Leo confided to Mabel Dodge. He left handwritten notes for Gertrude and Alice complaining about their habit of leaving the lights on downstairs, about their disproportionate use of the gas stove in the kitchen, about the high cost of coal for their linen service, and even about their supposed overuse of stamps. In private he was merciless about his sister's talent. "I can't abide her stuff and think it abominable," he wrote. "Her artistic capacity is, I think, extremely small. Gertrude's mind is about as little nimble as a mind can be." Both Gertrude and Picasso, he concluded, were "turning out the most Godalmighty rubbish that is to be found."[27]

Gertrude professed herself to be untroubled by Leo's opinions, saying merely that "he continued to believe in what he was saying when he was arguing, and I began not to find it interesting." Eventually, however, "it destroyed him for me and it destroyed me for him." In April 1914, Leo moved out of their Paris apartment, resettling near Florence, Italy, with Nina Auzias and his carefully divided share of the siblings' collected paintings. He took the Renoirs and the Cezannes; Gertrude held on to all but one of the Picassos. Except for a chance meeting six years later on a Paris street, at which time neither spoke, the previously inseparable duo never saw each other again. Gertrude had a simple if cold-blooded explanation for the break. "It is a funny thing being a genius," she wrote. "It was I who was the genius, there was no reason for it but I was, and he was not."[28]

Having outlasted her chief rival for Gertrude's affections, Alice soon confronted a dangerous new intruder—Mabel Dodge.

Working then on the second of four husbands, as well as a steadily rotating roster of lovers, including the revolutionary journalist John Reed, Dodge was an incorrigible flirt and an insatiable faddist. Her newest fad was Gertrude Stein. Bombarding Gertrude with letters and telegrams, each more fawning than the last, Dodge induced her to visit Dodge's Italian retreat, Villa Curonia, outside Florence. Alice, of course, went along, and the two rivals for Gertrude's attention immediately squared off.

Although somewhat chunky and plain looking in photographs, Dodge considered herself a femme fatale. Alice begged to differ. "She was a stoutish woman with a very sturdy fringe of heavy hair over her forehead, heavy long lashes and a very old fashioned coquetry," Alice recalled in a volley of well-considered adjectives. "She reminded me of a heroine of my youth, the actress Georgia Cayvan." It was not intended as a compliment. Cayvan was a big-eyed, round-faced actress of the late nineteenth century remembered mainly for being the only actress ever to wear a spun-glass dress on stage. (It proved too brittle to be long endured.) Dodge, for her part, reached even farther back in time to describe Alice. Gertrude's little friend, she said, was "like Leah, out of the Old Testament, in her half-Oriental get-up—her blues and browns and oyster whites—her black hair—her barbaric chains and jewels—and her melancholy nose." She was particularly fascinated by Alice's obsessive attention to her hands. "She was forever manicuring her nails," Dodge observed. "Her hands were small and fine and almond shaped, painted glistening nails[,] they looked like the hands of a courtesan. Every morning, for an hour, Alice polished her nails—they had become a fetish with her. She loved her hands."[29]

The private warfare between the two women flared into the open one day at lunch. Gertrude was in the process of writing a flattering if impressionistic profile of her hostess that she titled "Portrait of Mabel Dodge at the Villa Curonia," and Dodge responded to her fixed attention "in a sort of flirtatious way." That day, she remembered, Gertrude "sent me such a strong look over the table that it seemed to cut across the air to me in a band of electrified steel—a smile travelling across on it—power- ful—Heavens!" Alice, who missed very little where Gertrude was concerned, did not miss that look. Throwing down her napkin, she rushed out of the room. Gertrude ambled after her, returning alone a few minutes later to report neutrally that Alice "doesn't want to come to lunch. She feels the heat today." It was an art- ful use of words.[30]

Delighted to be the subject of a personal essay by the great Gertrude Stein, Dodge had three hundred copies of the work privately printed and bound in flowery Florentine paper. She returned the favor by writing a glowing appreciation of Gertrude in the next issue of *Arts and Decoration* magazine, which was devoted to the legendary Armory Show. Gertrude and Leo had loaned their Matisse painting *Blue Nude* and Picasso's *Vase, Gourd and Fruit on a Table* to the show, which Dodge in her fevered way declared "the most important public event since the signing of the Declaration of Independence." Her more mea- sured description of Gertrude's work was surprisingly acute and perceptive. "In Gertrude Stein's writing every word lives," Dodge wrote, "and is so exquisitely rhythmical and cadenced that if we read it aloud and receive it as pure sound, it is like a kind of sensuous music." Like Picasso, said Dodge, Gertrude's work functioned on a level beneath the merely rational. "Listening to Gertrude Stein's words and forgetting to try to understand what they mean, one submits to their gradual charm." Gertrude could not have agreed more. "I've just gotten hold of your article and I am delighted with it," she gushed to Dodge. "Really it is awfully well done and I am proud as punch."[31]

Eventually Dodge went too far, daring to lecture Gertrude on her decision to place a new collection of abstract poems, *Tender Buttons*, with New York publisher Donald Evans. Dodge had fallen out with Evans over some localized feud involving the poet Edwin Arlington Robinson, and she cabled Gertrude "not to publish with D. Evans [who] is absolutely third rate, & in bad odor here." Gertrude went ahead with her plans anyway, and the hothouse friendship between the two came to an end—much to the satisfaction of Alice, who long since had learned to keep her literary opinions to herself.[32]

Over time *Tender Buttons* would become one of Gertrude's best-known and best-liked works, its hard-to-characterize contents organized around a series of objects and the way in which the author looks at them. Many of the pieces seem to be disguised allusions to lesbian sex. *This is this dress, aider* plays off one of Gertrude's nicknames for Alice to describe an apparent orgasmic release: "Aider, why aider why whow, whow stop touch, aider whow, aider stop the muncher, muncher munchers. A jack in kill her, a jack in, makes a meadowed king." *Red Roses* observes "a cool red rose and a pink cut pink, a collapse and a sold hole, a little less hot." *A brown* describes "a brown which is not liquid not more so is relaxed and yet there is a change, a news is pressing." *A petticoat* may be a seduction: "A light white, a disgrace, an ink spot, a rosy charm." Similarly, in *A leave*: "In the middle of a tiny spot and nearly bare there is a nice thing to say that wrist is leading. Wrist is leading." It was all either domestically erotic or erotically domestic, depending on one's point of view. Journalist H. L. Mencken, reviewing the poems in his magazine *The Smart Set*, carped that Gertrude's greatest achievement had been to make English "easier to write and harder to read."[33]

▼ ▼ ▼

ALL FINE LITERARY DISTINCTIONS BECAME SECONDARY IN THE
summer of 1914, when war broke out in Western Europe for the
first time in four decades. Gertrude and Alice were visiting philosopher Alfred Lloyd Whitehead and his family in London when
the fighting began that August, and as the *Autobiography* noted
briefly but poignantly, "the old life was over." Whitehead's wife
was part French, and news of the German invasion of Belgium
struck them hard. "I can still hear Doctor Whitehead's gentle
voice reading the papers out loud and then all of them talking
about the destruction of Louvain and how they must help the
brave little Belgians," Alice recalled. "Gertrude Stein desperately
unhappy said to me, where is Louvain. Don't you know, I said.
No, she said, nor do I care, but where is it."[34]

Soon the entire world would know and care where Louvain
was, as the brutal rape of Belgium presaged the German march
on Paris. Marooned in England, Gertrude and Alice could only
watch from afar as French troops mustered for a last stand along
the Marne River northeast of the city. "The Germans were getting nearer and nearer Paris and the last day Gertrude Stein
could not leave her room, she sat and mourned," remembered
Alice. "She loved Paris, she thought neither of manuscripts nor
of pictures, she thought only of Paris and she was desolate. I
came up to her room, I called out, it is alright Paris is saved,
the Germans are in retreat. She turned away and said, don't
tell me these things. But it's true, I said, it is true. And then we
wept together."[35]

The Miracle of the Marne, as it came to be known, saved
Paris, but in doing so it doomed the contending armies to four
long years of trench warfare on the muddy plains of Belgium and
northern France. Buoyed by much-needed infusions of cash from

Alice's father and Gertrude's cousin, the couple returned to Paris in October 1914. The city's streets were largely unpopulated; food and fuel were in short supply. Many of their French friends were off serving in the military; Americans such as Alfy Maurer were hastily making plans to return to the States. Picasso, an unaffiliated Spaniard, remained in Paris, but he was increasingly preoccupied with the failing health of his new mistress, Eva Gouel, who would die of tuberculosis a year later. The war's first Zeppelin raid that winter literally scared Alice knock-kneed, which sent Gertrude into spasms of laughter. "I would not have believed it was true that knees knocked together as described in poetry and prose," Alice remembered ruefully, "if it had not happened to me."[36]

Bored and lonely in Paris, the couple decided to visit Spain. To finance their trip, Gertrude sold her Matisse painting, *Woman with a Hat*, to Michael and Sarah Stein. With the proceeds from the sale, Gertrude and Alice toured Spain for several weeks before sailing from Barcelona to the Mediterranean island of Mallorca. There they settled into a rented villa near Palma, where they consorted with their English, French, and American neighbors but refused to speak to German residents of the island. Instead, they carried on a stubborn war of nerves with a truculent German governess who persisted in flying her national standard whenever the Germans won another victory. "We responded as well as we could," Gertrude recalled, "but alas just then there were not many allied victories." That changed when the French army held at Verdun after a yearlong slaughter, turning the tide of war toward the Allies. Gertrude correctly intuited the victory before its official announcement when she noticed that the ordinarily industrious Germans had suddenly stopped repainting their marooned steamer in Palma harbor.[37]

Returning to Paris, Gertrude and Alice found a more effective way to serve the Allied war effort than draping a French flag over their balcony. Walking along the rue des Pyramides one day, they came upon a uniformed young woman driving a Ford truck with the legend "American Fund for French Wounded" painted on the side. "There," said Alice, "that is what we are going to do. You will drive the car and I will do the rest." The fact that Gertrude did not know how to drive was dismissed as being beside the point. The woman driving the truck directed them to the fund's director, Mrs. Isabelle Lathrop, who welcomed their offer of help but politely suggested that they might want to get a truck first. "But where, we asked. From America she said. But how, we said. Ask somebody, she said, and Gertrude Stein did, she asked her cousin and in a few months the ford car came." In the meantime, Gertrude took driving lessons from artist-friend William Cook, who was moonlighting in Paris as a taxi driver.[38]

As soon as their reconfigured vehicle arrived, the pair headed south to their assigned posting at the French officers hospital at Perpignan. Gertrude was immensely pleased with their new Ford, which she named "Auntie" after her Aunt Pauline, "who always behaved admirably in emergencies and behaved fairly well most times if she was properly flattered." Along the way they managed to combine business and pleasure, stopping to eat at various Michelin-starred restaurants, including one that employed, much to Alice's vocal displeasure, Kaiser Wilhelm's recently paroled head chef, who Alice thought belonged in an Allied prison cell rather than a French kitchen. Arriving at Perpignan in a late-spring snowstorm, the couple moved into their quarters on the ground floor of a local hotel. The next day they assumed their duties transporting supplies from the train station to various military hospitals in the region.[39]

It was a heady time for the pair, who had never been south of Fountainebleau. At Rivesaltes, the birthplace of French marshal

Joseph Joffre, the hero of the Marne, they were photographed sitting proudly in their truck outside the marshal's childhood home. They had the photograph made into postcards, which they sent to friends in America to solicit contributions for the fund. Not even the sweltering summer heat slowed them down, although Gertrude complained constantly that she felt like a pancake, trapped between "the heat above and the heat below." Their self-designed uniforms could not have helped. Gertrude wore a heavy Cossack coat and hat, while Alice favored a modified British officer's coat with extra pockets worn over a long skirt and a broad-brimmed hat described erroneously as a pith helmet. In full garb she looked a bit like Juliette Gordon Low, founder of the Girl Scouts of America.[40]

▼ ▼ ▼

THE ENTRY OF THE UNITED STATES INTO THE WAR IN 1917 delighted the couple. "Hurrah for America," Gertrude jotted at the end of a poem, noting that "the war was so much better than just going to America. Here you were with America in a kind of way that if you only went to America you could not possibly be." Transferred to Nimes to open a new supply depot there, they encountered the first arriving doughboys. It was the most Americans Gertrude had seen in one place since she left her homeland in 1903. One doughboy, William Garland Rogers of Springfield, Massachusetts, became a particular favorite. After meeting him in the dining room of their hotel, they took him on a guided tour of nearby Roman ruins. Like everyone who rode with Gertrude, Rogers did not find it a relaxing experience. "Though possessed with lightning-fast reactions and a knowledge of how to handle a Ford, she felt she owned the road," he reported. "She regarded a corner as something to cut, and another car as something to pass, and she could scare the daylights out of all concerned."

The Kiddie, as they nicknamed the youthful-looking Rogers, would recall that at their first meeting "they pumped me for all they were worth. One spelled the other, like police grilling a prisoner for hours on end, until they dragged my whole history out of me."[41]

When the war ended on November 11, 1918, Alice wept. "Compose yourself," chided Gertrude, "you have no right to show a tearful countenance to the French whose sons will no longer be killed." One of those surviving sons, a wounded soldier, put things into sober context. "Well here is peace," Gertrude said to him. "At least for twenty years," the soldier responded. Back in Paris, she and Alice joined the thousands of exultant citizens who thronged around the Arc de Triomphe for a victory parade. "Everybody was on the streets," Alice recalled, "men, women, children, soldiers, priests, nuns, we saw two nuns being helped into a tree from which they would be able to see. And we ourselves were admirably placed and saw perfectly." They were later awarded the Medaille de la Reconnaissance Francaise by the French government in recognition of their war service. Alice never tired of pointing out that while their citations were virtually identical, hers praised her for having performed her duties *sans relache*—without pause—while Gertrude, who had often threatened to abandon their stalled vehicle on the side of the road, was not so honored.[42]

▼ ▼ ▼

THE PARIS THEY RETURNED TO AFTER THE WAR WAS NOT the Paris they had left behind. "The city, like us, was sadder than when we left it," Alice reflected. Their old friend Guillaume Apollinaire was dead, one of the millions lost in the raging influenza epidemic. Henri Matisse had relocated to Nice, an ailing Juan Gris was seldom around, and Gertrude was temporarily on the outs with Pablo Picasso, whose Russian-born wife, Olga, she did not much like. Meanwhile, she and Alice continued visiting wounded soldiers in the Paris hospitals and dealing with lingering shortages of food, supplies, and—worst of all—servants. Alice had to cook and serve their food herself, while Gertrude functioned as their chauffeur.[43]

Day by day the war receded, grass grew over the old battlefields, and visitors began returning to the rue de Fleurus. Alfred North Whitehead's daughter, Jessie, in town to serve as a secretary at the Paris Peace Conference, dropped by frequently. Painter Marcel Duchamp, not a particularly close friend, also came to visit, and photographer Man Ray, a new acquaintance, took a series of snapshots of Gertrude and Alice, one of which was destined to serve as the cover for *The Autobiography of Alice B. Toklas*. Sculptor Jo Davidson enticed Gertrude to pose for a new piece. The finished product depicted a burly, peasant-like Gertrude, shoulders hunched and hands lying in her lap. It made her look, Gertrude complained, like "the goddess of pregnancy." New callers came and went. "You can tell that the war is over," Gertrude told American art critic Henry McBride in December 1919. "So many people knock at the old door instead of ringing the new bell." Some of the callers came only once; the privileged few were invited back. One in particular returned time and time again, and it was upon those visits, and their acrimonious aftermath, that the sepia-tinged legend of Paris and the Lost Generation is largely based, and a major reason why Gertrude Stein and Alice Toklas are still remembered today.[44]

Many Saints Seen

IF THE FIRST TWO DECADES OF GERTRUDE'S LIFE IN PARIS had revolved around French and Spanish painters, the third would revolve around English and American writers. For Gertrude it was a natural progression. The disintegration of her relationship with Leo had effectively ended her avocation as an art collector, and the cataclysm of World War I, coupled with steadily evolving artistic tastes and the unavoidable inroads of time, marked the end of an era in French painting. And as much as Gertrude liked "seeing painted pictures," as she modestly described it, she was ultimately a writer at heart. When the city began filling up with other writers after the war, she and Alice stood ready to receive them—as always, on their own terms and conditions. The *Autobiography* is full of them.[1]

An important gathering place for English-language writers at the beginning of the twenties was a compact little bookstore with the proudly expansive name Shakespeare and Company. It was owned and operated by Baltimore native Sylvia Beach, the daughter of a Presbyterian minister, who had moved to Paris at the end of the war to study French literature. In the course of her studies she had discovered a lending library-cum-bookshop, La Maison des Amis des Livres, in the rue de l'Odeon. She had also discovered the store's owner, a plump, fair-haired young Parisian named Adrienne Monnier, who would quickly become, much as Gertrude did for Alice, her muse, mentor, and longtime lover. "I like America very much," Adrienne told Sylvia when she first met her. "I like France very much," Sylvia replied.[2]

With the help of a $3,000 gift from her mother, Sylvia opened a lending library and bookshop of her own directly across the street from Adrienne's. Her first official subscriber was Gertrude Stein. Having heard about the new bookstore from friends, Gertrude paid it a visit in November 1919 and was gratified to find two copies of *Tender Buttons* on the shelf. Alice Toklas remembered that the bookshop, at first, was not much frequented by other Americans. Instead, she said, "there was the author of Beebie the Beebiest and there was the niece of Marcel Schwob and there were a few stray Irish poets." Undergraduates from Oxford also dropped by when they were in Paris, and through them Gertrude arranged to publish a couple essays, "More League" and "Portrait of Harry Phelan Gibb," in the May 7, 1920, issue of *Oxford* magazine. It gave her a lifelong liking for Englishmen.[3]

A few months later Sylvia Beach introduced them to a promising new American writer, Sherwood Anderson of Clyde, Ohio. Anderson was making his first visit to Paris, accompanied by his soon-to-be ex-wife, Tennessee Claflin Mitchell. A rising star in the literary world, Anderson had published two novels and a widely acclaimed collection of short stories, *Winesburg, Ohio*. He wanted to meet Gertrude, whose story "Melanctha" he considered an important early influence on his work. He also liked, somewhat counterintuitively for a writer of realistic fiction, the densely experimental *Tender Buttons*, which he said had "excited me as one might grow excited in going into a new and wonderful country where everything is strange—a sort of Lewis and Clark expedition."[4]

Sylvia Beach helpfully provided him with a letter of introduction to Gertrude. "He is so anxious to know you," she wrote, "for he says you have influenced him ever so much & that you stand as such a great master of words." Alice was off on some "domestic complication" when Anderson came to call, but when she returned she could clearly see that his visit had meant a great deal to Gertrude. "Gertrude Stein was in those days a little bitter, all her unpublished manuscripts, and no hope of publication or serious recognition," recalled Alice. "Sherwood Anderson came and quite simply and directly as is his way told her what he thought of her work and what it had meant to him in his development. He told it to her then and what was even rarer he told it in print immediately after. Gertrude Stein and Sherwood Anderson have always been the best of friends but I do not believe even he realises how much his visit meant to her."[5]

Anderson wrote glowingly about his visit in the October 11, 1922, issue of the *New Republic*, depicting Gertrude, with rather broad poetic license, as a cook making "handmade goodies" in her "kitchen of words." (Actually, she seldom darkened the door to the kitchen, which was Alice's jealously guarded province.) In her figurative cooking bowl, said Anderson, Gertrude was "laying word against word, relating sound to sound, feeling for the taste, the smell, the rhythm of the individual word. She is attempting to do something for the writers of our English speech that may be better understood after a time, and she is not in a hurry." He would amplify his admiration for Gertrude in another strained comparison a few months later—this time to a construction worker. "For me," wrote Anderson in an introduction to Gertrude's *Geography and Plays*, "the work of Gertrude Stein consists in a rebuilding, an entirely new recasting of life, in the city of words." Gertrude accepted the compliment.[6]

▼ ▼ ▼

MORE SIGNIFICANT THAN ANDERSON'S *New Republic* ARTI-cle or his introduction to *Geography and Plays* was his own let-ter of introduction to Gertrude of "a young man instinctively in touch with everything worthwhile going on here." The young man in question was Ernest Hemingway. Anderson had met his fellow midwesterner (Hemingway was a Chicago native, by way of Oak Park) a year earlier at the Division Street apartment of Hemingway's childhood friend Kenley Smith, where Hemingway also met his future wife Hadley. Alice Toklas, who for a number of reasons, good and bad, would never warm to Hemingway, described his memorable advent on the scene in the late winter of 1922. "He was an extraordinarily good-looking young man, twenty-three years old," she remembered (actually Hemingway was still twenty-two), "rather foreign looking, with passionately interested, rather than interesting eyes. He sat in front of Gertrude Stein and listened and looked." Gertrude, to Alice's barely concealed disapproval, looked back.[7]

Accompanying Hemingway to the rue de Fleurus that first day was his tall, soft-spoken, auburn-haired wife Hadley. The couple had only been married a few months, and the former Hadley Richardson of St. Louis, Missouri, was still getting used to their new life in Paris. While Ernest took a seat at Gertrude's feet, Hadley was ushered to the far end of the room by Alice. It was an invariable house rule: husbands talked to Gertrude, wives talked to Alice. "The geniuses came and talked to Gertrude Stein and the wives sat with me," Alice recalled. "I began with Fernande Olivier and then there were Madame Matisse and Marcelle Braque and Josette Gris and Eve Picasso and Bridget Gibb and Marjorie Gibb and Hadley and Pauline Hemingway and Mrs. Sherwood Anderson and endless other geniuses, near geniuses and might be geniuses, all having wives, and I sat and talked with them all."[8]

For modest, sweet-faced Hadley, it was a new experience. "With her brown [actually gray-green] eyes brightly glittering, she would dart questions like arrows," recalled Hadley of their first conversation, "and in three minutes, would know your place of birth, your environment, your family, your connections, your education, and your immediate intentions. And she never forgot what she acquired." (Among other things, Alice learned that Hadley, like so many of Gertrude's old Baltimore friends, had attended Bryn Mawr.) Alice, said Hadley, was "a little piece of electric wire. She was small and fine and very Spanish looking, very dark, with piercing dark eyes." Hemingway described her as having "a very pleasant voice, was small, very dark, with her hair cut like Joan of Arc, and a very hooked nose." Both husband and wife found Alice a trifle intimidating.[9]

From the start, Gertrude was taken with Hemingway. Besides his blazing good looks, she recognized, as had Anderson, a serious young man as obsessed with the act of writing as she was. Better yet, he was willing to take instruction, which Gertrude was ever willing to give. A few days after the Hemingways' initial visit, she and Alice made a rare house call to the young couple's crowded flat on the fourth floor of a seedy apartment building on the rue du Cardinal Lemoine. The apartment was scarcely large enough for a small chair and bed. Alice took the chair and Gertrude sat on the bed and read through Hemingway's apprentice work. The inevitable young-man-coming-of-age novel failed to move her. "There is a great deal of description in this, and not particularly good description," she said. "Begin over again and concentrate." The stories were better, although one titled "Up in Michigan" was problematic. The writing was fine—in fact it was a lot like hers—but the subject matter, a frank depiction of sexual assault, was coarse and salacious. Gertrude, using a French painting term, called it *inaccrochable*, meaning that it was too graphic to be hung publicly. "There is no point in it," she said. "It's wrong and it's silly."[10]

She was right about "Up in Michigan," not one of Hemingway's better stories, but her most salient piece of advice actually had to do with his choice of careers. Having started his professional life as a cub reporter in Kansas City before the war, Hemingway had quickly moved up the ladder to become European correspondent for the *Toronto Star*—a plum job for a young man not yet twenty-three years old. That was all well and good, Gertrude said, if Hemingway wanted to remain a reporter all his life, but "if you keep on doing newspaper work, you will never see things, you will only see words and that will not do." Hemingway got the message, conceding later that "the value of newspaper work stops at the point that it forcibly begins to destroy your memory. A writer must leave it before that point."[11]

Gertrude's advice was put on hold when Hadley became pregnant and the couple went back to Toronto to have the baby. When they returned to Paris in 1924 with their son, John Hadley Nicanor Hemingway, called Bumby, they asked Gertrude and Alice to be his godmothers. It was not a particularly congenial role for the couple, but they did their best. Alice knitted baby clothes for Bumby and embroidered a little chair for him to sit in, and they dutifully attended his baptism in the chapel of St. Luke's Episcopal Church. The choice of church was intentionally ecumenical: Gertrude and Alice were nonobservant Jews, and Bumby's godfather, Irish-born Captain Eric "Chink" Dorman-Smith of His Majesty's Fifth Fusiliers, was Catholic. Hemingway assured his devout Protestant parents that the baby's godparents had sworn to instruct him scrupulously in all religious things, which was rather stretching the point.[12]

Bumby's unusual third name was directly thanks to Gertrude and Alice, who had inspired his father's burgeoning passion for Spain and its national sport of bullfighting, which they had first witnessed in Valencia in 1915. (Nicanor Villalta was a Spanish matador whom Hemingway particularly admired for his courage.) Alice later felt guilty about encouraging Hemingway to visit her favorite Spanish village, Pamplona, which he would make his own for all time with his breakthrough novel, *The Sun Also Rises*, in 1926. After that, said Alice, Pamplona was ruined for her, though not for the thousands of readers who have followed in Hemingway's footsteps ever since.

Hemingway repaid the literary instruction, career advice, godmothering efforts, and bullfighting tip by finding a home for Gertrude's long-languishing *The Making of Americans*. As writer-editor Ford Madox Ford's unpaid assistant at the *transatlantic review*, he convinced Ford to serialize the novel. With Alice's help, Hemingway copied out the first fifty pages of the book (the only existing typed copy was making the publishing rounds with Carl Van Vechten in New York City), carried them back to the office, and personally corrected all the proofs, a chore that Gertrude avoided whenever possible. For the next nine months, from April to December 1924, the entire shelf life of the magazine, segments of the novel appeared regularly. In all, about one-sixth of the book found its way into the pages of *transatlantic review*. Hemingway's role in bringing *The Making of Americans* before the reading public was a major reason why Gertrude could never completely write him off as a person, even as she came to severely underrate him as a writer. "I have a weakness for Hemingway," she admitted to Alice, who most emphatically did not.[13]

▼ ▼ ▼

IF HEMINGWAY WAS GERTRUDE'S STAR PUPIL, OTHER OLDER, more established writers were not so well received. Two of the era's leading poets, Ezra Pound and T. S. Eliot, made less than favorable impressions on Gertrude and Alice. The bumptious Pound, like them, was a westerner, born in Hailey, Idaho. (He also shared Gertrude's Pennsylvania background, having moved to Philadelphia as a child and earned a master's degree from the University of Pennsylvania.) He was as committed as Gertrude to modernism. As one of the founders of the imagist movement, Pound championed a new approach to poetry that called for clarity, force, and originality. His 1912 poetic manifesto, "A Few Don'ts by an Imagiste," published in *Poetry* magazine, announced that he and other imagists were "concerned solely with language and presentation," a statement of intent that could have applied equally well to Gertrude's work. His artistic credo was "Make it new."[14]

Pound was neither as young nor as handsome as Hemingway—few were—and he had the added handicap, in Gertrude's eyes, of talking too much and listening too little. "Gertrude Stein liked him but did not find him amusing," Alice noted. "She said he was a village explainer, excellent if you were a village, but if you were not, not." The final straw came one night when Pound showed up at their apartment with Schofield Thayer, editor of the prestigious literary journal *The Dial*. Pound, according to his frequent sparring partner Hemingway, had "the general grace of a crayfish." Somehow, in the course of the evening, Pound tipped over backward in Gertrude's favorite armchair, one with Picasso-designed upholstery, breaking it. Gertrude was not amused. "Finally Ezra and the editor of *The Dial* left, nobody too well pleased," recalled Alice. A few days later Pound ran into the couple near the Luxembourg Gardens and asked if he could call on them again. Gertrude declined, saying that Alice had a bad toothache and, besides, they were busy picking wildflowers. Pound might well have wondered why someone with a bad toothache would be out picking flowers, but the underlying message was clear enough. He never saw them again.[15]

Through Pound, Gertrude became acquainted with the leading Anglo-American poet of the day. As Alice remembered, "Ezra also talked about T.S. Eliot. It was the first time anyone had talked about T.S. at the house. Pretty soon everybody talked about T.S." With good reason: Eliot's epic, enigmatic *The Waste Land* had transformed modern poetry as completely as Picasso's *Les Demoiselles d'Avignon* had transformed modern painting. In person, however, the starchy Eliot was a good deal less compelling than the live-wire painter. He dressed and spoke like an English banker and conveyed at all times a pursed-mouth disapproval of most things and most people. In the fall of 1924, Gertrude and Alice were invited to tea at the Paris apartment of Lady Mary Rothermere, the wife of a prominent London newspaper publisher, who was then underwriting Eliot's new literary magazine, *Criterion*. Gertrude wasn't overly anxious to go—it seemed a bit like a royal summons to her—but Alice insisted, despite having to make a new evening gown from scratch. Before she could finish her sewing, the doorbell rang "and in walked Lady Rothermere and T.S."[16]

For some reason Eliot held onto his umbrella the whole time, while regarding Gertrude with "eyes burn[ing] brightly in a noncommittal face." When he inquired on whose authority Gertrude used so many split infinitives, she replied tersely, "Henry James." Before he left, Eliot made a half-hearted offer to publish some of Gertrude's work in his magazine, but he warned her "that it would have to be her very latest thing." After the visitors left, Gertrude told Alice, "Don't bother to finish your dress, now we don't have to go." She immediately dashed off a portrait of Eliot that she puckishly titled "The Fifteenth of November," the date of Eliot's visit, "so there could be no doubt but that it was her latest thing." She sent the piece to Eliot, and "he accepted it but naturally he did not print it." It would be two full years before the piece finally ran. By then, of course, it was no longer the latest thing.[17]

Another important American poet also ran afoul of Gertrude during a visit to the rue de Fleurus. William Carlos Williams of Rutherford, New Jersey, mixed his poetry writing with his day job as a practicing physician. Given the similarity of their backgrounds, one might have thought that he and Gertrude would get along. But Williams, at forty-one, was a bit older than most of the young men and women who paid court to Gertrude, and his no-nonsense personal style, learned at the bedside of sick children and dying elders, did not equip him with the usual level of deference. During his visit, Gertrude pulled out a sheaf of her unpublished manuscripts and asked Williams what she should do with them. "If they were mine," said Williams, "I should probably select what I thought were the best and throw the rest into the fire." Gertrude froze. "No doubt," she responded icily. "But then writing is not, of course, your métier, Doctor." Williams soon left, and Gertrude instructed the maid not to let him in again. "There is too much bombast in him," she said. Williams later redeemed himself by writing a favorable magazine piece in which he compared Gertrude to Laurence Sterne and Johann Sebastian Bach—an altogether more appropriate response in Gertrude's eyes.[18]

A steady stream of English and American writers came to see Gertrude at 27 rue de Fleurus. She liked most of them, to varying degrees, but neither she nor Hemingway could abide the suave, epicene poet Glenway Wescott, who affected a world-weary style, an ever-present ascot, a silk cigarette case with his initials on it, and a tweedy English accent (he was from Wisconsin). The accent amused Gertrude and Alice, but Chicago-born Hemingway groused that "when you matriculate at the University of Chicago you write down just what accent you will have and they give it to you when you graduate." Gertrude quickly lost interest in Wescott, whom she later dismissed as having "a certain syrup but it does not pour." In *The Sun Also Rises*, Hemingway would skewer the unoffending poet as Robert Prentiss, a supercilious boulevardier whose flamboyant style and literary pretensions made the book's narrator, Jake Barnes, want to throw up.[19]

▼ ▼ ▼

ONE NOTABLE PARIS-BASED WRITER DID NOT COME TO SEE Gertrude in the twenties—or at any other time. Despite living in the same general neighborhood, James Joyce and Gertrude Stein kept a wary distance from one another. Joyce was preoccupied just then with finishing his revolutionary novel *Ulysses*, and all Paris was talking about the trailblazing book—with one exception. Gertrude studiously avoided any mention of Joyce, whom she regarded as her chief rival. Hemingway recalled that "if you brought up Joyce twice, you would not be invited back. It was like mentioning one general favorably to another general. You learned not to do it the first time you made the mistake." After Shakespeare and Company published *Ulysses* in 1922—no respectable publisher would touch the scabrous masterpiece— Gertrude was furious. She and Alice marched over to Sylvia Beach's bookshop to inform her in person that they were transferring their library subscription to the American Library. Beach would have done well to listen to Gertrude. Although she had bankrolled Joyce and published *Ulysses* at a great financial cost to herself, the writer repaid her loyalty by abruptly dropping her for another publisher, leaving Beach heavily in debt for years to come.[20]

But if Joyce was a no-show, a steady stream of other Anglo-American writers came to see Gertrude at the rue de Fleurus. Her clear favorite was F. Scott Fitzgerald. Hemingway first brought him round to meet them in 1925, but Gertrude and Alice had read his career-making first novel, *This Side of Paradise*, when it came out in 1920. Gertrude considered Fitzgerald "the only one of the younger writers who wrote naturally in sentences." Accompanied by his striking but troubled wife, Zelda, Fitzgerald came bearing an auspicious hostess gift—an advance copy of *The Great Gatsby*. Despite his well-deserved reputation as a lush, Fitzgerald was sober on this and subsequent visits to the rue de Fleurus. "There used to be a good deal of talk about his drinking," Alice recalled, "but he was always sober when he came to the house." A born writer, Fitzgerald made effortless what Hemingway made hard: lyrical, flowing sentences that shimmered on the page like the soft jazz played at one of Gatsby's fabulous lawn parties. Even Hemingway, later stridently estranged from Fitzgerald, conceded that his friend's talent "was as natural as the pattern that was made by the dust on a butterfly's wings," although, being Hemingway, he felt constrained to add that Fitzgerald "understood it no more than the butterfly did."[21]

Indirectly, Fitzgerald was responsible for the bitter break between Gertrude and Hemingway. Always a generous supporter of other writers, Fitzgerald had been talking up Hemingway to his legendary editor at Scribner's, Maxwell Perkins. Describing Hemingway as "one of the nicest young men I have ever known" and "the real deal," Fitzgerald told Perkins that Hemingway was unhappy with his current publisher, Boni & Liveright. Fitzgerald thought his young friend was ripe for poaching. To facilitate matters, Hemingway turned on his early benefactor Sherwood Anderson, Boni & Liveright's star author, and dashed off a supposedly humorous burlesque of Anderson's latest novel, *Dark Laughter*. Hemingway's book, puckishly titled *The Torrents of Spring*, dismayed and embarrassed Hadley, who "found the whole idea detestable," and naturally hurt the feelings of Anderson. It thoroughly enraged Gertrude, both by its mean-spirited attack on their mutual, unoffending friend and for its gratuitous potshots at her. Hemingway entitled one segment of the novel "The Passing of a Great Race and the Making and Marring of Americans." In it he mocked Gertrude by having the book's hero, Yogi Johnson, exclaim fatuously, in blatant Stein fashion, "Ah, there was a woman! Where were her experiments in words leading her? What was at the bottom of it? All that in Paris. Ah, Paris! How far it was to Paris now. Paris in the morning. Paris in the evening, Paris at night. Paris in the morning again. Paris at noon, perhaps. Why not?"[22]

Gertrude could take a joke, within limits, but like Hadley and other close associates of Hemingway, she felt that his brutal lampooning of Anderson had crossed the line. Hemingway brushed off her complaints, saying that it was his responsibility as a writer to "call" another writer when he had written, in his opinion, a bad book. The disagreement festered for several years before Gertrude revived it with a vengeance in *The Autobiography of Alice B. Toklas*. One day, she wrote, she and Anderson were talking and the subject of Hemingway came up. Gertrude observed that Hemingway had been a good pupil, but that both she and Anderson were "a little proud and a little ashamed" of their finished product. Still, it was flattering "to have a pupil who does it without understanding it, in other words he takes training and anybody who takes training is a favorite pupil." Not so, said Alice. Hemingway was a "rotten pupil."[23]

Not content to leave it at that, Gertrude hit Hemingway where it was most likely to hurt—in his hypermasculine pride. He was "yellow," she said. He might write a real story someday, "not those he writes but the confessions of the real Ernest Hemingway," but she wasn't holding her breath. "After all, as he himself once murmured, there is the career, the career." Even the famous Hemingway style came in for dismissal. Like the French painter Andre Derain, never one of her favorites, Gertrude said that

Hemingway "looks like a modern and he smells of the museum." Hemingway struck back in kind, noting in an essay on Joan Miro that while it had taken the painter nine full months to finish his masterpiece *The Farm*, "a woman who isn't a woman can usually write her autobiography in a third of that time. Of course, if you have painted 'The Farm,' or if you have written *Ulysses*, and then keep on working very hard afterwards, you do not need an Alice B. Toklas." When his next book, *Green Hills of Africa*, came out a year later, Hemingway sent Gertrude a copy with the inscription "A Bitch Is A Bitch Is A Bitch Is A Bitch. From her pal Ernest Hemingway."[24]

Hemingway's final word on the breakup would come in his beautifully written but factually challenged memoir of his Paris years, *A Moveable Feast*. In it he claimed that he had dropped by Gertrude and Alice's apartment unexpectedly one afternoon and overheard a bitter quarrel taking place upstairs between them. The shocking language, he said, made him slink away embarrassed. While it is entirely possible that Hemingway overheard Gertrude and Alice quarreling—a not infrequent event—his squeamish reaction does not ring true. The tone of the chapter seems to imply that Hemingway was only then discovering that the two women were lesbians, and that it was his first encounter with the exotic species. This belies the fact that he had already written *The Sun Also Rises*, with its various forms of sexual behavior, including the idealized nymphomaniac Lady Brett Ashley, and that his own mother, Grace Hall Hemingway, had lived for several years with a much-younger female companion after his father's suicide. More importantly, it moves back the timing of his break with Gertrude from its real genesis after *The Autobiography of Alice B. Toklas* to a more innocent time in the mid-twenties. In the end, such qualifications didn't matter much anyway. By the time *A Moveable Feast* appeared in 1964, both Ernest Hemingway and Gertrude Stein were dead.

▼ ▼ ▼

TO ESCAPE THE CITY'S HEAT AND THE EQUALLY HUMID LIT-erary infighting, Gertrude and Alice left Paris each summer for the French countryside. Their preferred destination was the department of Ain, which bordered western Switzerland and was the ancestral home of famed eighteenth-century gourmand Jean Anthelme Brillat-Savarin, who had been born in the village of Belley. "Tell me what you eat, and I will tell you what you are," he had promised. Alice took him at his word, and she found his native region, with its well-run farms, colorful gardens, teeming lakes, and trout-filled streams, "too good to be true." Each day was a quest for new, mouth-watering French cuisine.[25]

They made their headquarters at Belley's Hotel Pernollet, a small, family-run establishment on the Avenue d'Alsace-Lorraine with ivy-covered walls and an arched entryway. Madame Pernollet ran the front of the hotel while her husband, a fourth-generation cook, commanded the kitchen. According to Gertrude, Monsieur Pernollet, a veteran of World War I, was the true author of the phrase "*une generation perdue*," which Hemingway would quote at the front of *The Sun Also Rises*, citing Gertrude ("in conversation") as its source. She declined the honor. "It was this hotel keeper who said what it is said I said that the war generation was a lost generation," Gertrude wrote. "He said every man becomes civilized between the ages of eighteen and twenty-five. If he does not go through a civilizing experience at that time in his life he will not be a civilized man. And the men who went to war at eighteen missed the period of civilizing, and they could never be civilized. They were a lost generation."

Monsieur Pernollet spoke from experience, having fought for France in the front lines after staunchly rejecting the army's surprisingly sensible offer to let him serve his country as a cook.[26]

Alice, a strict judge, found the food at the hotel distinctly average, but Madame Pernollet was a gracious hostess who filled their room daily with enormous bouquets of flowers from her private garden. Much better meals were to be had at the nearby hotels Berrard and Bourgeois, the latter of which featured Madame Marie Bourgeois, a two-time award winner as France's top chef. Marie, said Alice, was a genius in the kitchen, and it was from her that she learned "much of what great French cooking was and had been," lessons she would pass along in her own best-selling cookbook two decades later. Thinking perhaps of Gertrude, Alice appended, "Because she [Madame Bourgeois] was a genius in her way, I did not learn from her any one single dish. The inspiration of genius is neither learned nor taught."[27]

In the midst of all the grand dining, Gertrude still managed to get a fair amount of work done. In the summer of 1927 she and Alice proofed and edited the entire 925-page edition of *The Making of Americans*. The task was tedious; the Dijon printing house they had selected, Maurice Darantiere, made hundreds of errors, even dropping whole lines of text. Given the intense repetition of the novel, such errors were understandable, but it all made for maddeningly slow editing. "What a summer it was," Alice shuddered. "All day we struggled with the errors of French compositors." In the *Autobiography*, Gertrude claimed that Alice had broken her glasses in the process, forcing Gertrude to finish the job alone. "Never," Alice scrawled angrily in red on the book's manuscript—one of the few tangible disagreements with Gertrude that she let stand on the permanent record.[28]

Other work was more pleasant. Gertrude's sunny stream-of-consciousness novel *Lucy Church Amiably* was largely written out-of-doors to the accompaniment of Belley's many creeks and waterfalls, while Alice sat nearby, contentedly working on her needlepoint. The full title of the book was a mouthful: *A Novel of Romantic Beauty and Nature and Which Looks Like An Engraving Lucy Church Amiably*. A typical passage was appropriately sylvan: "Very little daisies and very little bluettes and an artificial bird and a very white anemone which is allowed and then after it is very well placed by an unexpected invitation to carry a basket by an unexpected invitation to carry a basket back and forth back and forth and a river there is this difference between a river here and a river there." It all sounded a bit like James Joyce's equally impenetrable *Finnegans Wake*, minus the Norwegian. Literary scholar Donald Sutherland has called it Gertrude's most important novel, "a vital rediscovery of the pastoral, a reliving of the inside and outside realities that occasioned the first pastorals." His opinion seems to be in the minority, although the novel is undeniably pastoral.[29]

▼ ▼ ▼

FROM THE BEGINNING OF THEIR TIME IN BELLEY, GERTRUDE and Alice were on the lookout for a place of their own. One afternoon in the spring of 1928 they were out driving when they came upon a farmhouse perched on a steep hillside just outside of town. Gertrude was adamant. "I will drive you up there," she told Alice, "and you can go and tell them that we will take their house." Alice, as usual, showed more restraint. "But it may not be for rent," she said. "The curtains are floating out the window," said Gertrude, as if that somehow proved her point. All it proved, said Alice, was that "someone is living there." She was right. The two-story manor was indeed occupied by a French army officer, Gabriel Putz, and his family, but not for long. Depending on which version one believes—Gertrude and

Alice wrote slightly different accounts about the circumstances surrounding the acquisition of their famous summer home—they either did or did not pull strings with friends in the French war department to have Putz promoted and transferred to Morocco, where he either was or was not captured by the enemy and either did or did not die. (He did not.) Probably, they simply waited for his lease to run out, which was what a neighboring farmer had recommended they do in the first place. At any rate, they moved into their dream home later that spring. They would summer there, without fail, for the next fifteen years.[30]

While Alice took charge of the gardens, Gertrude worked at her writing. Her daily routine involved rising late, eating the breakfast Alice had prepared, playing with their newly acquired white poodle, Basket (named by Alice, who said he looked so elegant that "he should carry a basket of flowers in his mouth"), and wandering the grounds in search of nuts and mushrooms. At some point, the muse would strike and Gertrude would sit down to write—once, memorably, in the middle of a pasture—but never for longer than a half hour at a time. "I have never been able to write much more than a half hour a day," she admitted. "If you write a half hour a day it makes a lot of writing year by year. To be sure all day and every day you are waiting around to write that half hour a day." Afternoons were reserved for driving around the countryside, eating at choice local restaurants and dropping off Alice's extra vegetables with favored neighbors.[31]

A steady procession of visitors came to Bilignin. One of the most colorful was the painter Francis Rose, an independently wealthy young Scotsman who traveled about with his pet Chihuahua, Squeak, in his front pocket and a string of sexual conquests in his back. Rose smoked opium, wallpapered his Paris apartment in black, and painted at lightning speed, once completing eleven paintings in eight days. Picasso, for one, did not think much of Rose as an artist. After being shown a Rose canvas that Gertrude had purchased for 300 francs, he marveled, "For that price one can get something quite good." But Gertrude liked Rose, partly because, she rationalized, "anybody called Francis is elegant unbalanced and intelligent and certain to be right not about everything but about themselves." She eventually purchased 130 of his paintings, hanging them, much to his delight, alongside her Picassos. Rose floated in and out of their lives for years, even though they questioned his choice in men. "There is nothing the matter with him but his character," Alice lamented after Rose had been beaten up yet again by one of his violent lovers.[32]

Another louche young protégé was the fledgling writer Paul Bowles, whom they called Freddy because Gertrude felt that Paul was too romantic a name for the insouciant Bowles, who went around town in shorts and sneakers and "didn't have one ounce of romanticism in [him]." Before turning to writing, Bowles had studied music with Aaron Copland in New York and Berlin, and Copland brought him to Bilignin to meet Gertrude in the summer of 1931. She liked Bowles but found him lacking industry. "If you do not work now when you are twenty, nobody will love you when you are thirty," she warned. She made him eat whatever was put in front him—once a baked gray eel that not even Alice could make appetizing—and bathe each morning with hot water. Bowles's primary role during his visit was to exercise Basket after the dog's daily vinegar bath. Wearing a pair of thick lederhosen to protect the tender backs of his legs while Basket chased him across the yard, Bowles would tear off with Basket in hot pursuit as Gertrude called down from her second-story window, "Faster, Freddy, faster!"[33]

Bowles would survive his literary boot camp at Bilignin and move to Tangier, Morocco, which Alice had suggested was a more suitable place for his anarchic nature. (As with Hemingway and Pamplona, she seemed particularly adept at pairing young writers with congenial locations.) A notorious hive of outlaws, known for smuggling, spying, armed robbery, kidnapping, and murder, Tangier attracted artists and criminals in equal measure. Bowles and his wife, Jane, would become permanent fixtures in the city's drug-taking claque of English and American expatriates, which in time would include the Beat legends William Burroughs, Jack Kerouac, and Allen Ginsberg and, a bit later, the Rolling Stones. His 1938 novel about life in Tangier, *The Sheltering Sky*, has become an accepted literary classic.

Another talented young visitor, one who would prove pivotal to Gertrude's reputation in America, was composer Virgil Thomson. A native of Kansas City and a graduate of Harvard, Thomson had come to Europe in 1926, one year too late to meet his recently deceased musical idol, Erik Satie. Gertrude and Alice had known Satie through Pablo Picasso, with whom he had collaborated on a well-received ballet, *Parade*, a few years earlier. Brought to 27 rue de Fleurus by fellow composer George Antheil, Thomson got off to a rocky start with Gertrude, borrowing and promptly losing her autographed copy of Robert Coates's surrealistic novel *The Eater of Darkness*. He made amends by setting Gertrude's poem "Susie Asado" to music and leaving a copy of the score on her doorstep as a peace offering. It was an early inkling of the close but often fractious relationship between Thomson and Gertrude. "Alice Toklas did not on first view care for me," Thomson recalled. "But Gertrude and I got on like Harvard men."[34]

During a 1927 visit to Bilignin, Thomson suggested that he and Gertrude collaborate on an opera. He would compose the music and she would write the libretto. Given Gertrude's long-standing dislike of music—she considered it an art form for adolescents—the idea was not at first blush a natural one. Nor could they agree on a subject. Thomson envisioned something to do with pairs: "In letters, for instance, there were Joyce and Stein, in painting, Picasso and Braque, in religion Protestants and Catholics." (In his innocence Thomson overlooked the fact that none of his examples actually got along.) Gertrude countered with one of her recent enthusiasms—George Washington—but the composer disliked eighteenth-century costume dramas, which he said made everybody look alike. Eventually, though neither of them was particularly religious, they compromised on an opera about the lives of saints. The result was *Four Saints in Three Acts*, a joint production that would cause a serious rift between the collaborators but that would eventually make it to Broadway and help further both of their names in America.[35]

In true Stein fashion, the title was willfully misleading. The finished product actually included about fifty saints, give or take a couple, presented in four or five acts. The lead characters were based on real historical figures from the sixteenth century: the mystical seer of visions Saint Teresa of Avila and the former mercenary turned Jesuit priest Saint Ignatius of Loyola. Others included the playfully named Saint Settlement, Saint Plan, Saint Cardinal, Saint Answers, Saint Plot, Saint Martyr, Saint Two, Saint Ten, and One Saint. Like most of Gertrude's extreme literary experiments, there was a good deal more sound than sense. Stage directions included "Many saints seen," "Some and some," "This is a scene where this is seen," "Saint Therese in time," "Would it do if there was a Scene II," "Usefully," "Closely," "Many saints," "Could Four Acts be Three, "When," "Alive," "Saint Fernande singing soulfully," "Saint Therese deliberately," and "Last Act. Which is a fact." The most famous passage occurred in act 3, scene 2: "Pigeons on the grass alas," which was, in context, more straightforward than most of the play's other business. There was no plot.[36]

Thomson finished scoring *Four Saints in Three Acts* in early February 1928, but it would languish unproduced for six more years. Gertrude tried to find outside funding for the work, approaching various wealthy friends for contributions. Chicago heiress Emily Chadbourne Crane chipped in $1,000 for the project, and Monaco-based hostess Elsa Maxwell promised to arrange a production in Monte Carlo in the spring of 1929. But Maxwell ultimately reneged on her promise, and a private run-through of the opera by Thomson for Gertrude's old Baltimore friends Etta and Claribel Cone produced "no great cash result." In the aftermath of their funding problems, Gertrude and Thomson had a falling out over the planned publication of a volume of his music that was to include several other pieces based on Gertrude's work. When Thomson sent her an invitation to one of his Paris concerts in early 1931, he got back a terse card from the rue de Fleurus. "Miss Stein," it read, "declines further acquaintance with Mr. Thomson." There matters would stand for the next three years.[37]

▼ ▼ ▼

TIRED OF WAITING FRUITLESSLY FOR SOMEONE ELSE TO REC-ognize Gertrude's greatness, Alice decided to do it herself. "All that I knew about what I would have to do was that I would have to get the book printed and then to get it distributed, that is sold," she said, sounding very much like Gertrude. She would start her own publishing house, dedicated exclusively to one client. "Call it Plain Edition," Gertrude joked, and so Alice did. To finance the venture, they regretfully sold their 1905 Picasso painting *Woman with a Fan*, modeled by their old friend Fernande Olivier, to American collector Marie Harriman. With the proceeds from the sale they funded the printing and distribution of five books between 1931 and 1933. *Lucy Church Amiably* was the first, followed by a book of essays, *How to Write*; a poem sequence with the pretty wonderful title (supplied by Alice) *Before the Flowers of Friendship Faded Friendship Faded*; a collection of dramatic pieces, *Operas and Plays*; and a volume of impressionistic word portraits, *Matisse Picasso and Gertrude Stein*. The press runs, between one hundred and one thousand copies, were not designed to make them rich, but Gertrude was thrilled to see copies of her works displayed in the windows of Paris bookstores, which was reward enough, perhaps, for both women.[38]

Then, almost overnight, everything changed. *The Autobiography of Alice B. Toklas*, coming in the midst of their self-publishing venture, would fundamentally alter their lives and bring them far greater rewards—both personal and financial—than they could have imagined. It happened quickly in the autumn of 1932. Alice gardened, and Gertrude wrote. Sometimes Gertrude interrupted the gardening to compare memories of a specific person or event. Invariably, when there were discrepancies, Alice's version won out. "Who is winning," Gertrude wrote in another context, "why the answer of course is she is." As Virgil Thomson observed, "Every story that ever came into the house eventually got told in Alice's way." Perhaps, as much as anything, that explained the book's title.[39]

Returning to Paris for the winter in late 1932, Gertrude contacted her agent, William A. Bradley, a former doughboy who had married a Belgian girl and stayed on in Europe after the war, to tell him about the new book. "Of course I shall be delighted to see Miss Toklas' Autobiography," Bradley wrote, "and hope you will send it to me as soon as it is completely typed." Wild horses couldn't keep him from reading it, he said. Once he had read it, Bradley swiftly sold the *Autobiography* to Harcourt, Brace in New York and arranged for the book to appear in four monthly installments of the *Atlantic Monthly*, beginning the next spring. The prickly editor of *Atlantic Monthly*, Ellery Sedgwick, a man who in the past had proved notably resistant to Gertrude's charms, now sang her praises. "There has been a lot of pother about this book of yours," he wrote a bit fussily, "but what a delightful book it is, and how glad I am to publish four installments of it! During our long correspondence, I think you felt my constant hope that the time would come when the real Miss Stein would pierce the smoke-screen with which she has always so mischievously surrounded herself. Hail Gertrude Stein about to arrive."[40]

To a large extent, the book sold itself. If few Americans had read much of Gertrude's writings, they had been seeing her face in magazines and newspapers for two decades. Throughout the twenties, Gertrude was most often cited in connection to James Joyce, whose novel *Ulysses* was often linked with Gertrude's work—unfairly to them both—as an example of equally impenetrable prose. She was mentioned often enough that in January 1923 she was one of 112 writers, politicians, and celebrities included in a two-page cartoon spread in *Life* magazine captioned "Life's Birthday Party." Later that same year a rather unflattering illustration of a much-too-heavy Gertrude was used to illustrate poet Djuna Barnes's salute to Gertrude as "the spiritual mother of all the modernists" in the *New York Tribune*'s influential Sunday book review section. By the time Ernest Hemingway name-checked Gertrude on the title page of *The Sun Also Rises* in 1926, he could do so with full confidence that readers would know exactly whom he was talking about.[41]

▼ ▼ ▼

ALL THAT WINTER THE COUPLE DINED OUT ON THE BOOK'S prepublication buzz. "The life we were leading was not the same we had been leading," Gertrude would recall. "An awful lot happens in a year." For one thing, they discovered that they had become social lions. Instead of entertaining guests at the rue de Fleurus, they now were going to other people's parties. It was a marked change from their usual mode of socializing, and Gertrude admitted that "I rather liked doing what I had never done before, going everywhere." She was discovering, in late middle age, the joys of dining out at someone else's expense— hardly the first time that a newly successful writer had entered the roundelay of the rich and famous. "We did not yet use a tiny engagement book and look at it in a nearsighted way the way all the young men used to do as soon as they were successful," Gertrude reported, "but we might have. Being successful is all the same and we liked it."[42]

An unforeseen consequence of completing the *Autobiography* was a bad case of writer's block for Gertrude, combined with a dizzying loss of self-identity. Success, she said, was like "a green spider coming to you at sunset, a spider at night makes everything bright a spider in the morning is a warning." Always the most prolific of writers, she suddenly found that the words would not come. "I had written and was writing nothing," she recalled. "Nothing needed any word and there was no word inside me that could not be spoken and so there was no word inside me." In a short piece for *Vanity Fair*, Gertrude described the disorienting effects of sudden fame. "What happened to me was this," she wrote. "When the success began and it was a success I got lost completely lost. I did not know myself, I lost my personality." She took long walks through the Paris streets with Basket, attempting to reassure herself that, as she often said, "I am I because my little dog knows me." Basket did know her—dogs never forget—but she was not so sure she knew herself. "The minute you or anybody else knows what you are you are not it," Gertrude said, "you are what you or anybody else knows you are and as everything in living is made up of finding out what you are in it is extraordinarily difficult really."[43]

Gradually Gertrude recovered; her inherent sense of self was strong. With the advance money from Harcourt, Brace she bought a new eight-cylinder Ford and splurged on a fancy coat and two studded dog collars for Basket. "I had never made any money before in my life and I was most excited," she confessed. "It is funny about money. If you have earned money it is not the same thing as if you have not earned money. And now the time had come that I was beginning to earn some." She made the arguable observation that the concept of money was what really separated men from animals, since "most of the things men feel animals feel and vice versa, but animals do not know about money, money is purely a human conception and that is very important to know very very important." Basket reserved comment.[44]

The best way to get more money, Bradley argued, was for Gertrude to go on a speaking tour of America. He brought an experienced booking agent to meet with Gertrude at the rue de Fleurus. It was not a good fit. The man was a humorless publisher of religious books and school texts who in his spare time pursued and promoted European celebrities. Trebly named Princess Elizabeth Charlotte Lucy Bibesco, daughter of former British prime minister Herbert Henry Asquith, was his most recent client. The princess, a writer of middling novels, traveled in exalted circles; the dowager Queen Alexandra and George Bernard Shaw were among the guests at her 1921 wedding to a Romanian prince at Westminster Abbey, and Marcel Proust was an intimate friend in his later years. Bradley gamely told the promoter that Gertrude's upcoming autobiography would make her equally popular. "Interesting, if true," the man replied.

If all lecture agents were like that, Gertrude told Bradley after the man had left, she would never go on tour in America. "I told him not to bother." In due time she would revise her decision.[45]

The first unofficial review of the *Autobiography* came in the form of a negative reaction from Olga Koklova, Pablo Picasso's Russian ballerina wife, whom Gertrude and Alice had never liked. As soon as they returned to Paris, Gertrude telephoned Picasso and told him about the book. He brought Olga with him to the rue de Fleurus for a private reading. Aside from correcting a couple minor errors concerning the interior of his studio, Picasso liked the book, at least the parts that were about him, which was all he cared about anyway. Olga was another matter. Hearing the name Fernande Olivier one time too often, she announced unpersuasively that she "didn't know that woman" and flounced off, leaving her husband sitting alone on Gertrude's sofa. He motioned for her to continue reading, but Gertrude motioned for him to go after his wife. "Oh," said Picasso. "Oh," said Gertrude. It was the last they would see of the painter until he returned two years later, sans Olga, from whom he had since separated. "When I saw him again I said how did you ever make the decision and keep it of leaving your wife," Gertrude recalled. "I suppose he said when a thing is where there is no life left then you either die or go on living, well he said that is what happened to me." Picasso was nothing if not lively.[46]

Neither Gertrude nor Alice was sorry to see Olga go, but in consequence Gertrude found herself having to talk Picasso out of his impulsive decision to quit painting and become a poet. "What kind of poetry is it I said, why just poetry he said you know poetry like everybody writes. Oh I said." Very gently, for her, Gertrude tried to explain to Picasso the difference between the work of the writer and the work of the painter. "Certain descriptions that you make have the same quality as your painting," she told him. "Oh yes said Picasso." She left it at that. Thankfully, in the end he returned to his brushes, and the world lost a mediocre poet but regained a great painter. It was one of Gertrude's least heralded contributions to modern art.[47]

THREE

You'd Better Come Over

W HILE WAITING FOR THE *Autobiography* TO COME OUT in America, Gertrude and Alice returned to Bilignin in the spring of 1933. The usual run of visitors came and went. One of the most welcome was academician Bernard Faÿ, who had just translated *The Making of Americans* into French and was hoping to do the same for *The Autobiography of Alice B. Toklas.* Faÿ, the scion of a prominent, conservative Catholic family, was another of the talented young gay men who tended to cluster around Gertrude and Alice. An early friend and supporter of Virgil Thomson, Faÿ was a fan of all things American. He had written biographies of Benjamin Franklin and George Washington, done two years of postgraduate studies at Harvard, and made more than twenty visits to the United States in the past few years. He doted on Gertrude, whom he called "our lady" as though she were one of his Catholic saints, and was particularly insightful about her relationship with Alice. "Between the two women," Fay wrote, "one seemingly stronger and the other more frail, one affirming her genius and the other venerating it, one speaking and the other listening, only a blind man could ignore that the most vigorous one was Alice, and that Gertrude, for her behavior as much as for her work and publications, leaned on her, used her and followed her advice." For Gertrude, her relationship with Faÿ would remain one of "the four permanent friendships" of her life, and it would have life-or-death ramifications for her and Alice a few years hence.[1]

Monthly excerpts of the *Autobiography* began appearing in

Atlantic Monthly in May 1933. They were a revelation to American readers who only knew Gertrude as an expatriate bohemian and a writer of obscure experimental works. Long lines formed at corner bookstands in New York City on the day the next issue of the magazine was scheduled to appear. Her name was suddenly on everyone's lips—"like Greta Garbo," gushed Carl Van Vechten. In August, the book came out in hardback, selling all fifty-four hundred copies in advance. The Man Ray photograph on the book's cover perfectly captured the relationship between Gertrude and Alice. The photograph, actually taken a decade earlier, showed a slender, erect Alice standing in the doorway at 27 rue de Fleurus, her dark helmet of bangs and girlish shift backlit in a luminous rectangle of light. She was looking into the room but had not crossed the threshold. Gertrude, facing away from the camera, sat at her writing desk, pen in hand, solid and relaxed. The two women were looking at each other. There were paintings on the wall. Time, always a bugaboo for Gertrude, stood still.[2]

Much to the surprise of Alice, who initially thought that the book was not sentimental enough to succeed, the *Autobiography* quickly captured the imagination of the American reading public—at least those who could afford to pay $3.50 for a copy. It was the midway point in the Depression, and millions of people were out of work. In every city and town there were soup kitchens, bread lines, five-cent apples peddled by former bank presidents, and "forgotten men" shivering over Sterno fires in squalid cardboard Hoovervilles. Newly elected president Franklin D. Roosevelt, having narrowly survived an assassination attempt in Miami that winter, had begun the ambitious series of federal programs known as the New Deal, designed to lift the people out of the morass of poverty and hopelessness created by reckless Wall Street bankers and speculators. It would take time.

Gertrude, never much of a fan of FDR or his policies, had other things on her mind just then. With the help of news clippings supplied by friends such as Carl Van Vechten and Sherwood Anderson, she was following the rise of the *Autobiography* to best-seller status and her unlikely apotheosis as a newly minted culture hero. Cover stories on Gertrude appeared in *Time* magazine, the *Saturday Review of Literature*, and the *New York Herald Tribune Books*. The *Time* piece, written by James Agee for the September 11, 1933, issue, was not an unalloyed rave. Agee, a native Tennessean and recent Harvard graduate, would later win fame for the book *Let Us Now Praise Famous Men*, a documentary look at the hardscrabble life of sharecroppers produced in conjunction with photographer Walker Evans. Agee was not a Stein fan. In his piece he managed to be simultaneously sexist, ageist, sizeist, and anti-Semitic. He pictured Gertrude unflatteringly as a mountainous presence: "Like a huge squat mountain on a distant border of the literary kingdom...she has loomed from afar over the hinterland of letters, a sphinxlike, monolithic mass. Twenty years she has squatted there; eyes accustomed to the landscape are beginning to recognize something portentous in her massive outline." Calling her "Mountain Stein," Agee reviewed her looks rather than her work: "Never a beauty, she is now massive, middle-aged, 59, would strongly resemble a fat Jewish hausfrau were it not for her close-cropped head." It called to mind Ernest Hemingway's more elegantly phrased gibe that Gertrude "got to look like a Roman emperor and that was fine if you liked your women to look like Roman emperors." At least Hemingway had a reason for his grudge.[3]

In the drumbeat of favorable publicity, the *Time* article was an exception. Most pieces took a more welcoming, if occasionally bemused, tone toward Gertrude and her work. As biographer Lucy Daniel has noted, "Stein got in on the rising tide of celebrity culture, her talents as a raconteuse were made available to all the world; you no longer had to visit her salon to be party to the bitchy, clever, piquant wit." James Agee notwithstanding, Gertrude's new book was a runaway success. "Remarks are not literature," she had famously told Hemingway, but *The Autobiography of Alice B. Toklas* came close. For the price of a book, one could revisit the glories of the Lost Generation, swap bon mots with Gertrude at 27 rue de Fleurus, stroll with Alice in the Luxembourg Gardens, teach Hemingway how to write and Picasso how to paint. One could snub Ezra Pound, argue with William Carlos Williams, ignore James Joyce, make T. S. Eliot squirm, and pour Marie Laurencin into bed after an all-night bohemian birthday party. It was a good deal cheaper than the cost of a transatlantic steamship ticket.[4]

Positive reviews streamed in from all sides. Edmund Wilson, who not long ago had been confessing proudly that he could not bring himself to finish *The Making of Americans*, now praised the *Autobiography* in the *New Republic* for "its wisdom, its distinction and its charm." Readers of modern literature and collectors of modern art, he said, were beginning to realize how much they owed her. William Troy, in the *Nation*, compared Gertrude in one sweeping breath to Henry James, Edgar Allan Poe, Nathaniel Hawthorne, and Herman Melville—a virtual patriarchy of the American literary tradition. "Among books of literary reminiscences," he wrote, "Miss Stein's is one of the richest, wittiest and most irreverent ever written."[5]

Not everyone was so delighted. Influential critic Clifton Fadiman, in the *New Yorker*, chided Gertrude for being an intellectual snob. "She is the Radcliffe aesthetic bluestocking," he wrote, "very arty, very snobbish, totally sheltered from life with a dilettante passion for the 'advanced,' pathetically reminiscent of the most artificial gestures of the nineties." The *Autobiogra-*

phy, groused Fadiman, was "a high-water mark in the delicate art of self-appreciation." The *New York Herald Tribune*'s Isabel Paterson similarly judged the book "a wonderful self-portrait of a perfect egotist. If a baby could write a book it would resemble 'The Autobiography of Alice B. Toklas.'" Unfavorable reaction also came from those stung by Gertrude's sharp tongue. A colloquy of dissenting voices assembled in the pages of *transition* magazine to denounce the book's alleged errors of fact, fancy, and opinion. Dada creator Tristan Tzara, himself barely mentioned in the *Autobiography*, took revenge for being called a "not very exciting cousin." The book, he said, was "a clinical case of megalomania," and Gertrude and Alice were "two maiden ladies greedy for fame and publicity" who had produced "a considerable display of sordid anecdotes designed to make us believe that Miss Gertrude Stein is in reality a genius." It was hard to tell whether Tzara was angrier about being mentioned in the *Autobiography* or about not being mentioned more frequently.[6]

Other victims were more justified in their complaints. Henri Matisse was entirely within his rights, from both a factual and a matrimonial standpoint, in complaining about the book's low-blow description of his wife as a horse. He somewhat undercut his point by describing Madame Matisse in similarly equine terms as "a very lovely Toulousaine, erect, with a good carriage and the possessor of beautiful dark hair that grew charmingly, especially at the nape of her neck." Fellow painter Georges Braque challenged Gertrude's account of the Paris art world in the twenties. Gertrude, no admirer of Braque, had pictured him as a mere camp follower of Picasso rather than the Spaniard's closest colleague and virtual cocreator of cubism. "Braque was a man who had the gift of singing and like all who sing he could mistake what he sang as being something that he said but it is not the same thing," she wrote. "When I say he sang I mean he sang in paint, I do not believe he sang otherwise but he might have, he had the voice and the looks of a great baritone." Braque fired back, saying of Gertrude that "for one who poses as an authority on the epoch, it is safe to say that she never went beyond the stage of the tourist. We in Paris always heard that Miss Stein was a writer, but we had our doubts. Now that we have seen her book, nous sommes fixes."[7]

The American husband and wife team behind *transition*, Eugene and Maria Jolas, were the ringleaders of the Gertrude Stein roast. Having published *Tender Buttons* and *Four Saints* in their entirety, along with Gertrude's ineffable "As a Wife Has a Cow A Love Story," they felt an understandable lack of appreciation at Gertrude's dismissal of their magazine as "bulky." They had committed the unpardonable sin, in her eyes, of publishing parts of James Joyce's bewildering *Finnegans Wake*. Now they struck back. The *Autobiography*, said Maria Jolas, was "final capitulation to a Barnumesque publicity," striking in its ingratitude. "What we should have foreseen however, was that she would eventually tolerate no relationship that did not bring with it adulation. When the moment came to play the mad queen in public, our heads had to come off with the others, despite very real service we had rendered her." Her husband piled on. "There is a unanimity of opinion that she had no understanding of what really was happening around her, that the mutation of ideas beneath the surface of the more obvious contacts and clashes of personalities during that period escaped her entirely," Eugene Jolas wrote. "*The Autobiography of Alice B. Toklas* in its hollow, tinsel bohemianism and egocentric deformations, may very well become one day the symbol of the decadence that hovers over contemporary literature."[8]

With the possible exception of Hemingway, whose objections to the *Autobiography* have already been entered into the record, the person most justified in resenting his treatment—or non-treatment—in the book was Leo Stein. Largely absent from the narrative of Gertrude's and Alice's early days in Paris, and never once referred to by name, Leo had been effectively disappeared from Gertrude's history. He declined to respond publicly, but in private he railed about his mistreatment to anyone who would listen. "God what a liar she is," he wrote to his friend Mabel Weeks following the book's publication. "Practically everything that she says of our activities before 1911 is false both in fact and implication. I doubt whether there is a single comment or general observation in the book that is not stupid." And in a letter to New York socialite Ettie Stettheimer, whose sister Florine was designing the costumes for *Four Saints in Three Acts*, Leo complained, "Nothing of the pre-war period is accurately true, very little of the whole is accurately true, and very little of it is even approximately true." The bottom line, he said, was that Gertrude was "basically stupid and I'm basically intelligent." It was a position Leo would hold unshakably to the end of his life.[9]

▼ ▼ ▼

IN THE BLIZZARD OF BOOK REVIEWS, GERTRUDE RECEIVED some welcome if unexpected news from Virgil Thomson. After seeing their opera languish for years in theatrical purdah, he had managed at last to secure backers for a gala production of *Four Saints in Three Acts*. A. Everett Austin Jr., director of the Wadsworth Atheneum in Hartford, Connecticut, offered to host a production of the opera in the museum's newly completed auditorium that winter. Even better, a group of Austin's friends and backers, going by the puckishly provocative name the Friends and Enemies of Modern Music, agreed to fund the production to the tune of $10,000. Through Gertrude's agent Thomson offered to split the proceeds 50/50. Gertrude accepted and then held firm when Thomson had second thoughts and wanted to renegotiate their arrangement. "My dear Virgil," she wrote, "I wish to keep to the original terms of our agreement, half share of the profits. It is quite true that upon you falls all the burden of seeing the production through, but on the other hand, the commercial value of my name is very considerable and therefore we will keep it 50–50."[10]

As for Thomson's unorthodox ideas for casting the opera, Gertrude was willing to go along with his wishes. Influenced by the Harlem Renaissance, Thomson wanted to use an all-black cast in the play. "Negro singers," he told an interviewer for the *New York World-Telegram*, "have the most perfect and beautiful diction. I have never heard a white singer with the perfect singer diction and sense of rhythm of a Negro." Rehearsals began in the basement of St. Philip's Church on 134th Street in Harlem, the oldest black-designed church in the city, with the young actor-playwright John Houseman coming on board as the opera's director. It was the beginning of a long and storied career for Houseman, who would go on to join Orson Welles's influential Mercury Theatre and help produce the notorious *War of the Worlds* radio broadcast that would send all of America into a panic on Halloween Eve 1938 with its fake-news report of an alien invasion from Mars. Forty years later, Houseman would win an Academy Award as best supporting actor for the only slightly less terrifying law school drama *The Paper Chase*.[11]

Four Saints in Three Acts sneak-premiered at the Wadsworth Atheneum on February 8, 1934, in conjunction with the opening of a major Picasso retrospective at the museum. Despite icy streets and an inconveniently timed taxi strike, a large crowd turned out, helped appreciably by a private rail line run down from New York City by the New Haven Railroad. Celebrity architect Buckminster Fuller was there, accompanied by society mavens Clare Booth and Dorothy Hale. So too was Carl Van Vechten, in attendance as Gertrude's self-appointed eyes and ears. The opera, he reported back ecstatically, was "a knockout and a wow. I haven't seen a crowd more excited since Sacre du Printemps." In the casual if unintended racism of the time, he allowed that "the Negroes are divine, like El Grecos, more Spanish, more Saints, more opera singers in the dignity and simplicity and extraordinary plastic line than any white singers could ever be. And they enunciated the text so clearly you could understand every word." Insurance agent turned poet Wallace Stevens, a Hartford resident, also attended, reporting to a friend that the opera was "an elaborate bit of perversity in every respect: text, setting, and choreography," but also "a delicate and joyous work all around."[12]

Another opening-night attendee was William Garland Rogers, the well-remembered Kiddie from World War I. Rogers, now a full-grown reporter on the Springfield, Massachusetts, *Union*, had recently renewed his acquaintance in an out-of-the-blue letter to Gertrude after the *Autobiography* came out. "For perhaps 10 years I have been trying to write a letter to you," he wrote, "and I should probably not be doing it now if you had not, in The Autobiography, wondered how many of the soldiers you met in Southern France knew today who you are." In his review for the *Union* on opening night, Rogers struck a professionally nuanced note: "A perfumed air of chi-chi pervaded the opening, which had been preceded by the arrival of carloads of the fashionable from New York and festive doings in the best house in the Connecticut Valley. A ticket to the opera was, as well, a ticket to the event of the season."[13]

It was definitely an event. Beginning with a low rumble of drums, the red velvet curtain opened on a purple-clad Beatrice Robinson-Wayne, playing Saint Therese, intoning the show's first lines: "To know to know to love her so. / Four saints prepare for saints. / It makes it well fish. / Four saints it makes it well fish." The set, designed by Florine Stettheimer, was a feast for the eyes, featuring a blue cellophane sky, pink taffeta palm trees, a sea wall built of shells, a real white donkey (later dropped for hygiene purposes), a white and gold gauze desert tent, and black chiffon costumes highlighted with black ostrich plumes. One theatergoer called it "a sort of Scraft's candy-box version of the Baroque." The showstopper of the evening was Edward Matthews's turn as Saint Ignatius in act 3. Backed by a line of dipping chorus boys, he sang, "Pigeons on the grass alas. / Pigeons on the grass alas. / Short longer grass short longer longer shorter yellow grass. / Pigeons large pigeons on the shorter longer yellow grass alas." The line "pigeons on the grass alas" would become one of Gertrude's most recognized quotes, nearly equal to "rose is a rose is a rose is a rose" and having the added advantage of usually being quoted more correctly.[14]

After a successful run of six performances in Hartford, *Four Saints in Three Acts* moved to the 44th Street Theatre in New York City, where it had its Broadway debut on February 20. Among those attending were the heiress Mrs. William D. Rockefeller, fashion photographer Cecil Beaton, composers George and Ira Gershwin, and Algonquin Round Table wit Dorothy Parker, whose own production, *After Such Pleasures*, had just opened up the street at the Bijou Theatre. As might be expected, the New York critics were more demanding. "Pigeons on the grass, alas, was pigeon English," one noted, dismissing the show as "cheap vaudeville humor." "I should like to discourse easily and familiarly on the plot of Stein's piece," Kenneth Burke wrote in the *Nation*, "but I must admit that I cannot. The words show evidence of a private playfulness which makes them more difficult to fathom than if they were written under gas." An article in a medical journal put forth the notion—diagnosis at long distance—that Gertrude was a victim of echolalia, a form of speech disorder in which the sufferer compulsively repeats words, phrases, and sentences. Music critic Lawrence Gilman sourly opined that a PhD thesis or a wine list would have made just as good a libretto, and newspaper columnist Franklin P. Adams expressed his considered opinion that Gertrude's libretto, if not the entire opera itself, was "spinach."[15]

Other reviews were more positive. Paul Bowles reported to Gertrude that the smart young artists in New York City were aligning against the show, mostly in protest to Thomson "having had the audacity to give Gertrude Stein in modern dress." But, said Bowles, crowds of regular people were walking up and down Broadway, sitting in automats and talking excitedly about the opera while they worried about how to get tickets for it. *Autobiography* publisher Alfred Harcourt told Gertrude that on the night he saw the play, "Toscanini was in the orchestra chair behind me. He seemed completely absorbed in the performance and applauded vigorously." And Stark Young, drama critic for the *New Republic*, raved, "I wish I knew some way to make sure of being taken seriously when I say that 'Four Saints in Three Acts' is as essential theatre the most important event of our season. What a joke on the hard-working, hard-punching, expensive and self-evident aspect of the average musical show this whole event is! It is important because it is theatre and flies off the ground. It creates instead of talking about." The stolidly gray *New York Times* was less impressed. The newspaper's music critic, Olin Downes, complained that "a spirit of inspired madness animates the whole piece. The trail of foppishness and pose and pseudo-intellectuality is all over it. Every snob and poseur in town swelled the gathering." On balance, said Downes, the opera was "nine-tenths farce."[16]

Van Vechten snapped a photo of the theater's marquee showing Gertrude's name up in lights (and satisfyingly above Virgil Thomson's). As further proof of her cultural ascendancy, he took a second photo of a show window at Gimbels department store advertising "4 Suits in 2 Acts." Not to be outdone, Macy's would advertise its new fall line as "Four Suits in Three Acts." Bergdorf Goodman christened a new tea gown "Saint" in honor of the production and advertised "our newest bouquet bateau," a hat with a rose on the brim, with a drawing of a model surrounded by the circular phrase, "a rose is a pose is a rose is a pose." Another store, Wanamaker's, offered a line of red, white, and silver mandarin jackets it dubbed "4 Saints in Cellophane," in the ungodly combination of rayon and cellophane. A print ad for RCA Victor radios declared, "With a bow to Gertrude Stein, an RCA Victor…is an RCA Victor…is an RCA Victor."[17]

Gertrude, for her part, would not allow herself to believe entirely in the opera's success. "I rarely believe in anything," she said, "because at the time of believing I am not really there to believe." Still, her resistance was weakening. Before leaving for Bilignin for the summer, she granted a rare interview to *New York Times Magazine* contributor Lansing Warren, who happily reassured readers that Alice Toklas was indeed "a very real and efficient personality despite the doubts that were expressed as to her existence when the autobiography appeared." Also real was Basket the dog, who greeted the reporter with "rather friendly hostility." Gertrude made allowances. "Basket is a great watchdog when he thinks about it," she said. "But he doesn't always remember and so he has to be all the more demonstrative when he does." She was writing a new book, she told Warren, to be titled *Four in America*, about George Washington, Wilbur Wright, Ulysses S. Grant, and Henry James. In it, she said, she was depicting Grant as a religious leader and James as a general, which would have been news, no doubt, to them both.[18]

▼ ▼ ▼

SAFELY REMOVED FROM THE LONG-RANGE COMMOTION, ALICE placidly tended her gardens. By then she had learned the hard way to follow the folk wisdom of her French neighbors, who advised her never to plant on new or full moons, never to plant on Good Friday, never to transplant parsley, and always to use pig manure on her New Zealand spinach. Bilignin's relatively high elevation at the foot of the French Alps made the weather unpredictable; one year Alice lost an entire crop of string beans to an early frost, and the next year she lost a crop of green peas. "It took me several years to know the climate and quite as many more to know the weather," she admitted. "Experience is never at bargain price." Her Gallic neighbors—even helpful, watchful Madame Roux, who came to do the washing and ironing and stayed to advise on the cooking—obstinately refused to eat the American yellow corn that Alice grew, considering it literally chicken feed. "When it was known that we were growing it and eating it," remembered Alice, "they considered us savages." Undeterred, she continued to plant the American flag, or at least American corn, on French soil.[19]

It was a strange, disordered season at Bilignin—a "queer summer," in Gertrude's view. There was constant trouble with servants, who were forever quitting and leaving in the middle of the night. One collapsed in their hallway, and another apparently tampered with Gertrude's beloved automobile, stuffing a rag into the gas tank and tearing out several spark plugs. A Portuguese couple, before departing, took to sleeping outdoors like Gypsies, much to the vocal displeasure of the neighbors.

Gertrude's sculptor friend Janet Scudder, whose own automobile was also vandalized during a visit, warned her that it was hard enough to find one good servant, let alone a couple, particularly if they were married to each other. "Better give it up," Scudder advised. Gertrude finally settled on an old soldier and his wife from Lyon, who wanted new livery—"well he did not get them"—but who at least "knew how to polish furniture" since his brother was a carpenter.[20]

Alice, for her part, could never keep the servants straight. "The memory of some of them is vague," she confessed, "even of some of them who were satisfactory and stayed for quite a long time." There was Swiss-Italian Celestine; middle-aged Basque Maria; another Maria, who was Swiss; a Frenchwoman whom Gertrude dubbed Muggie Moll ("a handsome woman with a cast in one eye"); Jeanne, Leonie, a second Jeanne, an Austrian, three Breton sisters (Jeanne III, Caroline, and Margot); a "vigorous, cultivated, smartly dressed Finn" named Margit, who was so melancholy that their friends called her Mademoiselle Hamlet; and a young Polish-American woman, Agnel, who made "the best Southern fried chicken they ever ate" but was unable to write down the names of her dishes in either English or Polish since "she was illiterate in both languages."[21]

Without a doubt the strangest character to visit Bilignin that summer was the adventurer, travel writer, and consensual sadist William Buchner Seabrook, who called Gertrude one night out of the blue and invited himself and his wife over for a visit. A former *New York Times* reporter, Seabrook had driven ambulances for France in World War I, during which he was gassed at Verdun and later awarded the Croix de Guerre for his service. After the war he had wandered the world, experiencing and writing about his outré encounters with West African cannibals, Haitian zombies—he was the first mainlander to popularize the term—Arab whirling dervishes, Yezidee devil worshipers, and homegrown Satanists such as the notorious Aleister Crowley. He drank a quart and a half of whiskey per day and was now on the second of three wives. His current wife, novelist Marjorie Muir Worthington, accompanied him to Bilignin.

One night, said Gertrude, she and Alice had just sat down to dinner when they were interrupted by a telephone call from Seabrook, who said he had read the *Autobiography* and "it had done something to him. He said he wanted to see if I was as interesting as my book was. I said I was." Gertrude invited the Seabrooks to come over after dinner. "He looked like a south European sailor," she recalled. (Actually, he was a dead ringer for the horror-movie actor Lon Chaney Jr., circa *The Wolf Man*.) Marjorie "looked like a college woman and together they looked different from anything that we saw around here." Seabrook examined the numerous Francis Rose paintings at the farm and pronounced them works of black magic. "How do you tell?" Gertrude wanted to know. "Well he said you don't tell. Oh well I said." It was good to know.[22]

In her defense, Gertrude could not have known just how strange Seabrook truly was. She and Alice took the couple to dinner the next night at a lakeside restaurant in Aix-les-Bains and then sent them on their way. A few months later Seabrook checked himself into a mental institution in upstate New York for treatment of his rampant alcoholism. The ordeal gave him the inspiration for another best seller, *Asylum*, about his hair-raising progress through the institution's twelve-step recovery program. The cure didn't take, and Marjorie divorced him a few years later, after which she wrote a biography of her former husband, *The Strange World of Willie Seabrook*, detailing his sordid career as a practicing sadist. Seabrook, she said, liked to chain (consenting) women naked to walls, bedposts, and ceilings. He mail-ordered custom dog collars for his victims, whom he styled "apprentice witches," and kept them locked in cages for hours at a time. He was nice about it, one submissive participant said. In the end, exhausted from his various labors, Seabrook took a fatal overdose of sleeping pills after completing his final book, *Witchcraft: Its Power in the World Today*, which rather proved his point about the dangers of trafficking in the dark arts.[23]

▼ ▼ ▼

BESIDES HOSTING THE USUAL RUN OF VISITORS TO THE MANOR house, Gertrude had two unrelated murder mysteries to investigate that summer. The first involved their old hotel-keeping friend Madame Pernollet. Always overworked, the concierge told Gertrude and Alice that certain unexplained things were "overwhelming" her. She did not elaborate. A few days later she was discovered lying unconscious with a broken back in the hotel's concrete courtyard, having apparently fallen from an upstairs window. "They picked her up and took her to the hospital and no one staying in the hotel knew anything had happened to her," Gertrude reported, adding in a terse Hemingwayesque aside, "and then she was very religious she always had been and then she was dead." It was never determined whether Madame Pernollet, a devout Catholic, had intentionally leaped or fallen to her death. In a decidedly odd detective novel she wrote about the affair, *Blood on the Dining Room Floor*, Gertrude suggested that the victim had been pushed out of a top-floor window by a relative of a young serving girl with whom Monsieur Pernollet was having an affair. The girl's brother, a troubled war veteran, put out the ridiculous cover story that Madame Pernollet had sleepwalked to her death, which was enough to arouse Gertrude's, if not the authorities', suspicions.[24]

In *Blood on the Dining Room Floor*, in which there was neither blood nor dining room nor floor, Gertrude sought to explicate the case. Along with recounting the puzzling details of Madame Pernollet's death, the book also conflated the fatal event with a second suspicious death that occurred that summer at Bilignin. The English mistress of Gertrude's neighbor, Madame Caesar, had been found lying dead in a ravine with two bullet holes in her head, her invariably worn Basque peasant cap carefully laid beside her on a rock. Gertrude, playing detective, questioned the local coroner, who ventured the sensible professional opinion that no one shoots herself twice in the head. An unnamed veteran—Monsieur Pernollet?—told Gertrude that during the war soldiers who wanted to kill themselves sometimes did fire two bullets into their own heads, although he failed to explain how it was physically possible for them to do so.

Investigating further, Gertrude questioned Madame Caesar about her friend's mental state on the night before the tragedy. Everything was perfectly normal, Madame Caesar told her. In that case, said Gertrude, if the Englishwoman had simply wanted to kill herself, "she should have done it on the boat coming over and not waited until when she did do it it was most inconsiderate of her. Yes said Madame Caesar and she always had been so considerate of me." Gertrude concluded, "There was nothing further. It never bothered us any more but every time I wanted to write I wanted to write about what happened to her. Anyway there is no use in not forgetting what you know and we do not know what happened to her." She had reached a dead end. As she observed, it was a queer summer.[25]

▼ ▼ ▼

RETURNING TO PARIS FOR THE WINTER, GERTRUDE continued to be badgered by her agent to tour America. Didn't she want to be rich? William Bradley asked her. "Certainly I said I do want to get rich but I never want to do what there is to do to get rich," Gertrude replied, adding coquettishly, "There are some things a girl cannot do." Someone had suggested that she write cigarette ads, saying she could make a lot of money at it. "So naturally I began to write them, how can I not naturally begin to write them, that is what reading and writing is." For some reason, she did not send them in after she wrote them—perhaps they were not up to her idiosyncratic standards. Picasso, dropping by for a visit, said it didn't matter, anyway, since the same two or three people who had been interested in Gertrude's work before she became famous were the same ones who were still interested in it now. That was his idea, presumably, of a pep talk.[26]

Other friends were more encouraging. Sculptor Jo Davidson counseled Gertrude to strike while the iron was hot, noting that "one had to sell one's personality in order to succeed." Carl Van Vechten gushed that he had "nothing but words of praise" for the *Autobiography*. "It seems to me, indeed, that I have talked about nothing else since the first part appeared in the Atlantic," he wrote. "What a delightful book it is! I am showering copies on my happy friends. I think you'd better come over and take the tribute due you." And Sherwood Anderson, although worrying a bit about "that number when you took such big patches of skin off Hemmy with your delicately held knife," thought that the book as a whole was a great joy. "Why don't you and Alice come to America as a great adventure next summer," he suggested, "Ford around, come see us and others?" It would give them both the opportunity to have "one big taste of America."[27]

Gertrude was noncommittal. "After all," she said, "there is no sense in it because if it were not for my work they would not be interested in me so why should they not be more interested in my work than in me. That is one of the things one has to worry about in America." Nor was she convinced that a speaking tour was the best venue for her work. "I do not like it," she said. "I like to read with my eyes not with my ears." That was the problem with politicians and schoolteachers, Gertrude complained. "Everybody hears too much with their ears and it never makes anything come together, something is always ahead of another or behind, it does not even make any bother but it does nothing either but make a noise and a noise is always a confusion, and if you are confused well if you look at anything you are really not confused but if you hear anything then you really are confused." "That depends on who you are," muttered Alice.[28]

Gertrude made a trial run of sorts in January 1934 when she agreed to stand in for travel-delayed Bernard Faÿ at a scheduled meeting of the American Women's Club in Paris. She rightly suspected his motives for missing the dinner, believing he had maneuvered her into taking his place as a way to whet her appetite for public speaking. The topic of his speech, "Democracy and President Roosevelt," failed to excite her on either a general or specific level. Politics typically bored her. "The men in politics are like the women in dressing," Gertrude complained. "Sometimes the skirts are long and sometimes they are short." As for the new American president, she viewed Roosevelt's recent triumph as a bit of a fluke. Republicans, she said, "are the only natural rulers in the United States. When a Democrat gets in he only does so because of the singular seductiveness which he possesses. Cleveland had it and Wilson had it. Roosevelt was honestly elected, but he is not half as seductive as his predecessors, so I don't think he will be elected a second time." She was off by three reelections.[29]

Gertrude was on firmer ground when it came to art. In response to a complaint by a woman in the audience that modern writers and painters were uninspired and sought merely to "create a sensation," Gertrude retorted, "Don't be silly. Have you read my latest book?" "No," said the woman. "Well, you better go and read it," Gertrude advised. "Present-day geniuses can no more help doing what they are doing than you can help not understanding it, but if you think we do it for effect and to make a sensation, you're crazy. It's not our idea of fun to work for thirty or forty years on a medium of expression and then have ourselves ridiculed." Note her use of the word *genius*.[30]

Faÿ's plan worked, and Gertrude began reconsidering her objections to an American visit after she and Alice returned to Bilignin that spring. Carl Van Vechten came for a day and in a whirlwind of activity took ninety publicity photos of the couple, alone or together, posing on the terrace, in the garden, or on the wall beside the farmhouse. After nearly two decades as a successful newspaper reporter, music, dance, and literary critic, and best-selling novelist, Van Vechten had abruptly switched careers, becoming a portrait photographer of writers, artists, and actors. (At the time of his death he would leave behind nearly five thousand such portraits.) Alice wanted to know whether he could guarantee that Americans on the street would stop and say, "There goes Gertrude Stein," when they passed. "Oh, yes," said Van Vechten, "I think it will happen." "You mean you will hire some small boys to do it so as to give me the pleasure of it," Alice said skeptically. "Perhaps we will not have to hire them," said the photographer.[31]

William Rogers came to Bilignin for a four-day visit and added his voice to those urging Gertrude to make the tour. The Kiddie assured her that she would be a great success and that American newspapers "would be friendly, or at least curious, which from one point of view amounted to the same thing." He offered to board Basket and their new Chihuahua, Pepe, a gift from Cuban-French painter Francis Picabia, at his mother's farm in

Springfield, Massachusetts, but Gertrude and Alice were afraid the dramatic change in climate might make the dogs sick. If they came to America, they said, they would board the dogs with friends on the Left Bank in Paris, where the weather (and presumably the cuisine) would be better suited to their delicate canine constitutions.[32]

Gertrude had not seen Rogers for a decade and a half, but she trusted his judgment, experience, and goodwill. She decided on the spot—the tree-shaded station yard at Bilignin where they were waiting for Rogers to catch his return train—to do the tour. "We always believe everyone as we listen to them," she said. "We believed him." That was not always the case, but by then Gertrude was ready to be convinced. Not even an admonitory letter from old friend Janet Scudder could dissuade her. "I don't at all approve of your going to America," Scudder warned. "I think that you should follow your usual serene habits and allow America to come to you. In other words, the oracle on the mountain top should *stay* on the mountain top. Anyhow you have been away too long. You and Alice will be like two Rip van Winkles over there. It's too *late* to take this step." Actually, it was Scudder's advice that was too late—they were going. "Thirty years are not so much," Gertrude shrugged, "but after all they are thirty years."[33]

In preparation, Gertrude wrote six lectures to deliver: "What Is English Literature," "Pictures," "Plays," "The Gradual Making of *The Making of Americans*," "Portraits and Repetition," and "Poetry and Grammar." The essays were good, she told Rogers, "but they are for a pretty intelligent audience and though they are clear very clear they are not too easy." All the lectures were concerned in varying ways with three central questions: movement, repetition, and the concept of the "continuous present"—qualities Gertrude considered quintessentially American.

"This generation," Gertrude wrote, "has conceived an intensity of movement so great that it has not to be seen against something else to be known, and therefore this generation does not connect with anything...and that is why it is American." She would also stress the need to study American literature as an independent entity. For the time, it was a revolutionary notion.[34]

Gertrude, a reflexive agnostic, put herself squarely on the side of the gods, if not God, in her own writing. In her lecture "What Is English Literature," she observed, "The writer is to serve god or mammon by writing the way it has been written or by writing the way it is being written that is to say the way the writing is writing. If you write the way it has already been written then you are serving mammon, because you are living by something someone has already been earning or has earned. If you write as you are to be writing then you are serving as a writer god because you are not earning anything." It was a roundabout recapitulation of the eternal conflict between art and the marketplace—a conflict she would soon experience firsthand.[35]

Bernard Faÿ, visiting after Rogers, suggested that Gertrude engage his friend Marvin Chauncey Ross of the Walters Art Gallery in Baltimore to finalize arrangements for the tour. Gertrude gave Ross specific instructions about what she did and did not want on her tour. There were to be no more than five hundred people in the audience at a time, no more than three appearances a week, and a flexible schedule that would allow her and Alice to do whatever they wanted to do during their downtime. Additionally, Gertrude demanded not to be formally introduced at the lectures, not to be expected to attend dinners or luncheons in her honor—she disliked eating in public—and that no tickets be sold to benefit any fund or cause, no matter how worthy it was deemed to be. She wanted a fee of $100 from schools and $250 from private clubs, and whenever possible she wanted to lecture before mixed groups—not a purely women's club such as the site of her recent contretemps in Paris.

While Gertrude concentrated on her lectures, Alice saw to the specifics. "I now commenced to prepare the costumes for Gertrude's voyage," she recalled, "one to lecture in the afternoon, one to lecture in on evenings, one to travel in, an odd dress or two. Gertrude also had her leopard-skin cap from which she refused to be parted." For convenience sake, they decided to have all their clothes made in Belley rather than Paris. Alice had long since cut off Gertrude's thick, wavy braids and given her the severe butch cut that remains as much a part of her public image as anything she said or wrote. (Alice, on the other hand, never changed the page-boy bangs she had adopted as a young woman in San Francisco. She, too, had a signature look.) They had a special leather case made to hold Gertrude's lectures. Having confessed earlier to William Rogers that she got stage fright just thinking about her talks, Gertrude now was at peace with her decision. "Worry is an occupation part of the time," she said, "but it cannot be an occupation all the time."[36]

She committed her thoughts to paper in an uncharacteristically tentative essay, "Meditations on Being About to Visit My Native Land." "What will they say to me and what will I say to them," she wondered. "I cannot believe that America has changed, many things have come and gone but not really come and not really gone but they are there and that perhaps does make the America that I left and the America I am to find different but not really different.... One does not like to feel different and if one does not like to feel different then one hopes that things will not look different." Anticipating the give-and-take of her lectures, she wondered who would ask the most questions, or the first ones. "I love to ask questions and I do not dislike answering them," she said, "but I like to listen and I like to have others listen....I always listen to the answer after I have asked the question and I hope that in that as in other things I am a good American." Her openness would prove to be a consistent, and consistently appealing, aspect of her talks.[37]

Finally, it was time to go. Using his connections as a transatlantic traveler, Bernard Faÿ secured them discount first-class tickets aboard the SS *Champlain*, leaving out of Le Havre on October 17. Stepping onto the boat train in a drenching rain, Gertrude immediately lost one of the buttons from her new pair of shoes. Trac, the "insecure, unstable, unreliable but thoroughly enjoyable" Indochinese cook they had recently taken on at Bilignin, leaped to the rescue, sewing the button back on with needle and thread. "In this prosaic fashion," said Alice, "we went off on our great adventure." Due west, across the slate-gray Atlantic, America lay waiting.[38]

FOUR

Gertrude Stein Has Arrived

O NCE ON BOARD THE SHIP, GERTRUDE AND ALICE WERE treated like the transatlantic celebrities they had become. *Champlain*'s captain, William Vogel, invited them to dine at his table during the voyage, but Gertrude declined, preferring to select their own menus each morning and eat at their own private table each night. Inside their stateroom they found a large going-away bouquet from their old friend the Duchess of Clermont-Tonnere, whose flapper-style bob had inspired Gertrude's own severe haircut a few years earlier. The room was redolent of roses.

The uneventful crossing took a week. The 641-foot *Champlain*, built by the French line Chantiers et Ateliers de Saint-Nazaire, was one of three new luxury liners plying the Atlantic that autumn; the others were the *Colombie* and the *Lafayette*. Gertrude and Alice mingled freely with other passengers, including the widow of a French general killed at Touraine when they were there, and about whose accidental death Gertrude and Alice maintained a discreet silence. They also met a woman who read their horoscopes and told Gertrude, unsurprisingly, that her visit to America "would be of the greatest interest to her." "Everybody talked to us and we talked to everybody," Gertrude said. They met a prosperous-looking couple from Newark, New Jersey, Dr. and Mrs. Robert Wood, which would quickly prove useful after their arrival in America. And they renewed their acquaintance with Abbé Ernest Dimnet, the best-selling author of *The Art of Thinking*, a sort of self-help book for intellectuals that included one quote, in particular, that might have pertained to Gertrude: "Genius is not genius all the time, although it is superior all the time."[1]

The abbé made something of a spectacle of himself during the ship's mandatory lifeboat drills, complaining loudly that no one was actually getting into the boats. "Tell the captain," Gertrude said. He went off to do just that, but he returned to report furiously that the captain had told him, "You could not get into the boat unless the ship was stopped it would be too dangerous and to stop the ship was too costly. Yes that is the way it is they prepare they prepare and they never know whether they can do what they are prepared for." Dimnet had a point, as the doomed passengers aboard *Titanic* might have concurred, having never taken part in lifeboat drills themselves before the great liner struck an enormous iceberg in the early morning hours of April 15, 1912, sending more than twelve hundred passengers tumbling into the frigid waters of the North Atlantic.[2]

Champlain steamed into New York harbor unscathed on the morning of October 24. Seeing the Statue of Liberty moved Gertrude, but the famous New York skyline was less dramatic than she expected. "It did not look very high," she said, "and I was disappointed." A Coast Guard cutter hove up alongside, loaded to the gunwales with reporters and photographers eager to commemorate the arrival of Gertrude Stein. Gertrude met them in the ship's lounge while Alice attended to their luggage in customs. Carl Van Vechten, wearing an easily recognizable bright-green and purple shirt for the occasion, came aboard and assisted Alice with the bags. He was horrified when she went to tip the customs officials in the manner customary for French bureaucrats. "You will not be doing that here," he said firmly. "Don't even shake their hands."[3]

Back in the lounge Gertrude faced the American press for the first time. It was an equal match. William Rogers had whispered to Alice that he was worried about the number of questions they would ask Gertrude. "Oh you do not need to be," said Alice, "it will not disturb her." As usual, Alice was right; the press conference went surprisingly well. The hard-bitten New York reporters were charmed by Gertrude—New Yorkers always like someone who can take abuse and give it back. In short order, Rogers observed, "Miss Stein had the reporters frightened." Not that she was trying to scare anyone. "Everybody who has ever done anything has seen reporters," she remembered. "Well anyway there we all were and it was very lively and I liked it. I always like talking and I like asking questions and I like to know who everybody is and where they come from. This first lot asked me questions later on I was able to ask them."[4]

The reporters had done their homework and came prepared to interrogate Gertrude on the notorious difficulty of her style. "Why don't you write as you talk?" one wanted to know. "Why don't you read as I write?" she fired back. She went on to explain: "I do talk as I write, but you can hear better than you can see. You are accustomed to see with your eyes differently to the way you hear with your ears, and perhaps that is what makes it hard to read my works." What about all her repetitions? "No, no, no, no, it is not all repetition," she maintained. "I always change the words a little." One reporter asked if she had been upset by the comparisons of her writing style to the babbling of insane people. "No, not one bit," she replied, "because there is an important difference. You can continue to read me, but not the babblings of the insane. Besides, the insane are frequently normal in everything except their own phase of insanity."[5]

That last point was debatable, as she well knew from her time in medical school, but the reporters let it slide. The talk turned to politics—always a dangerous subject for Gertrude. Someone asked her about a recent speech by President Roosevelt. Only Lincoln Steffens wrote correctly about Roosevelt, she said, mixing her Roosevelt cousins. Theodore Roosevelt had been dead for several years, it was pointed out to her. "He may not be as dead as you think," she replied. What about President Coolidge—did she know he was dead too? "Of course he may have died while I was on the boat coming over," Gertrude said gamely, channeling Dorothy Parker's famous response to the news that the notoriously tight-lipped Coolidge had died: "How can you tell?"[6]

Fortunately for Gertrude, the reporters were more interested in her appearance than her politics. They cited her thick wool stockings, round-toed, flat-heeled Mary Jane shoes, cream-and-black-striped shirt, coarse tweed suit, and green cloth hat modeled after a Louis XIII–era hunting cap that Alice had seen at the Cluny Museum. The *New York Times* irritated Gertrude by describing her cap as "a gay hat which gave her the appearance of having just sprung from Robin Hood's forest." Others described it variously as "a braumeister's cap, a jockey's cap, a deerstalker's cap and a grouse-hunter's cap." "It's just a hat," Gertrude said with a trace of annoyance. They went back to their desks and wrote up her arrival for the morning papers, calling her "the Sibyl of Montparnasse" and "the Mama of Dada" and "the high priestess of the Left Bank." Headline writers vied for wit: "Gerty Gerty Stein Stein / Is Back Home Home Back," "Gertrude Stein Barges In / With a Stein Song to Stein," "Gertrude Stein, Stein / Is Back, Back, and It's / Still All Black, Black."[7]

Alice, when mentioned at all, was called "a queer, birdlike shadow," "an enigmatic bodyguard," "Miss Stein's constant companion," "a somewhat submerged heroine," and "Gertrude's Girl Friday." None of the descriptions were wrong. Evelyn Seeley of the *New York World-Telegram* reported that someone had asked Gertrude point-blank, "Is there an Alice Toklas?" to which Gertrude had responded happily, "Well, of course! There she is!" Capitalizing on the attention (or nonattention) paid to Alice, Harcourt, Brace took out a full-page ad in *Publishers Weekly* declaring tongue in cheek that "Alice B. Toklas really exists. She has been Gertrude Stein's intimate companion for 25 years." Stepping clumsily on the book's surprise ending, the ad went on to reveal, "You find out on the last page that Gertrude Stein wrote it." So much for the twist.[8]

▼ ▼ ▼

ALTHOUGH NO ONE MADE THE COMPARISON AT THE TIME, Gertrude's arrival was almost identical to the advent of the equally quotable and sexually ambiguous Oscar Wilde fifty-two years earlier—down to the gaggle of reporters racing across the harbor in a small boat to intercept his ship. The ineffable Oscar had arrived in New York Harbor on January 2, 1882, for a speaking tour of his own, and he had likewise jousted good-naturedly with the press. At the time, eight years before writing his classic horror novel *The Picture of Dorian Gray* and more than a decade before conquering the London stage with *The Importance of Being Earnest*, Wilde's genius was still more theoretical than actual. It consisted mainly of self-promotion, which was almost the exact opposite of Gertrude's situation. He made headlines while still on the high seas, announcing magisterially that he was "not exactly pleased with the Atlantic. It is not so majestic as I expected." A letter in the *Pall Mall Gazette* a few days later read, in full, "I am disappointed in Mr. Wilde," signed "The Atlantic Ocean." Unlike Gertrude, Oscar handled his own luggage in customs. "I have nothing to declare except my genius," he said—or is supposed to have said, since no one actually reported it at the time. Either way was fine with Oscar.[9]

But if Gertrude was a more accomplished writer than Oscar at the time of their arrivals in America, there were several notable similarities between the two. Both were noted wits, outlandish dressers, epigrammatic writers, and absolute originals. Both, too, were gay, although it was scarcely a subtext in the reporting of the time, perhaps because neither writer made it a point of emphasis. They simply were what they were, without explanation or apology. (Oscar, of course, would later go to jail in England for the crime, more or less, of being himself.) And finally, both had come to America with the declared purpose of educating Americans about art. Wilde came to lecture on the imprecise if not indeed contradictory topic "the science of the beautiful," of which he himself was the chief embodiment. Gertrude had come, she told reporters, "to tell very plainly and simply and directly, as is my fashion, what literature is." Oscar kept much the busier schedule—140 lectures in 260 days—but then he was also less than half Gertrude's age at the time.[10]

The two Americas that Oscar and Gertrude visited half a century apart were, in some ways, very different countries. America in 1882 was still in mourning for its popular young president, James A. Garfield, who had been assassinated the previous year by the madman Charles J. Guiteau. At the same time, it was a prosperous, energetic, forward-looking nation—at least in the North—having come through the Civil War, Reconstruction, and a severe financial panic to launch itself headlong into the Industrial Revolution upon an unexcelled system of railroads. Wilde made full use of the railroads during his tour, logging some fifteen thousand miles as he crisscrossed the country from Maine to California, from Canada to Texas.

In 1934 the nation still had its railroads, but a new bone-crushing depression was not quite at the midway point, with unemployment hovering around 22 percent and murderous labor strife erupting from New York to San Francisco. A colorful but deadly parade of bank robbers, kidnappers, bandits, and murderers—Bonnie Parker and Clyde Barrow, John Dillinger, Pretty Boy Floyd, Machine Gun Kelly, Baby Face Nelson, Ma Barker, Creepy Karpis—had spontaneously arisen, as if summoned by hard times from the very ground of the Dust Bowl itself. That same year the fledgling Federal Bureau of Investigation had set out on a relentless series of manhunts for the newly minted "Public Enemies" that amounted to little more than outright assassinations. In short order, Bonnie and Clyde and John Dillinger were tracked down, ambushed, and killed, without being given the option, admittedly slight, of surrendering. The others would soon meet similar fates.

American movies reflected the public's fascination with gangsters. Such top grossing films as *Little Caesar*, *The Public Enemy*, *Scarface*, *White Heat*, *The Roaring Twenties*, and *Manhattan Melodrama* made huge stars of tough-guy actors Edward G. Robinson, James Cagney, Paul Muni, and Humphrey Bogart. Even the reigning movie heartthrob, Clark Gable, whose box office hit *It Happened One Night* would win all five major Academy Awards, was something of a tough guy himself, a man's man who bore a certain resemblance to John Dillinger with his dazzling smile and dapper mustache. (Coincidentally, Dillinger had attended another Gable movie, *Manhattan Melodrama*, on the night he was shot down by FBI agents outside the Biograph Theater in Chicago that July.) Only America's favorite moppet, Shirley Temple, bucked the trend of crime movies, debuting her signature tune "On the Good Ship Lollipop" in the musical *Bright Eyes*. She would win an Academy Award too.

Even the national sport of baseball mirrored the roughneck tenor of the times. The same month that Gertrude and Alice arrived in New York, the St. Louis Cardinals, bearing the gangsterish nickname "the Gas House Gang," won the World Series over the Detroit Tigers in a notably fight-filled, beanball-marred series. The gang's leader was a rawboned, wisecracking pitcher from backwoods Arkansas, Jerome Hanna "Dizzy" Dean, who, along with his brother Paul "Daffy" Dean and teammates Pepper Martin, Ducky Medwick, and Frankie "the Fordham Flash" Frisch, captured whatever headlines the nation's real gangsters left them. They even managed the improbable feat of overshadowing the sport's long-reigning king, Babe Ruth, who somewhat quietly finished his legendary career with the New York Yankees that same summer. Gertrude would be competing for attention with world-class headline grabbers—gangsters, G-men, movie stars, and athletes. Fortunately for her, she was up to the task.

▼ ▼ ▼

AFTER THE REPORTERS LEFT, GERTRUDE MADE A SHIP-TO-shore radio broadcast—sadly, no transcript survives—and then joined Alice, Carl Van Vechten, William Rogers, and Random House publisher Bennett Cerf for an automobile ride into the city. Cerf, in the best tradition of New York publishing, had poached Gertrude from Harcourt, Brace by promising to publish whatever she wrote, one book per year—a bold promise given Gertrude's enigmatic history. He had already brought out a new edition of *Three Lives*, her well-respected trilogy of short stories, and *Portraits and Prayers*, a grab bag of earlier pieces on artists and writers ranging from Matisse and Picasso to Hemingway, Edith Sitwell, Jean Cocteau, Max Jacob, and Basket the dog. Seeing Gertrude in action with the press gave Cerf a good feeling about their future endeavors. She was, he said admiringly, "the publicity hound of the world—simply great."[11]

Alice had booked them into a three-room suite at the Algonquin Hotel on West 44th Street. The Algonquin, of course, was famous for its Round Table of wits, including Dorothy Parker,

Robert Benchley, Alexander Woollcott, George S. Kaufman, Robert Sherwood, Marc Connelly, Harold Ross, and Haywood Broun. The group had broken up by the time Gertrude and Alice arrived, which was too bad: with their own lengthy salon experience in Paris, the couple would have fit right in. As it was, their suite was so filled with cameras and recording equipment that Alice could not unpack their suitcases. "The reporters had come back to the rooms," she complained; "there were wires, there were coils, there were all sorts of impedimenta. I could not open my bag, I could not open my trunk. I could do nothing."[12]

Pathé News was there to film a newsreel of Gertrude introducing herself to movie-going audiences, and Joseph W. Alsop Jr., a young reporter for the *Herald Tribune*, had followed them from the ship to continue his interview. Alsop, a relative of the Roosevelts, was favorably known to Gertrude for having written positively about the rehearsals and debut of *Four Saints in Three Acts* the previous February. That earned him a private interview with Gertrude, during which he asked again why she did not write as clearly as she talked. "I do write clearly," she said. "That is not the answer that is a fact. I think I write so clearly that I worry about it." Alsop reported the dialogue word for word the next day and continued to report, more extensively than anyone else, on Gertrude and Alice's progress across America.[13]

William Rogers, a newsman himself, carefully counted the column inches and placement devoted to Gertrude's arrival. There were front-page articles in the *New York Sun*, the *Post*, the *World-Telegram*, and the *Brooklyn Eagle*, as well as long pieces in the *Times* and the *Herald Tribune*, accompanied by several photos of Gertrude and one of Alice. "Even if I had been too sleepy to glance at the newsstand in the lobby," wrote Rogers, "the headlines would have shrieked up at me. There were Miss Stein and Miss Toklas on every single front page. Twelve columns of space were devoted to her in New York City alone within twenty-four hours of her arrival. There and then she was promoted from curiosity to celebrity."[14]

Not until late that afternoon were Gertrude and Alice finally free to go for a walk. They quickly realized they were special visitors. A clerk in a fruit shop asked Alice, "Miss Toklas, how are you liking New York?" "How did he know who I was?" Alice wondered. "Everybody knows us on the street," Gertrude replied happily. The headline crawl on the New York Times Building ceaselessly proclaimed "Gertrude Stein Has Arrived...Gertrude Stein Has Arrived...Gertrude Stein Has Arrived"—to which Alice deadpanned, "As if we did not know it." She wondered aloud why Paris called itself the City of Light, since New York clearly outshone it in numbers and brilliance. Gertrude replied that when Paris gave itself that title, "there were more lights there than anywhere, you cannot blame them that they all think so although there are more lights here than anywhere." Alice wasn't convinced. "She always prefers that anything should be American," Gertrude noted.[15]

The couple went back to their hotel for dinner. Gertrude and Alice had been forewarned by French friends that American food was moist in comparison to French food, which typically was served dry with complementary sauces. Gertrude would posit that American food was moist because the heat was dry—more or less the reverse of French cuisine. Jacques, the headwaiter at the Algonquin, did his best to reintroduce them to American fare. They had T-bone steaks, green-apple pie, and "ineffable ice creams." Georges, the Greek maître d', contributed his personal recipes for cream of mushroom and cold chicken curry soups. Gertrude particularly liked the hotel's honeydew melons, but Alice, whose tastes were more refined, thought melons should be eaten outdoors—and anyway, she preferred the ones that came from Spain. "From the beginning," she said, "the ubiquitous honeydew melon bored me." Gertrude, thinking ahead, decided that she should have the same light meal before each lecture: honeydew melon, oysters, an egg, and corn muffins. Alice, for her part, would stick to steak and ice cream.[16]

Gertrude's first lecture, sponsored by the Museum of Modern Art, was scheduled for November 1 at the Colony Club at Park Avenue and 66th Street. A minor crisis arose when Gertrude, suffering from stage fright (or the fear of stage fright), became convinced that there was something wrong with her throat. She called her *Champlain* friend Dr. Wood. "Hearing his voice was already soothing," Gertrude remembered, "but having him come and feel my pulse was everything and he was there at the first lecture and so was my voice." The museum offered to send a limousine to pick them up, but Gertrude and Alice walked the twenty-two blocks to the club. A large, sophisticated audience had gathered for her talk. As per her instructions, there was no introduction. "It was silly," Gertrude said, "everybody knew who I was and if not why did they come and why should I sit and get nervous while somebody else was talking." She wore a new brown silk dress and diamond brooch for the occasion.[17]

Her talk was on "pictures, that is about paintings," she began. "Everybody must like something and I like seeing painted pictures." When she first came to Paris, she recalled, she had spent more time at the Louvre looking at the gold picture frames than at the paintings themselves. That drew a laugh from the crowd and launched Gertrude into the subject of framing and movement. Leonardo da Vinci's *Virgin and Child with Saint Anne*, she said, had first made her aware of the sense of movement within a painting. In it, the infant Christ playfully grappled with a lamb while his mother, sitting on her own mother's lap, attempted to restrain him. There was a lot going on inside the frame, said Gertrude. "Before this the moving in a picture was the effect of moving, that is, the depiction of figures in more or less violent action, but in this picture there was an internal movement, not of the people or light or any of these things but inside in the oil painting. In other words the picture did not live within the frame." Subsequent painters, from Rubens and Velasquez to Seurat and Picasso, had tried to capture the sensation of movement, and "modern pictures have made the very definite effort to leave their frame." She expressed the hope "that some picture would remain out of its frame"—a very modern concept that Jackson Pollock and other abstract expressionists would explore—and explode—in the next decade.[18]

▼　▼　▼

AS REPORTERS HAD DONE HALF A CENTURY EARLIER AFTER Oscar Wilde's first New York appearance, they reviewed the audience as much as they did the speaker. The *New York Times* thought there was "no unanimity of opinion among the audience" about the meaning or significance of Gertrude's talk, but her "straightforwardness and amiability" had gone a long way toward winning over the crowd. The ubiquitous Joseph Alsop reported that Gertrude had "variously pleased, mystified and infuriated her audience," winning several rounds of applause. Despite reading her remarks "in the same slightly monotonous voice that mothers use to read to sick children," Gertrude had carried the night, said Alsop. "The truth is that with Miss Stein there is never a dull moment."[19]

Things got even livelier the following night at Gertrude's next appearance, at Columbia University's McMillin Theater. Not understanding the distance involved, Gertrude and Alice had walked all seventy-two blocks from the Algonquin to the college at 116th Street. There had been a nasty contretemps earlier concerning her talk. Learning that seventeen hundred people were expected to attend, as opposed to the mandated limit of five hundred, Gertrude, through Alice, put her foot down. Contacting Dr. Russell Potter, the director of the university's Institute of Arts and Sciences, which was sponsoring the lecture, Alice demanded an explanation. "I asked him if he had not received word from Paris about the number of people to be admitted to each lecture. Oh, he said, I did not think you meant it. Why did you suppose, I said, that it was said and not meant." Suitably chastened, Potter sent out an emergency notice to members that "Miss Stein refuses—flatly, adamantly, steadfastly, definitively, unconditionally, and absolutely—to address more than 500 persons at any one time." It sounded very much like a direct quote.[20]

Vindicated, Gertrude went through with her lecture "The Gradual Making of *The Making of Americans.*" It did not go over as well as her first. The press counted twenty-five people walking out before the lecture was over, and during the question-and-answer segment after the speech one audience member stood up to complain that he had not understood a thing Gertrude was talking about. "You don't need any special preparation to understand," she responded. "A child could understand it. Some children read my work and like it. Some adults like it. I like it." As she explained it, the title of her lecture referred not to the three years it had taken her to write *The Making of Americans,* but rather to the lifetime it had taken her to live it. Like much of her work, it involved both talking and listening—often simultaneously. "I began very early in life to talk all the time and to listen all the time," she said. "I cannot remember not talking all the time and all the time feeling that while I was talking while I was seeing that I was not only hearing but seeing while I was talking." Perhaps it made sense to the audience.[21]

At a second Columbia lecture, "Poetry and Grammar," Gertrude turned to the nuts and bolts of composition, painstakingly parsing the use of nouns, pronouns, verbs, adverbs, adjectives, conjunctions, articles, and prepositions. She came down on the side of verbs and adverbs, which "are lively because they all do something and as long as anything does something it keeps alive." Nouns, on the other hand, were inert. "A noun is a name of anything," she said, "why after a thing is named write about it." Slang existed to change nouns, "which have been names for so long," into something else. The shadow of her notable rose hung over her. She saved her special scorn for the "servile" comma, arguing that "commas have no life of their own, and their use is not a use, it is a way of replacing one's own interest and I do decidedly like to like my own interest in what I am doing. A comma by helping you along holding your coat for you and putting on your shoes keeps you from living your life as actively as you should lead it and to me for many years and I still do feel that way about it only now I do not pay as much attention to them, the use of them was positively degrading." It was a lot to put on the humble comma. The *New York Times* drily wondered "why apostrophes and periods escaped her critique."[22]

In the fallout from the Columbia controversy, Marvin Chauncey Ross was fired as tour manager, with Alice taking over his role. Henceforth she would handle the bookings, the travel arrangements, the theater owners, and the press. An example of the latter occurred when a reporter from the Columbia University student newspaper, the *Spectator*, arrived at the Algonquin to interview Gertrude. Although the interview had been prearranged, Alice kept the young man waiting for twenty minutes before coming downstairs to tell him that Gertrude, as it happened, was unavailable for comment. Alice would speak in her place. Wearing a feathered hat and speaking "a little jumpily," she insisted that "Miss Stein thinks that newspapermen are very nice, very kind and gentlemanly," but she admonished, "You people should have interviewed Miss Stein many years ago when she was not so well known and not so busy." Later she brusquely told a reporter for *Art News*, "Miss Stein has no desire to speak of art or artists, painting or aesthetics. Miss Stein feels she has been occupied with art most of her life and in this time a great deal has been said on the subject." The fact that Gertrude had just given a lecture on that very subject at the Museum of Modern Art was not discussed.[23]

William Rogers wondered at Gertrude's approach to publicity and her handling, or mishandling, of potential supporters. "People wanted to talk to her, and she would not be bothered; wanted to wine and dine her and she would have few of their dinners and none of their wine," said Rogers. "Spread the most delectable tea before her, and she would ask for a glass of Vichy water, the one thing her embarrassed hostess was certain not to have; offer her the fanciest dessert and she would prefer, please, a plain red apple." Rogers watched with dismay when she refused to meet privately with supporters after her lecture at Pittsfield and told officials at the windowless Springfield Museum that she preferred windows in her art galleries "so that she could take a look outdoors between paintings." In Hartford, Connecticut, she spurned an invitation from some of the same people who had sponsored the first public performance of *Four Saints in Three Acts*. "No professional manager would have countenanced this highhanded treatment of audiences and sponsors," said Rogers, "and few publicity-mad writers would have behaved as she did, either. It was not a smart thing for her to do. Many friends and admirers whom she might have won, she simply didn't. She wasn't putting on an act, or being rude; she simply did not like parties, and she had her integrity to maintain."[24]

Her natural warmth and openness worked with audiences, if

not always with white-tie donors. In Pittsfield, Massachusetts, she won over the crowd by responding to a question about what she thought of celebrated artist Thomas Hart Benton, who had just appeared, like her, on the cover of *Time* magazine. She had never heard of him, said Gertrude, but "the chances are he's not great." It got a big laugh. "Gertrude Stein made a great many new friends last night," reported the local newspaper. "There are two human characteristics which are irresistible, kindliness and sincerity. And Miss Stein has both." Thomas Hart Benton had no comment.[25]

As she had done for the past twenty-five years, Alice controlled private access to Gertrude. When Mabel Weeks, an old friend of Gertrude's from Baltimore, kept demanding to know when she could see Gertrude, Alice cut her off. "I am sorry," she said, "but I do not know." And when the mother of California playwright Carley Mills, Francis Rose's erstwhile boyfriend, telephoned the hotel to invite them to dinner, Alice "regretted it was not going to be possible." Gertrude, she explained, needed to conserve her strength for the stage. Besides, although Alice was too polite to say it, they did not much like her son anyway.[26]

▼ ▼ ▼

WITH THE ALGONQUIN SERVING AS THEIR HEADQUARTERS, Gertrude and Alice traveled by train and automobile to various sites in the Northeast. On November 3, they joined publisher Alfred Harcourt and eighty thousand other sports fans for the Yale-Dartmouth football game in New Haven, Connecticut. Each team's head coach was in his first year: Raymond "Ducky" Pond for Yale and Earl "Red" Blaik for Dartmouth. Pond's nickname might have seemed like a no-brainer, given his last name, but in reality he had been dubbed "Ducky" by the famous sports-writer Grantland Rice after returning a fumble sixty-three yards for a touchdown against Harvard in 1923 through "seventeen lakes, five quagmires and a water hazard." Blaik, whose teams later would win three consecutive national championships at the United States Military Academy at West Point, owed his more prosaic nickname to his reddish hair. Yale won the game that day by a baseball-like score of 7–2. Two weeks later the Bulldogs would upset undefeated Princeton, ending its fifteen-game winning streak and becoming the last team in football history to play only eleven starters for all sixty minutes of a game.[27]

Gertrude, of course, knew nothing about the teams' history, but she enjoyed the game as spectacle. "We did see them playing football," she recounted in *Everybody's Autobiography*, "not very well it must be said not very well." The sport interested her, she said, with the players alternately kneeling, crouching, squatting, and blocking each other up and down the field. She liked football, Gertrude said, because "nothing happened—it was a spectacle, a landscape, and a ritual, like dancing, war, bull-fighting and theatre." Fans kept interrupting to ask her to autograph their programs, and one very drunk man told her that he just had to see her. "And I just had to see him," Gertrude replied. "I did see him and he did see me." The football players reminded her of Native American dancers. "It proves that the physical country that made the one made the other and that the red Indian is still with us," she observed. "They just put their heads down solemnly together and then double over, while on the sidelines the substitutes move in a jiggly way just like the Indians. Then they all get down on all fours just like Indians…and then there is that little brown ball they all bend down and worship." The game hasn't changed all that much since then.[28]

On November 5 they went to Princeton, F. Scott Fitzgerald's alma mater, for Gertrude to lecture at McCosh Hall on *The Making of Americans*. The stricture on audience size seemed

like "a great joke" to the head of Princeton's English department, Robert Kilburn Root, who told Gertrude he usually had
to bribe students to round up as many as two hundred for a
speaker. This time, he said, he'd had an awful time keeping the
size down to five hundred. Gertrude remained "very solemn" in
the face of Root's hilarity. One "young and very good-looking"
student, Donald Sutherland, previously had sent Gertrude some
of his manuscripts. Now, introduced to her at a faculty reception, he found her almost God-like in her majestic sweep and
laser-focused attention. Sutherland would keep in touch with
Gertrude and Alice for the rest of their lives, and in 1951 he would
produce the first scholarly study of her writings, *Gertrude Stein:
A Biography of Her Work*, in which he ecumenically compared
her work to that of Catholic poet-priest Gerard Manley Hopkins
in its violent wrenching of syntax and word order.[29]

At Bryn Mawr, the alma mater of so many of Gertrude's
old Baltimore friends, she and Alice stayed overnight at the
Deanery, the former residence of Martha Carey Thomas, the
formidable spinster president of the college. Thomas had served
as the barely disguised model for the predatory headmistress
of Gertrude's early novel *Fernhurst*, in which the headmistress
steals the affections of a younger woman from her husband,
much as Mabel Haynes had stolen May Bookstaver's affections
from Gertrude. That, at least, was how Gertrude remembered
it. She had no recourse to more direct aides-mémoire: Alice had
made her burn all her letters from Bookstaver after discovering
Gertrude's manuscript of the lesbian-triangle novel *Q.E.D.* at
the bottom of a desk drawer. Romance of another sort—the love
of language—was on Gertrude's mind in her Bryn Mawr talk,
when she told the audience at the Agassiz Theater that "poetry
is really loving the name of anything. One can love a name, and

if one does, then saying it over and over only makes one love it more. Being in love makes for poetry." It was a revealing choice of words by a woman who generally chose her words with care.[30]

At Vassar, where the smartly dressed young women at Avery Hall all looked like Katharine Hepburn, the local press carefully appraised Gertrude's appearance. "The writer heralded as 'eccentric,' appeared as a wholly normal person, free from any oddities of personality," the *Poughkeepsie Courier* reported. "She wore a dark woolen skirt, a silk open at the throat blouse of simple cut, and low heeled red kid sandals. Her only bit of jewelry was a brooch at the neck of her blouse. Her voice, while exceedingly low pitched, was audible to everyone in the hall, and her manner was enthusiastic and agreeable. In spite of her stock, middle aged figure, Miss Stein appears of indeterminate age. Although her close-cropped hair is gray, her face is unlined." Alice would judge the Vassar women "beautiful and very smartly dressed" but rather rowdy in the dining hall. "The dining-room was really a huge mess hall with acoustics that made a pandemonium of the thousands or was it only hundreds of voices," she recalled. "It was the beautiful young women students who were making this demoniacal noise. No wonder we had always thought of the graduates of the college as sirens, tragic and possibly damned."[31]

Gertrude's return to Radcliffe understandably attracted a great deal of local media attention. "Radcliffe's most famous daughter," the *Boston Sunday Post* announced, "will come to Boston this winter to tell the Athenians of America all about the strange conglomeration of words she turns out in prolific fashion at her Parisian home on the Rue de Fleurus." She would be accompanied, said the newspaper, by one "Annie B. Toklas," who ran "the domestic affairs" for Gertrude and risked her life daily by riding with Gertrude, whom the paper called "the worst automobile driver in the world." About Gertrude herself the paper observed, "Her eyes are like those of a jolly teddy bear, brown and shiny. Her outfit, from hat to skirt, is made of some overcoat-tweed material. She looks as if she expects it to rain at any moment and acts as if she hopes it won't." One reporter tried to bait her by quoting a famous anecdote about Robert Browning, who, when asked what a line of poetry meant, replied, "Madame, when I wrote that God and I knew what it meant. Now only God knows what it means." Gertrude bristled at the implied comparison. "Every line I have ever written means exactly what I meant it to mean," she declared. "It means the same thing now as when I wrote it." God didn't enter into the equation.[32]

Accustomed to scrappy, combative characters, the Boston press approved of Gertrude. "Put away any notion that Gertrude Stein is either slightly cracked, or a literary sideshow faker of the kind Barnum liked to handle," said the *Boston Evening Transcript*. "This pleasing, thick woman with the close-cropped iron-gray hair, the masculine face and the marvelously pleasant smile, voice and manner, is doing something she thinks is good and no abracadabra, simon-pure, could come from her wittingly." With the reporter's question fresh in her mind, Gertrude kept asking the students, "Do you see what I mean?" When they laughed, she added, "Maybe you will but I doubt it." She helpfully condensed for them her thoughts about the difference between hearing and understanding. "The essence of intelligence," she said, "is that you know it before you know it." After her lectures at Radcliffe and the Signet Club at Harvard, Gertrude showed Alice around her old undergraduate haunts. She was dismayed to find Cambridge more changed than any other place they had visited, "so different that it was as if I had never been there. I lost Cambridge then and there." It was a harbinger of an even more depressing homecoming in Oakland a few months later.[33]

▼ ▼ ▼

THEY RETURNED TO NEW YORK FOR THREE LECTURES AT
Brooklyn's Academy of Music. At one of them Gertrude met
the feminist poet Marianne Moore, which in itself might have
been adventure enough for one night, but then an "attentive
young man"—one assumes she was being ironic—closed a door
on Gertrude's finger, and she was taken to a nearby drugstore
for treatment. "It was dirty the drugstore," she scoffed.

> One of the few things really dirty in America are the drugstores
> but the people in them sitting up and eating and drinking milk
> and coffee that part of the drugstore was clean that fascinated
> me. After that I was always going in to buy a detective novel just
> to watch the people sitting on the stools. It was like a piece of
> provincial life in a real city. The people sitting on the stools and
> eating in the drugstore all looked and acted as if they lived in a
> small country town. You could not imagine them ever being out
> in the streets of New York, nor the drugstore itself being in New
> York. I never had enough of going into them.

Five-and-dime stores were a different matter; Gertrude found
them disappointing. "There was nothing that I wanted and what
was there was not there for ten cents."[34]

Carl Van Vechten and his curvy second wife Fania, a Russian-
born actress whom they privately called "Madame Bottoms,"
hosted a series of parties for Gertrude and Alice at their home
on West 55th Street. One of the most memorable was an all-
black event attended by Walter White, head of the National
Association for the Advancement of Colored People, poet James
Weldon Johnson, and the current cast of *Four Saints in Three
Acts*. Gertrude, noting their preference for the descriptor *colored*, took the opportunity to argue for the more formal if less

favored designation *Negro*. "I know they do not want you to say Negro but I do want to say Negro," she said. "I dislike it when instead of saying Jew they say Hebrew or Israelite or Semite, I do not like it and why would a Negro want to be called colored. A Negro is a Negro and he ought to like to be called one if he is one." Times have changed.[35]

At another party Gertrude inadvertently offended actress Mary Pickford, "America's Sweetheart." Pickford had ventured the wish that "she knew more French and I said I talked it all right but I never read it I did not care about it as a written language she said she did wish she did know more French." Pickford, nonplussed perhaps by the attitude of a woman who had lived in France for the past thirty years, backed out of a planned publicity photo of the two of them shaking hands. Gertrude, equally flummoxed, wondered "just what it was that went on inside Mary Pickford. It was her idea and then when I was enthusiastic she melted away." Pickford, of course, did not need any more publicity.[36]

There were other parties hosted by the Van Vechtens, the Bennett Cerfs, the Alfred A. Knopfs, and various high-level New York scenesters. Accustomed to being the center of attention, Gertrude accepted it as her due, meeting and greeting everyone cordially, even regally. "Each aspirant," she said, "was led to the footstool like a mule to a well." Best-selling novelist Louis Bromfield, a frequent visitor to Bilignin, brought his parents east from Mansfield, Ohio, to meet her. During a lull in the conversation, the elder Bromfield was heard to say, "I didn't quite catch the gentleman's name, Mama." He was talking about Gertrude. The only time Gertrude was thrown off stride occurred when Alice, in a rare example of either poor judgment or random kindness, invited a strange young man to one of the Van Vechtens' parties. After several cocktails the man knelt at Gertrude's feet and kissed the hem of her garment, which was a bit much even for Gertrude. He was ushered out of the royal presence.[37]

The *New Yorker* took note of the illustrious visitors in one of its "Talk of the Town" columns, describing the good life at Bilignin, where Gertrude rose late, bathed long, and wandered the estate looking under rocks while Alice busied herself "dusting and fussing around." It was a fairly accurate depiction of their daily life in France—one wonders where the writer got his details—and sketched them as a pair of lovable eccentrics. The *Journal of Medical Opinion*, less charmed, quoted an unnamed psychiatrist who judged Gertrude to be schizophrenic. It was similar to other long-distance diagnoses that claimed she suffered from such speech disorders as palilalia or echolalia, which were in no way the same conditions. The first involves the involuntary repetition of words, phrases, or sentences; the second refers to the repetition of someone else's words. Gertrude said very little that wasn't voluntary, and what she did say was always unmistakably her own. As for her own public speaking, Gertrude allowed, "I never really did care very much about hearing any one lecture. My eyes always have told me more than my ears....Speaking voices always go at a different tempo than when you listen to them...and they always go on at the wrong tempo."[38]

Whatever the tempo, she soldiered on, appearing with Virgil Thomson on November 16 at a charity event for the New York Christmas Fund at the Ritz Tower Hotel and following that appearance with a return engagement at Columbia, where she chided the inattentive students for giggling during parts of her talk on English literature. "Slowly you will see what I mean," she admonished them. "If not, why not?" It being the traditional season of giving, Gertrude attended another charity event at the Barbizon Plaza Hotel to benefit "needy authors and painters." The auction was sponsored by the Artists' and Writers' Dinner

Club, whose very existence proved perhaps that not all authors and painters were needy. For those who were, Gertrude auctioned off copies of *Portraits and Prayers* ($22), *Four Saints in Three Acts* ($8), and *Three Lives* ($9).[39]

More satisfying was her speech to the Dutch Treat Club, an exclusive men's club for writers, illustrators, and show business performers. The club had met every Tuesday since 1905 at a different restaurant, where members paid for their own meals—hence the name—and stayed to be amused by the week's guest speaker. Among the hundreds of club members were actors James Cagney and Bob Hope, heavyweight boxing champion Gene Tunney, illustrators Norman Rockwell and James Montgomery Flagg (Uncle Sam), and humorists Robert Benchley, George S. Kaufman, Rube Goldberg, Ogden Nash, and Ring Lardner. The club barred women, partly because their higher-pitched voices were judged to be irritating, but Gertrude, who spoke at a lower timbre, was exempted from the exclusion. While waiting to be introduced (a club tradition she had to allow), she was amused to see that her introducer was too nervous to eat his lunch. "He was pale and his hands were shaking," she recalled. "What is it. I am nervous, he said. I said, you are making believe being nervous in order to be effective, I said, aren't you. I don't know he said. Are you always like this, I said, always he said and how long have you been doing it, for three years once a month, he said. Dear me, I said." There was no mention of who the nervous emcee was, or whether Gertrude was given one of the club's notorious yearbooks, which featured naked drawings of the members' favorite hat checkers, coat checkers, and waitresses. No one bothered to sketch Gertrude.[40]

On November 12 she did a rare book signing at Brentano's, where the *New Yorker* reported that "one confused man somehow found himself standing in front of Miss Stein without a book, so he shouted at a clerk, 'Three Saints! Three Saints! Give me a Three Saints!' The right title is 'Four Saints,' a clerk corrected the gentleman coldly. Miss Stein just laughed. She doesn't get peeved about things like that." A few days later, in Philadelphia, she did get peeved, treating one insistent audience member at the Barclay Ballroom, reported the *Philadelphia Inquirer*, "like a none too intelligent school boy. While her questioner fumbled in confusion she upbraided him for using words which, she said, he didn't know the meaning of himself, among others, 'meticulous' and 'cosmic.' " Despite the uncharacteristic blowup, Stein got a good reception from other audience members. Local attorney and art enthusiast R. Sturgis Ingersoll felt moved to insist, "I hope you come back often, because you are a damn good thing for Philadelphia."[41]

Back in New York, Gertrude sat down for a radio interview at NBC with a skeptical broadcaster named William Warner Lundell. The veteran newsman, a native of Minneapolis, actually had things in common with Gertrude. Like her, he had graduated from Harvard (or Harvard Annex, in her case) and had lived for a time in Paris. During his career at NBC, he had carved out a niche interviewing such artistic sorts as Mary Pickford, journalist H. L. Mencken, and Austrian composer Arnold Schoenberg. But Lundell, a part-time minister when he wasn't broadcasting, was also a practical-minded inventor of electrical gadgets who in 1931 had become the first person to do a live radio broadcast from an airplane. He was not, perhaps, the ideal representative of Gertrude's target audience. The first substantive question he asked, after the usual get-acquainted chitchat, concerned the "absurd" *Four Saints in Three Acts*. "Many American people doubt your ability to speak intelligibly," Lundell said. He wondered what the opera had to say about her scheme of lecturing, "which, if it is to be successful, must at least be understandable, which is more than most of us can say for your opera."[42]

Gertrude, to her credit, kept her poise. "Look here," she responded, "being intelligible is not what it seems, after all these things are a matter of habit. When you say they do not understand *Four Saints* what do you mean, of course they understand or they would not listen to it. If you enjoy it you understand it, and lots of people have it enjoyed it so lots of people have understood it." Lundell asked her about her habit of eliminating capital letters and question marks, baiting her to admit that punctuation marks were "crutches for the mentally crippled." "That is it exactly," Gertrude said, "they are a help to some people but the average reading mind does not need them." What about slang, he wondered. "Your study in these slang phrases, it would seem to me, must be rather limited. In your literary circles you don't meet much new and vigorous slang." "Oh, don't I?" she fired back. "How do you know I do not? And what makes you think I only talk to literary circles? I talk to and listen to anybody." As for her well-known quote, "Pigeons on the grass alas," Gertrude explained that she had written the line while walking in the Luxembourg Gardens in Paris, repeating the phrase in various forms "until I had emptied myself of the emotion." Lundell concluded that many of her lines were "rather hard for us normal Americans to see." "What is a normal American?" Gertrude asked. "There are lots of quite normal Americans who do see. And how. But after all you must enjoy my writing and if you enjoy it you understand it. If you did not enjoy it why do you make a fuss about it? There is the real answer." She seemed, as usual, to enjoy the debate. So did Lundell, who rendered his considered opinion, "She's not so crazy. She's smart."[43]

▼ ▼ ▼

ONE MONTH INTO THEIR VISIT, GERTRUDE AND ALICE already felt like native New Yorkers. "Everybody knows us on the street," Gertrude told William Rogers, "and they are all so sweet and kind it is unimaginable and you go into a store anywhere to buy anything and they say how do you do Miss Stein and Alice goes anywhere they say how do you do Miss Toklas and they so pleasantly speak to us on the street, it is unbelievable." Just that day, she continued, "One man said to the woman who was with him, there goes your friend Gertrude Stein as if he had had enough and more than enough. I too thought I might be news but not like that." In her own letter to Rogers, Alice was positively gushy. "Everything has been wonderful," she wrote, "we are making plans for a leisurely tour of the whole country, by air of course. I want to stay in the U.S.A. forever. And I'm not discovering it, it's always been like that only now, it's more so."[44]

They may not have been discovering America, but America was discovering them. The Pathé newsreel of Gertrude explaining why she had come to America had made its way into the nation's movie theaters and currently was being seen by tens of thousands of viewers from coast to coast. In it she announced hopefully, "My lectures are to be a simple way to say that if you understand a thing you can enjoy it and if you enjoy a thing you can understand it. And in these lectures I want to tell so simply that anybody will know it and know it very well that you can enjoy all the things I have been writing. And since you enjoy them you can understand them." That was her hope, at any rate.[45]

The *New York Times* printed a tongue-in-cheek letter to the editor after the newsreel appeared. "It was interesting to hear Gertrude Stein in the news reel express her reaction to 'pigeons

in the grass, alas,' " the reader wrote, misquoting the preposi-
tion. "May I suggest that Miss Stein throw a handful of seeds to
the pigeons? It would then be still more interesting to note her
reaction. Think how pleased the pigeons would be!" *New Yorker*
humorist James Thurber complained, tongue more or less in
cheek, "I saw Gertrude Stein on the screen of a newsreel theatre
one afternoon and I heard her read that famous passage of hers
about pigeons on the grass, alas. It is neither just nor accurate
to connect the words alas with pigeons. Pigeons are definitely
not alas." Ornithological questions aside, it was clear that people
were reading and discussing Gertrude as never before. As biographer Lucy Daniel has noted, "For the newspapers Stein was
the light relief. Her own life, and the lives she wrote about that
intersected her own in *The Autobiography*, were the celebrity
lives that represented a distraction from the grinding hardships
being faced by many of her readers."[46]

If Gertrude resented being comic relief, she kept it to herself.
She was having too much fun to begrudge anyone else having
fun, even at her expense. She laughed as loudly as anyone when
the *New Yorker* reported her embarrassing wardrobe malfunc-
tion at a Virgil Thomson concert at the Hotel Majestic. Gertrude, said the magazine, wore "extraordinary blue-and-white
striped knickers for underwear, and somehow stepped out of
them and left them lying there on the floor. She thought it was
very funny." Taking its cue as always from publisher Harold Ross,
who tersely declined an invitation from Bennett Cerf to attend
a dinner in Gertrude's honor, the magazine took regular potshots at Gertrude, most of it notably less witty than their target
herself. Only Alexander Woollcott, who had a top-rated radio
show along with his *New Yorker* column, bucked the official line.
Gertrude, he said, was "a very beautiful woman" and, like him, a
lover of French poodles. Their friendship became so well known

that it was later spoofed in the hit Broadway comedy *The Man Who Came to Dinner* by George S. Kaufman and Moss Hart. In it the curmudgeonly protagonist, stranded in a boring midwestern home over the holidays, takes a transatlantic telephone call. "Hello, Gertie!" he shouts. "How's my little nightingale?" She always calls him at Christmas, the character explains to his baffled hosts.[47]

Bernard Faÿ, watching Gertrude's progress from afar, wrote from France, "I feel that what is going on now in America—what this trip of yours is doing is tremendously important to the mental life in America. What you bring them, nobody had brought them since Walt Whitman." He had been watching Americans closely since 1919, Faÿ assured Gertrude, "and seen them get excited over all kinds of things: the new Ford cars, Mr. Hoover, Al Smith, air travel, the Queen of Rumania, speak-easies, etc.; but I have never seen them act as they do now with you. It is something deeper and more personal."[48]

Comic poet Ogden Nash, author of the immortal couplet "Candy is dandy / But liquor is quicker," felt moved to dissent. He wrote a new, slightly longer couplet for the *New York American*: "The fault I'm sure is solely mine, / But I cannot root for Gertrude Stein." In that sentiment he found himself distinctly in the minority. Gertrude may not have been the queen of Rumania, but, for a season at least, she was the queen of New York. And Alice, as always, was the power behind the throne.[49]

FIVE

Yes Chicago Too

I N THE MIDST OF THEIR MANHATTAN SOCIALIZING, GER-
trude and Alice caught a plane to Chicago for the opening-
night performance of *Four Saints in Three Acts*, to be conducted
personally by Virgil Thomson at the Louis Sullivan Auditorium.
Neither woman had ever been on an airplane before, and they
approached it as a grand adventure. Carl Van Vechten, worrying that they might be frightened, volunteered to go with them
to hold their hands. He needn't have bothered. Carrying special
cloth Indian totems he gave them for protection, they thoroughly
enjoyed the experience. "It was nice," said Gertrude. "I know of
nothing more pleasing more soothing more beguiling than the
slow hum of the mounting." Looking down at the ground passing beneath them, Gertrude viewed it as a giant cubist painting.
"It was then in a kind of way that I really began to know what
the ground looked like," she recalled. "Quarter sections make
a picture and going over America like that made anyone know
why the post-cubist painting was what it was. The wandering line
of Masson was there and the mixed line of Picasso coming and
coming again and following itself into a beginning was there,
the simple solution of Braque was there and I suppose Leger
might be there but I did not see it." When Alice leaned over to
ask Gertrude how she was doing, Gertrude told her brusquely,
"Do not interrupt my pleasure."[1]

They were met at Midway Airport by their local hostesses,
Fanny Butcher and Elizabeth "Bobsy" Goodspeed, who would
facilitate their entrée into Chicago society. Butcher, the literary

critic for the *Chicago Tribune*, had long championed Gertrude's books, even though she confessed she understood them "only in flashes…as a child reads." Bobsy Goodspeed was a force on the local arts scene, serving as president of the Arts Club of Chicago and, most recently, as the organizer of the art exhibition at the Chicago World's Fair. Her husband, Charles "Barney" Goodspeed, was a leader in Republican Party politics and a trustee at the University of Chicago. The wife of the university's president, Robert M. Hutchins, was rumored to be Bobsy Goodspeed's lover. Whatever the truth to the rumors, it was widely agreed that willowy, ethereal Maude Hutchins was one of the prettiest women in Chicago. Maude, a scion of the blueblood Phelps family from New York State, was something of a rebel, announcing early on that she had no intention of being a tame little faculty wife, hosting teas and serving cookies. Instead, she became a fixture in the high society columns of the newspapers, invited male and female undergraduates to pose for her in the nude, and scandalized the university by sending out Christmas cards to board members and trustees with a nude drawing of her barely pubescent but easily recognized fourteen-year-old daughter Franja on the front in an arrestingly suggestive pose.[2]

Gertrude and Alice would spend a good deal of time with Fanny and Bobsy during the course of three separate visits to Chicago, but it would still not be long enough to work out all the complex personal and sexual relationships among the players in whose elevated circles they now moved. On their first whirlwind stopover, they sat in Bobsy's private box seats for their first-ever viewing of *Four Saints in Three Acts*. Alice found the opera enchanting, but Gertrude was on the fence. "I was less excited about it than I expected to be," she would recall. "It was my opera but it was so far away." The singers at least "said all the words." To the *Chicago Tribune* she allowed, "I am completely satisfied with it. Before it was inside me and now it is outside me." After the performance they went backstage and Gertrude signed photographs for the cast. Alice, ever the epicurean, long remembered Bobsy's delicious clear turtle soup, which she would memorialize in her best-selling cookbook (p. 126) two decades later.[3]

The Chicago press, on first encounter, found Gertrude refreshingly warm and humorous. When a *Chicago News* reporter prodded, "Now Miss Stein, can you tell us just when buttons are tender?" she quickly replied, "I don't know, you will have to ask the buttons." Another reporter wanted to know if she was pulling the public's leg. "I don't know anything about the public's leg," she said, "and I'm too old to pull a leg if I wanted to." The *Tribune* printed an old photograph of Gertrude, Alice, and Basket under the caption, "The Toklas Family Complete." So positive and wide-ranging was the coverage that one promoter complained loudly that he couldn't sell tickets for recent Pulitzer Prize–winning poet Robert Hillyer. "Gertrude Stein comes out here preaching the gospel of obscurity and is a riot," said the promoter. "And here's Hillyer, writing, beautiful, limpid, lucid prose, coming to read his poetry, and I can't make anybody care. You can't get near Stein, but I've got plenty of tickets for Hillyer."[4]

▼ ▼ ▼

THEIR FIRST VISIT WENT SO WELL THAT GERTRUDE AND ALICE returned to Chicago for a two-week stay on November 24. Once again Bobsy Goodspeed was their hostess, putting them up for four days at her Lincoln Park townhouse before they checked into the landmark Drake Hotel facing Lake Michigan. The Drake, at the time, was one of Chicago's two leading hotels (the Palmer House was the other). Renowned for its daily afternoon tea in the all-white Palm Court, the Drake was also home to the city's chief mobster, Frank "The Enforcer" Nitti, who had succeeded his boss Al Capone after Capone's conviction for tax evasion three years earlier. It is unlikely that Gertrude crossed paths with Nitti; they both had crowded social schedules.

Bobsy hosted several tea parties of her own for Gertrude and Alice, including one at which they were delighted to reunite with the former Hadley Hemingway. Hadley had married local architect Paul Scott Mowrer a few months earlier, and if she bore any resentment toward Gertrude for the rough treatment accorded to her first husband in the *Autobiography*, she was too polite to say so. Hadley, as always, was effortlessly nice to everyone. As for the complaints of other alleged victims of the book in the current issue of *transition* magazine, Gertrude brushed them off in the press as "babyish" and "infantish." Her comparison of Amelie Matisse to a horse was meant as a compliment, Gertrude maintained. "I'm crazy about horses," she said. "You know there are many beautiful horses." It was not, perhaps, her finest moment. Fanny Butcher loyally put the best construction on the controversy by noting that it had served to increase the public's interest in the *Autobiography*. "They do this sort of getting worked up over literature so well in Paris," she claimed. Gertrude appreciated the gesture. When she left Chicago, she gave Butcher a copy of *Four Saints in Three Acts*, inscribed a bit naughtily to "the best of the famous fans and...the very best of Fannies."[5]

Gertrude soon found herself embroiled in another quarrel. The setting was the President's House on the University of Chicago campus, where she and Alice were the guests of honor at a dinner hosted for them on November 25 by Robert M. Hutchins. Known variously as "the Boy President" and "the most dangerous man in American education," Hutchins propounded a new approach to college education, deemphasizing vocational training and specialization in favor of having students learn how to think for themselves by studying the great thinkers of the past. To that end he brought in writer-philosopher Mortimer Adler from New York City to help him develop a "Great Books" program at the university. Hutchins and Adler were winding up a class that evening, and in her husband's absence Maude Hutchins presided as hostess. Ordinarily, this would not have been a problem, but Gertrude had apparently tired of the nonstop round of dinners, cocktail parties, and opera performances that Bobsy Goodspeed had orchestrated for them in the past three days. When Hutchins and Adler walked in, she demanded to know where they had been and what they had been doing. "The energy Gertrude exuded in a small room hit one like Niagara Falls," Adler remembered. Hutchins started to apologize to "Miss Stein." "Don't call me Miss Stein," she said. "Call me Gertrude Stein."[6]

Things went downhill from there. Hutchins began explaining the Great Books program, and Gertrude, in her own words, "began to get excited." She noticed, she said, that there were no books in English on the list he handed her. "No," said Hutchins, "in English there have really been no ideas expressed." "Then I gather," she said, "that to you there are no ideas which are not sociological or government ideas." He allowed that was so. "Government is the least interesting thing in human creation," responded Gertrude heatedly. "Creation and the expression of that creation is a damn sight more interesting. Naturally you are teachers and teaching is your occupation and naturally what you call ideas are easy to teach and so you are convinced that they are the only ideas but the real ideas are not the relation of human beings as groups but a human being to himself." Adler jumped in, determined, he said, to give her "a dose of her own medicine." In her later account, Gertrude claimed to have forgotten exactly what she said or did next, but Bobsy Goodspeed reported that Gertrude had pointed to Adler's "narrow" forehead and shouted, "With your dialectics, you could *prove anything* to me but, of course, you would be *wrong!*" and whacked him on the head. Alice, as always a silent onlooker to the altercation, said only that "the discussion was fairly lively."[7]

At that moment, the Hutchinses' maid burst in and announced formally, "Madame, the police." Adler turned white, as anyone would, but everyone else burst out laughing. Fanny Butcher, using her newspaper contacts, had arranged for two Chicago homicide detectives to take Gertrude and Alice on a tour of the local underworld. Their ride had come. "The way I felt about her at that moment," remembered the still-embittered Adler four decades later, "I wished they could have arrived earlier and taken her for a ride Chicago-style." Despite his ungallant wishes, there would be no Valentine's Day Massacre in their immediate future. Alice paused in the doorway. "This has been a wonderful evening," she told the room. "Gertrude has said things tonight that it will take her ten years to understand." How long it would take the others to understand was anyone's guess.[8]

The memorable evening continued. The two detectives drove their guests around Chicago's less upscale neighborhoods, which Alice politely termed "various parts of doubtful respectability." Because of the bad weather, one of the cops explained, there was unlikely to be much for them to see. "The sergeant said he was afraid not much would happen," Gertrude recalled, "it was raining and when it rained nobody moved around and if nobody moved around there could not be any homicide unless it was a family affair." They had just missed one such killing, but "it had not been interesting as it had been a family affair and everybody could understand everything." For the celebrities' benefit the detectives stopped at an apartment house and rousted a group of unoffending African Americans, telling the residents they were looking for a man who had stolen a purse earlier that night. It made the people uneasy, Gertrude reported, as well it might, but everyone relaxed long enough to tell them that they were all from the South, except for one Canadian. Gertrude, Alice, and their guides moved on to another rooming house, this one full of Chinese men who likewise were doing nothing overtly suspicious. Gertrude asked one of the detectives, a bit skeptically, if he could always tell "which ones were the bad men in a town." He could, said the detective, although he admitted that he was still troubled by the unsolved killing of an elderly black man on a street corner in Chinatown a few years earlier. "Somebody shot him and nobody heard anything nobody knew anything nobody saw him or anything, he was shot down dead," said the detective. "I will never know why anybody shot him."[9]

That was "the night they caught Baby Face," Gertrude remembered, and they heard numerous radio calls reporting the search. Earlier that day, Lester Joseph Gillis, aka Baby Face Nelson, had been killed in a gunfight with FBI agents Herman Hollis and Samuel Cowley in Barrington, Illinois, thirty-two miles northwest of Chicago. Although the gunfight took place in broad daylight, Nelson's body was not found until later that evening, wrapped in an Indian blanket and left on the front steps of a Lutheran church in Skokie by his wife Helen and his right-hand man, John Paul Chase. Baby Face had already killed a third FBI agent in a separate shootout, officially making him the most lethal Public Enemy in bureau history. Agent Hollis was nearly as lethal himself, having brought down Nelson's former partner John Dillinger outside the Biograph Theater in Chicago four months earlier. Fortunately for Gertrude and Alice, their guides did not happen upon Baby Face while the women were in the backseat of the squad car. They did, however, manage to get lost at one point, which greatly amused Gertrude, who wondered how two Chicago policemen could get lost in their own hometown. She promised not to tell anyone.[10]

They continued their tour, looking in at dawn on a local dance marathon, which disturbed Gertrude more than any of the night's other tawdry sights and sounds. The marathons, vividly evoked in Horace McCoy's 1935 novel *They Shoot Horses, Don't They?*, were a ghoulish by-product of the Depression and the economic anxieties unleashed upon the common people. Dubbed "bunion derbies" and "callus carnivals," and more elegantly described by dance historian Sonny Watson as "pageants of fatigue," the marathons peaked in popularity in the early years of the thirties, when as many as twenty-five hundred people at a time took part in contests across the country. Rules varied from event to event, but all required some form of continuous motion by the contestants, who danced in pairs for weeks, sometimes months, for a chance to win a few hundred dollars in cash and prizes. Members of the public paid twenty-five cents apiece for the dubious privilege of gawking at the exhausted dancers as they stumbled, lurched, clutched, grabbed, and fell against each other in varying states of unconsciousness. Professional ringers, called "horses" because they could go the distance, mixed with local entrants and usually came away with all the winnings. Physical injuries, mental breakdowns, comas, hysteria, even death occurred among the sleep-deprived contestants. One Seattle man dropped dead of a heart attack after dancing nonstop for eighty-seven hours.[11]

To Gertrude, the Chicago marathon seemed like something out of Dante's *Inferno*. "Here there was nothing neither waking nor sleeping, they were all young ones and they were moving as their bodies were drooping," she recalled. "They had been six weeks without sleeping and some no longer had another one with them they were moving and drooping alone but when there were two of them one was more clinging than moving and the other one was supporting and moving. There was plenty of light and a little noise." The organizer of the marathon, sensing some free publicity, invited Gertrude and Alice to pose with one of the bedraggled couples. Gertrude, horrified, declined. Years later, surrealist filmmaker Jacques Viot described to Gertrude the difference between movies and plays. "The film audience is not an audience that is awake," he said, "it is an audience that is dreaming it is not asleep." Viot's comment made her think of the Chicago dance marathon, she said. She never went to another.[12]

Despite such disconcerting sights, Chicago would prove to be the couple's favorite city during their tour. Having never seen a true midwestern winter, Gertrude spent hours looking out the window at the Drake Hotel. "Yes Chicago too was good to look at," she recounted. "I had not seen winter for many years and Alice Toklas had never seen it. We liked it." The skyscrapers in particular fascinated Gertrude. "They told us that the modern high buildings had been invented in Chicago and not in New York," she wrote. "It is interesting that it should have been done where there was plenty of land to build on and not in New York where it is narrow and so must be high of necessity. Choice is always more pleasing than anything necessary." She liked the illuminated signs on the roofs of buildings advertising dances. "I never tired of seeing them," she said, "the somber gray light on the buildings and the simple solemn mechanical figures dancing, there were other things I liked but I liked that the most." Alice, as usual, had her own distinctive way of looking at things. "It is not the way they go into the air but the way they come out of the ground that is the thing," she observed. "European buildings sit on the ground but American ones come out of the ground." They agreed that America had no sky, only air, and because of that "there is no lid on top of them and so they move around." It was an interesting take on the frontier thesis first advanced by historian Frederick Jackson Turner, coincidentally, in Chicago four decades earlier.[13]

Between the police rides and the window gazing, Gertrude found time to conduct a two-hour seminar on epic poetry at the University of Chicago on December 4. Robert Hutchins, showing an admirable disinclination to hold a grudge, invited Gertrude to teach one of their Great Books classes. "Of course I will," she responded. Her appearance was kept secret by the university to ensure that only those students already enrolled in the seminar would attend. On the day in question Gertrude was in good form, much to the surprise of Hutchins and Adler. They were all sitting around a long table. "I began to talk and they not Hutchins and Adler but the others began to talk and pretty soon we were all talking about epic poetry and what it was," remembered Gertrude. "It was exciting we found out a good deal." Afterward, Hutchins marveled at the way in which Gertrude had been able to engage the students in a lively give-and-take. "You did make them all talk more than we can make them and a number of them talked who never talked before," he said graciously. Gertrude was not surprised.

> You see why they talk to me is that I am like them I do not know the answer, you say you do not know but you do know if you did not know the answer you could not spend your life in teaching but I really do not know, I really do not, I do not even know whether there is a question let alone having an answer for a question. To me when a thing is really interesting it is when there is no question and no answer, if there is then already the subject is not interesting.

Overlooking the dig at his chosen profession, Hutchins gamely invited Gertrude to come back any time.[14]

▼ ▼ ▼

USING CHICAGO AS THEIR BASE, GERTRUDE AND ALICE ventured into the greater Midwest, often traveling by airplane, their
new favorite way to travel. On December 6, they took a flight
to Madison, Wisconsin, where Gertrude delivered two talks on
the topic "What Is English Literature" at the University of Wisconsin. It was already deep winter in Madison, which pretty
much qualified it as deep winter anywhere this side of Siberia,
and Gertrude walked around carefully in the ice and snow. At a
house party that evening she ran into an old acquaintance from
her years at Johns Hopkins medical school, Dorothy Reed Mendenhall. Gertrude suggested they find a quiet corner to catch up,
but they were interrupted by the arrival of famed architect Frank
Lloyd Wright, who also wanted to talk to Gertrude. Unfortu-
nately, the two modernist giants never got the chance to converse.
Gertrude wanted to eat first and promised to see Wright after
her talk, but he left before she could meet up with him.

The next morning Mendenhall drove them to the airport to
catch a flight to St. Paul, Minnesota. Mendenhall, said Gertrude, was "the same as she had been" at medical school—not
necessarily a compliment—and Gertrude mostly looked out the
car window. "It had not snowed," Gertrude observed a bit puz-
zlingly, "but there was certainly more snow and it was whiter."
Thirty-seven years later, remembering even further back in time,
Mendenhall would tell Edmund Wilson that Gertrude had been
hopeless in medical school—clumsy, untidy, careless, and arro-
gant. "At medicine, she worked only in a half-hearted way," said
Mendenhall, now a doctor herself, "and her grades were always
poor." Perhaps it was late revenge for their less than collegial
reunion in Madison.[15]

Gertrude and Alice flew into Minneapolis in a three-seater

Gypsy Moth airplane, skimming low over the mounded snow banks. Gertrude was enchanted. "It was unbelievably beautiful, and the symmetry of the roads and farms and turns make something that fills me," she wrote to William Rogers, "and the shadows of the trees on the wooded hills, well the more I see the more I do see what I like, I cannot tell you how much we like it, last night my eyes were all full of it." In Minneapolis they stayed at the home of Quaker Oats heiress Mahala Dutton Douglas, a survivor of the *Titanic* disaster, which had claimed the life of her husband, Walter. Mrs. Douglas was a childhood friend of Carl Van Vechten's, whose 1924 novel, *The Tattooed Heiress*, was reputedly based on her early life in Cedar Rapids, Iowa. Her stately home, "Walden," on the bluffs above Lake Minnetonka, was modeled after a French palace and was indirectly the cause of her widowhood. Her husband had retired at the early age of fifty, and they had traveled to France in early 1912 in search of furnishings for their new residence before heading home aboard *Titanic*.[16]

Mrs. Douglas did not share details of the *Titanic* sinking with Gertrude and Alice on their visit, but she did serve them "a superlative lunch" in a dining room filled with flowers, including the first Tiepolo blue orchids Alice had ever seen. Alice later commemorated both the table setting and Mrs. Douglas's recipe for Lobster Archiduc in her published cookbook: one three-pound lobster, boiled alive and then cooked in eggs, brandy, port wine, whisky, heavy cream, lemons, and butter, seasoned with salt and cayenne pepper. The dish, she said, had "an illusive flavor."[17]

That night Gertrude appeared before the Women's Club of St. Paul, where she made a comment that might well have applied to hometown boy F. Scott Fitzgerald: "Even a slow catastrophe is quite fast." Fitzgerald was not around—he seldom revisited St. Paul—but Gertrude and Alice were soon reunited with another old friend, Sherwood Anderson. Someone told them that Anderson was visiting family in nearby Stillwater. "Ah if he was we would see him certainly we would," Gertrude directed. "Someone find him and someone did." Actually, according to Alice, Anderson found them, calling them up and offering to drive them to his sister-in-law's house for dinner. "It was the happiest of meetings," Alice said, noting that she was served mint jelly—also a first. Gertrude said Anderson was "traveling around to write what he thought everybody felt about farming that is the farmers." An unregenerate city girl herself, she was not much interested in rural life, but the food was good—"a very good Virginia dinner"—and afterward Anderson's in-laws cheerfully helped shovel them out of the snow and put them back on their way.[18]

Usually Gertrude refused all invitations to dinner parties and receptions at local homes, preferring "not being entertained because I like a quiet life and do not like to go out to dinner and above all not to a reception certainly not when I am not to know any one, so the social life I preferred in traveling was the life with reporters and I did enjoy them." She backed up her words when she came to the rescue of a young St. Paul reporter after reading his humorously critical account of her lecture. "The reporter had reported my talk as if it were a wrestling match and it was very well written and of course any author would have noticed that every paragraph or so he introduced one of the best sentences I had written and it came in well. It pleased me I like good writing." At lunch she mentioned the article to the woman who had organized the lecture. "I said I was much taken with the way my lecture was written up...but she said everybody is furious because it reflects so on the taste of this city not at all I said he writes well and what is more he understood what I said which is to me a pleasant thing and does not often happen that is not by reporters reporting, well she said there is his editor over there, everybody has been complaining to him so that he was going to fire the young fellow who did it." At Gertrude's intercession the young man's job was saved, and he dissolved into tears upon hearing the news. "He said you saved his life," Gertrude was told. "I hope he will go on," she replied.[19]

Their newfound love of air travel was not without complications. Leaving St. Paul on December 9 for Chicago, where they were supposed to catch a connecting flight to Iowa City, their plane was diverted by bad weather to Milwaukee. The painter Grant Wood (*American Gothic*) had arranged for Gertrude to speak to a Gertrude Stein Club he had organized in Iowa City, but flying conditions made it impossible. There had already been engine trouble on the ground, causing them to transfer to a second plane. It was a clear, starlit evening, and as they began to descend, they were savvy enough to know they were not landing in Chicago. "Alice Toklas began to say what are they doing we must get to Chicago to catch the plane for Iowa City and she called the second pilot and she told him. No he said we can't get to Chicago we are coming right down in Milwaukee and there if you want you can get the train for Chicago." Alice indignantly demanded to know "why do you start a plane if it cannot go where it is supposed to go." The plane could go there all right, the pilot said, but not that night. "Why not," said Alice, "it is a lovely night." "Maybe so," said the pilot, "but lady wouldn't you rather be in Milwaukee than in your coffin?" For once Alice was at a loss to reply.[20]

While taking a commuter train back to Chicago, Gertrude noted that their fellow passengers were engrossed in newspaper stories about the newly arrived Dionne quintuplets. The five babies, born on May 28 in Ontario, Canada, would become the first quintuplets to survive infancy and live to adulthood. It was interesting, thought Gertrude, that the Dionne story "was really the only thing in the paper that was really real" to the passengers. She was not all that interested in babies herself. By the time they reached Chicago it was snowing so hard that they could not locate the chauffeur Bobsy Goodspeed had sent to pick them up. They slogged back to the Drake Hotel on foot, and Alice was forced to admit that their erstwhile pilot had been right, "no plane could get into Chicago." Gertrude's appearance in Iowa City was canceled as well.[21]

They had better luck flying to Detroit two days later in a new Douglas airplane, the largest plane they had yet ridden in. Gertrude told Carl Van Vechten that she thought they should go in together and buy their own secondhand plane. They could emblazon it with their family crest, a champagne bottle and a corset over the motto "We do what we do which is a pleasure." They had taken to calling themselves the Woojums family—Mama, Papa, and Baby Woojums—and Papa Woojums thought it was a fine idea. Mama Woojums (Alice) was unconvinced. After arriving in Detroit, Gertrude wanted to find the factory where they made the Fords she had driven exclusively since World War I. She found the streets foreign and frightening, with a policeman on every corner calling out directions through a megaphone. A loudspeaker blaring out the news that a crazed gunman was on the loose did nothing to lessen her anxiety. Back at the hotel, she and Alice were further disconcerted by all the comings and goings through their room by the cleaning staff. After three days they put in an emergency call to their old friend Joseph Brewer, then serving as president of Olivet College. Brewer, who had published Gertrude's collection *Useful Knowledge* in 1929, sprang to their rescue, organizing a relief party of virtually the entire Olivet faculty. "They took us away with them," said Gertrude, "and that was a pleasure."[22]

After a couple days at Olivet, Brewer took them on to Ann Arbor, where Gertrude was scheduled to speak at the University of Michigan on December 14. Along the way she saw numerous roadside billboards for Burma-Shave. The Minneapolis-based company had devised a nationwide advertising campaign that took advantage of the vast increase in motorists and their necessarily brief attention spans. A series of six wooden billboards spelled out in white letters on a red background a rhyming jingle, followed by a giant sign reading "BURMA-SHAVE." A typical jingle declared, "Pity all / The mighty Caesars / They pulled / Each whisker out / With tweezers." Gertrude, always easily amused, found the signs "a whole lively poem" in themselves.[23]

Her talk at Ann Arbor was sponsored by the university's Hopwood Award Committee, which oversaw the annual Avery Hopwood and Julie Hopwood Creative Writing Awards, established by their late friend the playwright Avery Hopwood, who had suffered a fatal heart attack in 1928 while wading in the surf at Juan-les-Pins on the French Riviera. (Prominent recipients of the award, which is still ongoing, have included Arthur Miller, Theodore Roethke, Frank O'Hara, Edmund White, John Ciardi, Robert Hayden, and Marge Piercy.) Known as the Playboy Playwright because his frothy plays were considered risqué by the standards of the time, Hopwood once had four shows running simultaneously on Broadway. Among his works were *The Demi-Virgin*, *Getting Gertie's Garter*, *Gold Diggers of Broadway*, *Gold Diggers of 1933*, and his best-known if somewhat uncharacteristic play, *The Bat*, cowritten with mystery novelist Mary Roberts Rinehart. Gertrude and Alice had first met Hopwood, another close friend of Carl Van Vechten's, in 1915. They liked him, even when he broke glasses and spilled wine on their guests—unlike the long-banished Ezra Pound. "We adored him," said Gertrude, describing Hopwood as having "the air of a sheep with the possibility of being a wolf."[24]

Despite her friendship with their benefactor, the Michigan faculty did not take to Gertrude. One called her "a terrible bore" who produced nothing but "automatic writing." Another said she was unintelligible, and a third cautioned students—who were always more receptive to her work than their professors—to guard against "a quick enthusiasm for her work until they have balanced it with an understanding of what other artists have already accomplished." Gertrude, for her part, negatively contrasted the enormous university with the "little country village" at Olivet. The chief difference was Brewer himself, who Gertrude said was very serious about his duties as president. "Any American can be serious when he is serious about it," she reasoned, "and almost any American can be serious about it, some English people can be serious about what they are serious about but more Americans can be and are and Joe Brewer is." Michigan's president, Alexander Grant Ruthven, was mostly serious about garter snakes, of which he was the world's leading authority (he eventually identified sixteen new subspecies). He was also serious about cracking down on bootleggers at the school's fraternities, which cannot have endeared him much to the brother Wolverines.[25]

In Indianapolis, Gertrude gave her lecture "The Gradual Making of *The Making of Americans*" to the Contemporary Club at the John Herron Art Institute. She and Alice squeezed in a visit to Stephen Foster Hall, whose unlikely provenance there was the result of an inextinguishable fascination with the great songwriter's work by Josiah Kirby Lilly, president of the locally based pharmaceutical giant Eli Lilly and Company. Gertrude, with her characteristic disinterest in both popular music and the place of her birth, neglected to mention that Foster hailed from the same suburb of Pittsburgh—Allegheny—that she did. Her own taste in music ran to "On the Trail of the Lonesome Pine" and a new jingle she had been taught by Mildred Weston Rogers, "Yo ho yo ho yo ho yo ho for we are the makers of Wonder Bread."[26]

Gertrude and Alice had been urged to visit the museum by New York acquaintance Alexander Woollcott. The museum, said Gertrude, contained everything Foster had ever done, along with records of all his songs and even "the purse that was on him when he was dead"—a purse that contained all of thirty-eight cents and a scrap of paper with the title, or beginning, of a new song, "Dear friends and gentle hearts," that he never got to finish. (Tin Pan Alley tunesmiths Sammy Fain and Bob Hilliard eventually completed the song eighty-five years later, and "Dear Hearts and Gentle People" was a massive hit for Dinah Shore.) The Foster museum was about to be moved to Pittsburgh, Gertrude said, "another city where they could build a museum that would look more like a church." She was more interested in their tour of Indianapolis's famous Indian mounds, where archaeologists were busily slicing into the mounds. "I suppose they have to slice them if they want to know what is inside in them," Gertrude shrugged, "and of course they do want to know what is in them and each one might be different from the one they had had open." On the whole, she judged Indianapolis "not in any way a disappointment." It was not exactly billboard-worthy praise.[27]

From Indianapolis they flew to Columbus, Ohio, where Gertrude gave her lecture "Poetry and Grammar" to the Chi Delta Phi Honorary Literary Society at Ohio State University. They found the Ohio state capital another pleasant place, with a nice climate—at least when compared to the Arctic cold of Minnesota and Wisconsin. Alice said she wanted to come back and live there, but then she also wanted to live "in Avila and New York and New Orleans and California." Gertrude preferred Chicago and Texas, but she didn't want to live there, she said. "I like to live in Paris." Columbus interested her, particularly after she found a room devoted to cubist paintings at the local museum, including several "really good" Picassos. The museum had been funded by a local businessman who had never owned a painting until he went to New York at the age of seventy and discovered the cubists. In the next ten years the man bought enough paintings to fill a new room at the museum. The paintings were all "very lovely," Gertrude said, unlike most American art, which she judged "not awfully good." Of course, she had high standards.[28]

A former professor at Ohio State, Clarence Andrews, had been one of the first academics to teach Gertrude's work in his classes. Andrews had died of pneumonia two years earlier, but one of his former students, Samuel Morris Steward, carried the Stein torch westward with him to Carroll College in Helena, Montana, and Washington State University in Pullman. At WSU, Steward ran afoul of the school's fundamentalist president by publishing a novel, *Angels on the Bough,* that contained a sympathetic portrait of a prostitute. Steward sent a copy of the novel to Gertrude, which she read and liked. "You have really created a piece of something," she told him, "you have succeeded in reaching a unity without connecting." E. M. Forster might have disagreed.[29]

Steward went on to have a career that was almost too outlandish to be believed. Leaving academia in protest over the declining quality (as he saw it) of his students, Steward went to work with pioneering sex researcher Alfred Kinsey, for whom he recorded his multifarious sexual encounters in his "Stud File," performed extreme bondage and sadomasochistic acts on camera, and personally introduced Kinsey to the gay demimonde in Chicago. He became a tattoo artist—he was the Hell's Angels' official tattooist during the 1960s—and wrote numerous pornographic novels and one thankfully nonpornographic novel, *Murder Is Murder Is Murder*, which featured Gertrude and Alice as amateur detectives. Among his many sexual conquests, so he claimed, were Lord Alfred Douglas, Oscar Wilde's young lover, and Glenway Wescott, Gertrude's syrupy Paris visitor. Gertrude and Alice, unaware of Steward's more outré accomplishments, continued to correspond with him for many years and hosted him twice at Bilignin in the late thirties. Gertrude even included him in her children's book, *Alphabets and Birthdays*, observing gnomically, "He could eat the candles but not the cake."[30]

From Columbus they went to Toledo, where Gertrude indulged in one of her favorite new pastimes—rubbernecking. American houses fascinated her. "The wooden houses of America excited me as nothing else in America excited me," she wrote. "I never stopped being excited by the wooden houses everywhere. I liked them all." One house in particular interested her, the home of Champion Spark Plugs founder Robert A. Stranahan. The Harvard-educated Stranahan was not home that day, but his wife, Page, was there and received them graciously. Gertrude introduced herself and told Mrs. Stranahan about faithfully using her husband's products during the war. Mrs. Stranahan passed along the compliment, and a short time later Gertrude received in the mail a small stainless steel charm in the shape of a spark plug, which the company handed out to favored customers. She would have preferred one of the original silver charms, Gertrude confessed privately, but they had been discontinued by Champion during the Depression.[31]

Gertrude was fascinated by the windows in the houses they passed. "That is one thing any American can do," she observed, "he can put windows in a building and wherever they are they are interesting." Many of the windows were curtainless, a fact that Gertrude ascribed to characteristic American openness.

"Everybody in America is nice and everybody is honest except those who want to break in," she reasoned. "If they want to break in shutters will not stop them so why have them. Why shut the shutters and the curtains and keep anyone from seeing, they all know what they are going to see." Whether anyone saw Gertrude Stein looking through their windows was not reported.[32]

▼ ▼ ▼

FOLLOWING A TWO-MONTH-LONG SWING THROUGH THE NORTH-east and the Deep South (detailed in the next chapter), Gertrude and Alice returned to Chicago in late February so that Gertrude could conduct two weeks of seminars at the University of Chicago. For the duration of their stay they moved into the Drexel Avenue apartment of another newfound friend, Pulitzer Prize–winning novelist Thornton Wilder. Shy, soft-spoken, buttoned-down, and closeted, Wilder was an unlikely candidate to become a dear friend of Gertrude and Alice, but he did. They met him at one of Bobsy Goodspeed's parties, and Wilder graciously turned over the key to his apartment and moved into the Quadrangle Club. The two-bedroom flat had a small kitchenette, "no larger than a dining-room table," Alice observed, but it was a welcome respite after four months on the road, eating in hotels, restaurants, private homes, and drugstores. With meats, vegetables, cream, butter, milk, and eggs delivered to their door, Alice prepared home-cooked meals for Gertrude, herself, and assorted dinner guests. She marveled at the way the milkman slipped the bottles invisibly through the milk door in the wall. It was, said Alice, "my ideal of happy housekeeping."[33]

Wilder remains the only writer to win Pulitzer Prizes for both fiction and drama: *The Bridge of San Luis Rey*, *Our Town*, and *The Skin of Our Teeth*. The first two are still on many high school reading lists, and virtually every American student has seen and/or performed in the shamelessly sentimental *Our Town*. Wilder was so modest about his own achievements that he neglected to tell Gertrude and Alice that he had a new novel, *Heaven's My Destination*, about to be published. That novel, considered by many critics to be his best, was a comic picaresque about a traveling textbook salesman, George Marvin Brush, at large (like Gertrude and Alice) in Depression-era America. "An earnest, humorless, moralizing, preachifying, interfering product of bible-belt evangelism," Brush spent his time doing good deeds for unappreciative recipients and getting arrested repeatedly under false pretenses. Wilder based the character on his own domineering father, Amos Parker Wilder, a minister, newspaperman, and onetime diplomat who stigmatized his teenage son by sending him to work on farms every summer as a way "to rid him of his peculiar gait and certain effeminate ways." Gertrude could sympathize—her own father, Daniel Stein, had been an equally humorless authoritarian. "There is too much fathering going on just now and there is no doubt about it fathers are depressing," she observed a few years later, noting that "Thornton Wilder writes to us these days and says he is shamelessly happy...now he has no father." Neither, of course, did she.[34]

Gertrude wrote four new lectures to give to Wilder's handpicked classes. The most interesting was the first, in which she brilliantly differentiated between English and American literature on the basis of geography. English writing, she said, had developed as a way to communicate "the daily island life" of a literally insular people. It was cozy, self-satisfied, and slow, as opposed to American writing, which had to be quicker and more immediate to keep up with the expanding borders of its restless, adventurous pioneers. Americans, she argued, responded to language that gave them a sense of forward movement, like the Burma-Shave signs she was so fond of reading. "The pressure of the non daily life living of the American nation has forced the words to have a different feeling of moving," she said. "Words left alone more and more feel that they are moving and all of it is detached and is detaching anything from anything."[35]

Gertrude delivered her lectures informally to the students. She helpfully provided a list of supplemental readings, including *Jane Eyre*, *The Scarlet Letter*, *Robinson Crusoe*, *Paradise Lost*, *The Vicar of Wakefield*, *Henry Esmond*, Caesar's *Gallic Wars*, *The Mysteries of Udolpho*, and assorted works by Carlyle, Dickens, Emerson, Poe, Whitman, James Fenimore Cooper, Henry James, Mark Twain, various Romantic poets, and Dashiell Hammett. Class size was limited to thirty students, with Wilder acting as combination proctor, referee, and bodyguard. Once, when the class got rowdy and he went to calm them down, Gertrude waved him off—she could take care of herself. Three of the students, who were committed Marxists—she called them "fans of proletarian literature"—came into class one day with their heads shaved. They were anticipating summer, they said, which made her laugh. Other students insisted on reading long poems or discussing history instead of literature. Gertrude let them; she was enjoying herself. "I liked all of them," she said; "Thornton had chosen them not only those who were interested in literature, but those interested in philosophy and history and anything, which made it much more varied and interesting."[36]

Inevitably, someone asked her one day about her most famous phrase: "Rose is a rose is a rose is a rose." Her response has since become almost as famous as the line itself. "Now listen," she told the students. "You all have seen hundreds of poems about roses and you know in your bones that the rose is not there. All those songs that sopranos sing as encores about 'I have a garden; oh, what a garden!' Now I don't want to put too much emphasis on that line, because it's just one line in a longer poem. But I notice that you all know it; you make fun of it, but you know it. Now listen! I'm no fool. I know that in daily life we don't go around saying 'is a…is a…is a….' Yes, I'm no fool; but I think that in that line the rose is red for the first time in English poetry for a hundred years." No one cared to challenge the assertion.[37]

Wilder, like his students, was impressed by Gertrude, both personally and professionally. Years later he would say of her influence on him, "She cracked the sky open." At his strenuous urging, the University of Chicago Press agreed to publish a bound volume of Gertrude's lectures. *Narration*, as it was titled, featured an admiring introduction by Wilder. Other faculty members were not so favorably impressed. Professor Robert Lovett of the English Department expressed the viewpoint held by many. "I do not agree with my colleague's, Mr. Thornton Wilder's, appreciation of these utterances," he wrote. "I think, however, that they may be properly published as part of literary history. Gertrude Stein is a fact, as Dadaism is a fact, and records of both ought to be preserved." His colleague Edith Foster Flint was even less impressed. Gertrude's lectures, she said, left her with "a feeling of extreme irritation. I can see no virtue whatever in the manner of expression. And the ideas conveyed—so far as I am able to penetrate to them—do not seem to me so profound or novel as to necessitate, or warrant, the creation of a new medium, to me a grotesque medium." Gertrude would not have seen the private reports, but in a way she had already answered such criticism in her book-length poem *Stanzas in Meditation*. The final stanza reads, in part, "I call carelessly that the door is open / Which if they can refuse to open / No one can rush to close." She had opened many of those doors herself.[38]

After her triumph with Wilder's students, Gertrude wound up her formal lectures in Chicago during the first three weeks of March 1935. She found time to dine with various society mavens and to attend performances of *H.M.S. Pinafore* and *Iolanthe* mounted by Oscar Wilde's old theatrical sponsor, the D'Oyly Carte Company. At *Pinafore*, which she attended with Wilder and journalist-historian Lloyd Lewis, Gertrude was delighted when Lewis leaned over and whispered to her that the uniforms worn by the play's midshipmen were identical to the one worn by Union admiral David S. Farragut as a young sailor. "Pinafore was a nice thing," she allowed, "but Farragut was more thrilling." She had wanted to collaborate with Lewis on a new biography of Ulysses S. Grant and had let him read the section on Grant in her unpublished manuscript *Four in America*. She considered Lewis one of the most promising young writers in Chicago—he was forty-three at the time—and praised his breakthrough book, *Myths after Lincoln*, as the best "history of a dead man" she had ever read.[39]

Gertrude continued her efforts to persuade Lewis to collaborate with her. "I like the word collaboration," she wrote, "and I have the kind of imagination of how it could take place." Despite the success she shared with Virgil Thomson in creating *Four Saints in Three Acts*, it was debatable how well she actually collaborated with others. Generally, she preferred to go it alone. At any rate, Lewis was too busy completing a doorstop-size biography of Oscar Wilde and working as the drama critic for the *Chicago Daily Times* to consider working with Gertrude on the Grant project. "With my situation what it is and my plodding scheme of research what it cannot help but be," he advised her, "I see time as the great obstacle." Gertrude continued to exchange letters with Lewis and eventually reviewed his Wilde book favorably, saying, "Anything that is American is in him and he is in it." Whether or not Gertrude planted the seed, Lewis returned to Grant as a subject, completing the first volume of a planned trilogy on the general, *Captain Sam Grant*, before dying of a heart attack in 1949 at the age of fifty-seven. Fellow Civil War historian Bruce Catton was personally selected by Lewis's widow, Kathryn, to complete her husband's work, which he did with the books *Grant Moves South* and *Grant Takes Command*. For Catton, if not for Lewis, it was a good career move.[40]

When she was not lecturing, Gertrude rented a Drive-Your-self-Car—"I adore the words," she told a reporter—and took Alice for rides around the city. As always, her driving was determinedly unique. She was unfamiliar with common road signs. "In France it is all done with drawings," Gertrude said, while in America it was mostly done by words of one syllable. "No left U turns, that took me some time so much so that I did one," she recalled. Pulled over while driving her rental car by a policeman who demanded, "Where do you think you are going?" Gertrude responded matter-of-factly that she was trying to turn. "I guess you are a stranger," the policeman said. Gertrude admitted as much. "Well, go on," he said, "but you will most likely get killed before you leave town." One day she left her car keys with the doorman and asked him to call a garage to fix a flat tire. When she and Alice came back from lunch, an entirely new car was waiting for them. "Everything in America is just as easy as that," she beamed. No wonder Chicago was her favorite American city. As she told Thornton Wilder afterward, "I love Chicago and I guess I liked the two weeks there in your apartment and with all your family the best of everything...we did have a most awfully good time there."[41]

SIX

Naturally the Northern Girls
Came South

BETWEEN THEIR BOOKENDED VISITS TO CHICAGO, GER-
trude and Alice spent the Christmas holidays and the better
part of the next two months in the Northeast and the South. It
would be their first extended venture below the Mason-Dixon
line, and they would enjoy it immensely. Bur first came the holidays, which they spent with Gertrude's cousin Julian Stein and
his family in Pikesville, Maryland, just outside of Baltimore. Julian, the son of Gertrude's uncle Samuel Stein, had visited them
at the Hotel Pernollet in 1927 with his wife, Rose Ellen, and her
two children from a previous marriage. Somewhat inconveniently
for all concerned, Julian now was bedridden, recovering from a
recent heart attack, but Gertrude and Alice gamely pitched in,
helping the family hang stockings and decorate the house. On
Christmas morning they all trooped into Julian's bedroom to
open gifts. Gertrude was amused and pleased by hers—a packet
of bobby pins for her hair and a bound copy of comic books from
the local five-and-dime.

Julian's three-year-old granddaughter sat on Gertrude's lap
during the visit, and after they left she was asked how she had
liked Cousin Gertrude and her friend. She "liked the man part,"
said the little girl, "but why did the lady have a mustache?" (Alice
had a pronounced shadow on her upper lip.) In her childish way,
the little girl had posed a question that went largely unasked, and
certainly unanswered, during the entirety of Gertrude and Alice's
American tour: what was the exact nature of their relationship?
Were they friends, partners, roommates, business associates,

traveling companions—what? The answer, of course, was that they were all those things. But the more subtle and subversive aspect of their relationship, their long-standing lesbian couple-dom, was almost entirely overlooked by both the public and the press. Gertrude and Alice, for their part, went to no great lengths on the tour either to advertise or to hide their essential natures. By then they had lived openly as a gay couple for nearly three decades in France; it was literally second nature to them. At the same time, they had both come of age in America at exactly the same time that Oscar Wilde was being tried and convicted of consensual homosexual acts in England. They had excellent memories. In a much less sexually obsessed and inquiring era, they were perfectly willing to keep their inmost proclivities to themselves. It was both good manners and good common sense.[1]

▼ ▼ ▼

THEIR FLIGHT TO BALTIMORE, VIA WASHINGTON, PASSED over Gertrude's hometown of Allegheny, Pennsylvania, leading her to reminisce about her family and place of origin. "If I wanted to have it be anything it really was not," she said about Allegheny. "Anyway the river winds and I can remember my mother said that it was very dirty and everything was black in a few hours naturally we were dressed in white as babies and children but it did not look black anymore not as we went over it and the sky was blue and the air was clear. And the mountains separating it from Washington were the straightest line of mountains I ever saw." As for Baltimore, where she had spent the longest stretch of time before going to Paris, she observed, "At every station I knew the name of everything and the woods looked as I remembered them." Everybody had to come from somewhere, she said. "Nobody thinks about that enough now to be a bother but sometimes they think about it enough to be a pleasure." Her mother had been born in Baltimore, and her father had immigrated there as a child; they had gotten married there. "I used always to say to French people who lived in the provinces that I perfectly understood their family life and their feelings of differences and what happened to everyone because that was the way they lived in Baltimore," Gertrude reasoned. "They still do nothing really can stop anyone living and feeling as they do in Baltimore." Whether or not that was a bad thing, she did not say.[2]

Before giving her only lecture over the holidays at the Baltimore Museum, Gertrude inadvertently snubbed her old friend Etta Cone by pleading exhaustion and declining her offer to use Etta's apartment in Marlborough. "My dear Etta," Gertrude wrote, "Thanks so much for your invitation, but I am not accepting any invitations. There is so much more happening than in our wildest dreams—I am simply seeing no one except for a few very dear friends. With lecturing, broadcasting, cinema newsreels and newspaper people and my editors, I must in between go very easy." Etta, who had loyally purchased a ticket for Gertrude's museum lecture, suddenly found herself called away to North Carolina and gave the ticket to her niece instead. It is doubtful that Alice, who had disliked Etta ever since they quarreled over a lunch bill in Florence in 1908, regretted her absence. They would never see Etta again.[3]

Gertrude did manage to find time to look in on her eighty-year-old aunt Fanny Bachrach and her uncle Ephraim Keyser, the sculptor-brother of her late mother who had helped Gertrude and Leo find their famous apartment at 27 rue de Fleurus three decades before. They were doing well, which was more than could be said for the hosts of Gertrude's next visit. Scott and Zelda Fitzgerald were spending a lonely Christmas together in an apartment on Baltimore's Park Avenue, where they had moved after Zelda nearly burned down the Towson, Maryland, mansion they were renting at the time. Scott had recently finished what he hoped to be his masterpiece, *Tender Is the Night*, after nine long years of trying. Zelda, too, had written a novel, *Save Me the Waltz*, covering much of the same territory—unhappy couples in Paris and on the French Riviera—while undergoing treatment for schizophrenia at the Henry Phipps Psychiatric Hospital at Johns Hopkins University. After her husband, in a drunken rage, dismissed her fledgling literary efforts as "plagiaristic" and "third-rate," Zelda turned to painting for self-expression.[4]

Accompanied by Julian Stein's stepdaughter Ellen and son Julian Jr., Gertrude and Alice called on the Fitzgeralds on Christmas Eve. Scott was already drunk, and the fragile Zelda, at home on leave from the hospital, seemed "thin, eerie and fey" to Alice. Gertrude, accustomed to dealing with troublesome artists, ignored Fitzgerald's drunkenness and chatted pleasantly with the couple over old times. Zelda brought out several of the paintings she had done at the sanitarium. Gertrude selected two to take home with her. The couple's thirteen-year-old daughter Scottie was brought in to meet their guests. Not expecting Scottie to be there, Gertrude apologized for not bringing her a gift. Reaching into the pocket of her dress she pulled out a hazelnut, which she had picked up while coming across the lawn, and autographed it at Scottie's request. All in all, despite the gaily decorated Christmas tree in the living room, it was a fairly gloomy visit.[5]

Fitzgerald, as usual, was better behaved in his prose than in person. He immediately penned a thank-you note to Gertrude, saying a little awkwardly (since she was Jewish), "Having you come to the house was like—it was as if Jesus Christ had stopped in!" Fitzgerald apologized for his state when he received them. "I was somewhat stupid—got with the Christmas spirit," he wrote, but I enjoyed the one idea that you *did* develop, and like everything else you say, it will sing in my ears long after everything else about that afternoon is dust and ashes. You were the same fine fire to everyone who sat upon your hearth—for it was your hearth, because you carry home with you wherever you are. It meant so much to Zelda, giving her a tangible sense of her own existence, for you to have liked two of her paintings enough to want to own them. Everyone felt their Christmas eve was well spent in the company of your handsome face and wise mind and sentences "that never leak."[6]

▼ ▼ ▼

WITH CHRISTMAS, THEIR FAMILY, AND THE SADLY FADED Fitzgeralds behind them, Gertrude and Alice had another stop to make before New Year's. When they first had landed in Washington, Gertrude noted, "Some reporters were there. Are you going to see the President they asked me. That is up to the President I answered them." Or the president's lady, as the case may be. On December 30 they were invited to a private tea with Eleanor Roosevelt at the White House. The invitation was a bit surprising since Gertrude, while generally apolitical, was no fan of the new president. Franklin Delano Roosevelt, she once said, reminded her of Louis Napoleon—Napoleon III—whom she judged to have "no personality but a persistence of insistence in a narrow range of ideas." (It was that third Napoleon about whom Karl Marx famously observed that history repeats itself "first as tragedy, the second time as farce.") As a shorthand description of FDR's governing style, Gertrude's observation was surprisingly accurate, although she greatly underestimated the president's personal and political appeal, considering that he would be elected four times—and probably would have been elected a fifth time had he not died of a brain hemorrhage shortly after beginning his fourth term in office.[7]

It is doubtful that either the president or the First Lady was familiar with Gertrude's unenthusiastic opinion of FDR, or else she and Alice probably would not have been invited to the White House in the first place. As it was, they were taken upstairs to the First Couple's living quarters—no Oval Office visit for them. The president was "indisposed," Eleanor told them. "Yes," Gertrude responded noncommittally. Actually, he and his aides were working on the annual State of the Union address, his second, to be delivered five days later to the joint houses of Congress. It was an important speech, one in which FDR would lay out the groundwork for a multimillion-dollar plan to put the nation's five million unemployed citizens back to work through an Emergency Relief Appropriation Act and the creation of the Works Progress Administration and the Public Works Administration. Many of the president's top aides were working on the speech, including his chief advisor, Louis Howe, who looked in on Eleanor and her guests but declined to join them for a cup of tea. Other aides scurried about, "coming from somewhere going to somewhere. They were all writing the message to Congress," remembered Gertrude, "and each one and anyone was changing it." As a writer herself, Gertrude was interested in the speechwriting process, but she made no offer to help with the speech herself—a shame, really, if one imagines Franklin D. Roosevelt delivering the State of the Union address in Gertrude Stein's prose. It might have shaken things up even more than he did.[8]

A much warmer welcome was accorded them when they visited recently married William Rogers and his wife, the poet Mildred Weston, in Springfield, Massachusetts. Alice had scheduled a heavy round of lectures for Gertrude in New England, and Rogers, despite editing his hometown newspaper, the *Union*, offered to drive them around to the meetings. Rogers didn't own a car at the time, so he borrowed one from his neighbor Mrs. Wesson, somewhat formally described by Alice as being "of the family of the manufacturer of the revolver." Gertrude recalled that her own family had always had a Smith & Wesson revolver handy at their home in California. The New England winter was grueling, but they borrowed scarves, coats, and caps and went for an old-fashioned sleigh ride, looking "as round as big and little barrels." They also toured the cabin once belonging to Puritan minister John Williams, Jonathan Edwards's uncle, which still bore the tomahawk marks from the infamous Deerfield Massacre perpetrated on the settlers by Iroquois Indians and their French allies during Queen Anne's War. Alice, in a rare burst of lyricism, said that the New England churches "in their white coats were like postcards."[9]

Gertrude, for her part, was surprised by the plethora of New England schools and universities. "I did not know that New England had become like Switzerland," she said, "where there are nothing but schools and colleges and hotels and houses." She was particularly struck by the sheer number of private schools in the region. When she was a student in California, she said, nobody went to private school "unless you were defective in some way or came from South America or something." The privileged students of the Ivy League and its feeder schools were not so disadvantaged. At tony Choate, in Wallingford, Connecticut, they printed the text of her December 12 lecture, "How Writing Is Written," in their school magazine alongside some of their own work. "It is striking how well they are writing," Gertrude said of the students, adding with a mock sigh, "It is a bother." She worried, though, that the well-intentioned faculty was over-nurturing the boys, preventing them from "ever com[ing] to be themselves." That would not prove a problem for one Choate student on campus at the time of Gertrude's visit—future president John F. Kennedy. There is no reason to believe that JFK attended Gertrude's lecture—he generally skipped most of his classes and skated through Choate with a gentleman's B—but it was one more indication of the remarkable range of Gertrude's associations during the tour, from the great to the small. One Hartford cab driver amused William Rogers by asking whether his recent fare had been "the famous Stein. [He] said he missed Four Saints in Hartford and guessed he'd 'wait till it gets in the movies, because the movies make them easier.' "[10]

At nearby Wesleyan, students tried to trip up Gertrude by asking cheekily whether she considered herself a greater genius than Shakespeare. "I don't care to say whether I'm greater than Shakespeare," she told them, "and he's dead and can't say whether he's greater than I am. Time will tell." She questioned why the male students were so obsessed with success "when they know that eighty percent of them are not going to succeed more than to just keep going." And she wondered why "they do not keep on being interested in the things that interested them when they were college men." It was one reason, she said, why American men, unlike English men, did not get more interesting as they got older. Of course, Gertrude had entertained a weakness for English men ever since some Cambridge students took her up at Sylvia Beach's bookshop in Paris in 1919. At Amherst—"awfully nice," said Gertrude—student reporters went around asking faculty members for their opinions of the famous visitors. The football coach ungallantly allowed that he could use Gertrude at tackle but doubted whether she would be of any use calling signals. He guessed Alice could do that. One attendee at her lecture was more impressed by Gertrude's words than her athletic skills. "She knows what she's doing," he said. "I was dead set against her, and I just went to see what she looked like and then she took the door of my mind right off its hinges and now it's wide open."[11]

Of all the schools she visited on her northeastern swing, Gertrude liked Wesleyan and Mount Holyoke the best. She found it curious that these two colleges, with their strong emphasis on producing Christian missionaries, nevertheless seemed to have the most forward thinking students. At Mount Holyoke, she remembered, they mostly talked about the theater. Elsewhere, she found the students depressingly similar. "A certain kind of woman either goes to or comes out of Smith or Bryn Mawr or Radcliffe or Vassar or Wellesley," she said. "Anybody can almost know just what is all their life after going to happen to them and it almost does." She had gone to school with the same sort of young women when she was at Radcliffe. "No they had not changed not any one of them." She wondered if it was something in the food or the climate. Smith College, she told Carl Van Vechten, she did not like. "I didn't when I was at college at Radcliffe and I didn't at all when I was over there lecturing." She didn't say why.[12]

Something else that Gertrude wondered about—she was a naturally inquisitive person—was the high number of inebriated men she and Alice saw in New England. "We had not seen men drunk much anywhere else," she observed. As a writer herself, Gertrude viewed the problem through the lens of regional writers such as W. D. Howells and Louisa May Alcott, and "how they worried about offering anyone a drink and even about communion wine, anyone in that way might suddenly find that they had a taste for drink." Howells and Alcott were very genteel; their middle- and upper-class characters moved in proper circles, although occasionally one of them, like Howells's businessman-hero Silas Latham, drank too much for his own good.[13]

Gertrude was not much of a drinker herself, but she recalled that "in California we had all had wine to drink like any Latin and drinking wine can make you drunk but not so very likely." New England was another matter. It may have been the weather, or it may have been the times—there was a Depression going on, after all, although there was not much evidence of it in either Gertrude's or Alice's subsequent accounts of their American trip. Not everyone trod the varnished halls of the Ivy League or fluttered pink-cheeked across the snowy commons of a Seven Sisters school. The closest Gertrude came to seeing the other side of America was the dirty drugstores and disappointing five-and-dimes she occasionally looked into. Perhaps it was just as well, since, as physician-poet William Carlos Williams observed, "the pure products of America go crazy," and Gertrude was already on record as disliking contact with crazy people.[14]

After lectures at Brown University and the Kimball Museum of Fine Arts in Springfield, Gertrude spoke at the Wadsworth Atheneum in Mark Twain's adopted hometown of Hartford, Connecticut. (One wonders what the thin-skinned Twain would have made of the *Washington Post*'s headlined assertion that "Gertrude Stein Has Mark Twain Backed off the Map" and the claim that she was now "one of our prime humorists.") From Hartford, Gertrude and Alice took the train back to New York City to reunite with Carl Van Vechten for the first leg of their southern tour. Accustomed by now to air travel, Gertrude took a jaded view of American trains. "The train went along," she told William Rogers, "but that is about all that it did, but gradually it got here." In *Everybody's Autobiography* she would observe that many things about America had changed since she was last there three decades earlier, but "the trains have not changed, they make up the berths exactly as they did all the gestures were familiar. I found that train traveling was as bad as it had been thirty years before it had not changed, we had to wait and the train was late and coming back it was worse." Soon, train travel in the United States would be supplanted by Gertrude's beloved automobile—a change not entirely for the better.[15]

Back at the Algonquin, Gertrude and Alice resumed their swing through high society, lunching with the Van Vechtens and Bennett Cerf, taking dinner with Mary and Louis Bromfield, and attending a Broadway performance of Katharine Cornell in *Romeo and Juliet*, followed by a midnight dinner at Cornell's home. Cornell, called by a smitten George Bernard Shaw "the gorgeous dark lady" of the theater, had become famous as one of the foremost interpreters of Shaw's work, but her favorite role was that of Elizabeth Barrett Browning in *The Barretts of Wimpole Street*, which she had performed more than seven hundred times. Renowned for her low, rich voice and regal bearing, she was addressed by most people as Miss Cornell. Gertrude called her Kitty. A more or less open lesbian, Cornell was married to her gay theater director, Guthrie McClintic, an arrangement commonly known as a "lavender marriage," a social fiction designed to fool the closed-minded public. She had just completed a much-heralded cross-country tour of her own, appearing as Juliet to Basil Rathbone's Romeo, along with alternating performances of *The Barretts of Wimpole Street* and Shaw's *Candida*. Befitting her title of "First Lady of the American Theater," Cornell's tour dwarfed Gertrude's. In seven months she gave 225 performances before five hundred thousand people, including a legendary late-night performance as Juliet in McClintic's hometown of Seattle before a throng of fans who had waited for hours in the pouring rain for the weather-delayed troupe to arrive.[16]

On January 30, Gertrude visited the ERPI recording studio on West 57th Street to make a series of short records on aluminum disks for the National Council of Teachers of English. The recordings were made with the help of two Columbia University professors, George W. Hibbitt and W. Cabell Greet, resident lexicologists with a special interest in preserving American dialects. After thirty years in France, Gertrude had no particular accent; she spoke and read in a pleasant, musical way, exhibiting a trace of cultured Harvard burr. Throughout the tour, reporters commented approvingly on her American accent. "Foreign parts of speech have not affected her at all," T. S. Matthews of the *New Republic* observed. "She talks in as flatly sensible an American tone as any Middle Western aunt." The *Daily Oklahoman* concurred: "Her speech, her accent is like that of your next door neighbor. She prides herself on being the most ordinary American." When someone asked her in California, "How come you lived thirty years abroad—to acquire the American tempo?" she drawled, "I'm Amurrican." At the recording studio she read selections from *The Making of Americans*, her portraits of T. S. Eliot, Pablo Picasso, Henri Matisse, George Hugnet, and Christian Berard, and her dispassionate poetic account "How She Bowed to Her Brother." She described the last piece as a good example of "the new use of periods in which I use periods to break up the line rather than commas, because periods bring a more complete stop"—just like her relationship with Leo had done.[17]

▼ ▼ ▼

ACCOMPANIED BY VAN VECHTEN, GERTRUDE AND ALICE headed to Virginia by train to begin their long-anticipated tour of the South. Gertrude was looking forward particularly to visiting various Civil War battle sites. "After all," she wrote, "There will never be anything more interesting in America than the Civil War never." Neither she nor Alice, being the offspring of comparatively recent European immigrants, had relatives who had served in the Civil War, but Gertrude was so fascinated by the war that Alice sometimes called her a Civil War general herself. "I am always telling Bernard Faÿ and any other Frenchman that if they did not know the America that made the Civil War they do not know about America," Gertrude declared. Looking out the train window, she was startled by the lack of people or houses in the Virginia landscape. "The first thing to see was that there did not seem to be any inhabitants in Virginia," she wrote. "It was the only place in America where there were no houses no people to see, there were hills and woods and red earth out of which they were made and there were no houses and no people to see. Of course when they fought there it had been called the Wilderness, the campaign in the Wilderness but I had no realization that almost all Virginia was that."[18]

The Battle of the Wilderness to which she was alluding was fought on May 5–7, 1864, ten years before Gertrude was born, by the Confederate Army of Northern Virginia, led by Robert E. Lee, and the Union Army of the Potomac, led by Ulysses S. Grant. It was not, strictly speaking, a campaign, but the beginning of the much-longer Overland Campaign, a grisly bloodbath in which Grant inflicted disproportionately high losses on Lee's forces and drove the Confederates into a fatal siege at Petersburg. A staggering twenty-five thousand combatants were killed or wounded in the battle, the major significance of which was the discovery—news to both sides—that Grant was not planning to retreat, as his predecessors had done, but intended instead to head south and keep heading south until the war was over. As Grant's prewar friend from the United States Military Academy, Confederate general James Longstreet, warned Lee, "This man will fight us every day and every hour until the end of this war." He was not wrong.[19]

Gertrude and Alice had already taken a day trip with their friend Ellen Lamotte to Fredericksburg and down to the James

River outside Richmond, where they ate spoon bread and pork tenderloin on the riverbank. Reading the stone that marked the spot seven miles below the Confederate capital where Union general George B. McClellan had unaccountably halted his advance in 1862, Gertrude wondered, as Abraham Lincoln had wondered at the time, why McClellan had stopped. "It was unbelievable," she said, "to get within seven miles and to go away again. I had never really believed that it was so until I saw it there where it said it." Grant, she said, had served with McClellan in Mexico and knew what he was like. Lincoln had to learn it the hard way.[20]

Gertrude and Alice's own advance continued to Richmond, where Van Vechten introduced them to the well-known novelist and society doyenne Ellen Glasgow. The unmarried Glasgow, who suffered intermittently from what was politely called "nervous invalidism," came from one of Richmond's first families. There were Virginia colonists, Confederate generals, US congressmen, and West Point graduates in her background, and her family had acquired most of its fortune through the Tredegar Iron Works, the Confederacy's primary arms manufacturer during the war. She was best known for her 1902 novel, *The Battle-Ground*, which depicted the Civil War from a Southern point of view. A former suffragist who had marched in the celebrated London protests in 1909, Glasgow wrote novels featuring heroines who bravely set out on their own, abandoning weak-willed or overcontrolling husbands or lovers in a quest for self-sufficiency. This might have inclined her favorably toward Gertrude Stein, but Glasgow sourly told Van Vechten that she had qualms about meeting her fellow author. "Usually I avoid modern fads and people who lecture," she wrote, "but I have nothing against Miss Stein except her 'influence.' My private opinion is that the people she has influenced (especially Hemingway) couldn't have been much worse if she had left them alone."[21]

A bit grudgingly, then, Glasgow agreed to host a dinner for Gertrude and Alice at her columnated Victorian mansion on Richmond's exclusive West Street. Among the invited guests was her longtime friend and fellow novelist James Branch Cabell. Finding himself seated next to Alice at dinner, Cabell leaned over and asked, "Is Gertrude Stein serious?" "Desperately," said Alice. "That puts a different light on it," said Cabell. "For you," said Alice, "not for me." It was pretty rich for Cabell to ask if another writer was serious. His best-known novel, *Jurgen: A Comedy of Justice*, sent its titular hero on a picaresque journey to heaven and hell, where he eventually seduced the devil's wife. Noted Satanist Aleister Crowley unsurprisingly considered the book "one of the epoch-making masterpieces of philosophy." Gertrude mentioned neither Glasgow nor Cabell in her published memoir of the tour, but Alice made sure to reference her verbal swordplay with Cabell in her 1963 memoir, *What Is Remembered*.[22]

For Gertrude, no visit to Richmond would have been complete without a tour of its Civil War sites. After visiting the site of Libby Prison, where more than six thousand Union prisoners—all officers—had died during the war, she and Alice strolled down the city's ghost-haunted Monument Avenue, where a crowd of one hundred thousand people had turned out in 1890 to see the first and largest of the monuments there dedicated to General Robert E. Lee. "The Confederacy and Mr. Lee are as present and familiar as a newsreel," Alice told William Rogers. Gertrude was an outlier—or perhaps merely ahead of her time—in rejecting the romantic image of the Gallant Lee. To her he was a weak man who had knowingly led his countrymen to defeat because he lacked the moral courage to tell them the truth, "that the South could not win." Others might idolize him, Gertrude said, but she "could never feel that anyone could make a hero of him.

I could not." She was surprised to find the city of Richmond more midwestern than Southern. "It was not really as Southern as Baltimore or even Philadelphia," she judged, "and there did not seem to be many old houses in it." Of course, that was mainly because much of the city had burned to the ground on April 2, 1865, a few hours after Lee, Confederate president Jefferson Davis, and other high-ranking officials had fled the scene. Arriving Union soldiers helped put out the blaze.[23]

Before going to Richmond, Gertrude and Alice stopped off in Charlottesville, home of the University of Virginia. They were met at the train station by university president Dr. John Lloyd Newcomb and a delegation of balloon-waving students from the Raven Society. The next morning they were taken on a tour of the Thomas Jefferson–designed campus, his home at Monticello, the estate of fellow president James Monroe, and other elevated sights. Gertrude found the campus interesting enough, she said, if you liked columns. "If you can have enough columns and they are all over then a place is interesting," she wrote. "There never were as many of them anywhere as there were at the University of Virginia."[24]

That night she presented her lecture "Poetry and Grammar" to the Raven Society in honor of Edgar Allan Poe, "who of course I had always liked." The society honored Poe in its own way by awarding an annual prize to faculty, students, or alumni who particularly embodied "scholarly pursuits and their dedication to University ideals"—all things that their namesake had honored in the breach, if at all, during his one brief year at the university. Before she left, Gertrude was given a commemorative key to Poe's old room on the university's West Range, appropriately numbered 13, by President Newcomb. "Perhaps he gives it to everyone but I do not think so," said Gertrude, who proudly kept the key, embossed with a raven on one side and the state seal of Virginia on the other, in her billfold for the rest of her life.[25]

Their last stops in Virginia were at the College of William and Mary in Williamsburg and at Sweet Briar College near Lynchburg on February 8–10. On a tour of colonial Williamsburg Gertrude criticized the Rockefeller-funded restoration, saying of the refurbished buildings, "If they are not there and you want them there they have to be done over. You put new where the old was and old where the new was and that makes restoration." A visit to Yorktown, scene of Cornwallis's surrender to George Washington in 1781, was not particularly exciting to Civil War buff Gertrude. At William and Mary she gave her lecture "Portraits and Repetition" to the Phi Beta Kappa Society, foreshadowing the counterculture movement of the 1960s by asking the students "what was the use of their being young if they had the same opinions as all of them who were eighty and a hundred then what was the use. Somebody has to have an individual feeling."[26]

Sweet Briar, a women's college with pretensions of being "the Vassar of the South," had been founded in 1901 in the foothills of the Blue Ridge Mountains. Red brick buildings topped by blue-gray roofs stood on property willed to the college by Mrs. Indiana Fletcher Williams in honor of her daughter, Daisy, who had died at the age of sixteen of antitrypsin deficiency, a genetic lung disorder. Mrs. Williams, by then a widow, took the death of her only child hard. She preserved the girl's room exactly as it had been at her death and had her servants deliver breakfast daily to Daisy's grave. She had Daisy's favorite pony trotted back and forth through the cemetery with the girl's riding clothes lying across the pommel, and she personally read the mail aloud to her each day. Sixteen years later, devoted to the end, Mrs. Williams dropped dead at the foot of Daisy's bed. Given all the postmortem attention, it is perhaps not surprising that Daisy's ghost was unquiet. She was (and is) said to haunt the college, twirling around and around in mirrors, floating restlessly through campus on a cloud, and riding the attic elevator up and down in the president's house. Apparently there were no sightings of Daisy during Gertrude's visit, although Gertrude did report talking to one young woman who believed she could see the ghost of a tree still standing where a building now stood in its place. Gertrude, at any rate, did not believe in ghosts.[27]

The girls at Sweet Briar were "very good-looking," Gertrude noticed. (And Alice noticed that Gertrude had noticed.) The students, coming from various regions of the country, had quickly become assimilated. "Naturally the Northern girls came South," Gertrude wrote, "but once there they might as well have come from there, it was charming." Walking the grounds with a student reporter for the *Sweet Briar News*, Gertrude took an indirect jab at Ellen Glasgow and James Branch Cabell:

> Take that tree for instance. You see it and I see it. You can write about it because it is true. But if, because your parents and grandparents have decided it would be better that no tree should appear there, you decide to write as if it weren't there your writing will not be true. It won't convince me or anybody. That's what Virginia is still trying to do and has been ever since the Civil War. They ought to be producing fine writers but they aren't. They are still trying not to see the tree but they know down deep inside that it's there. You can't get away from it.

Gertrude judged that Sweet Briar and Mount Holyoke girls were the only college students who were not typecast. "Vassar, Wellesley and Smith girls will be Vassar, Wellesley and Smith girls all their lives," she told the Sweet Briar reporter. She was a Radcliffe girl herself.[28]

▼ ▼ ▼

VAN VECHTEN RETURNED TO NEW YORK CITY ON FEBRUARY 11, and Gertrude and Alice rode to Chapel Hill, North Carolina, with two Sweet Briar faculty members and their wives. It rained during the ride—welcome to winter in the South—but Gertrude at least found the region better populated than Virginia. "There were farms and people on them and there were no more hills and woods covering them," she wrote. "They told me that North Carolina was not like Virginia and South Carolina it was not." Along the way she and Alice saw their first cotton fields, "small and simple and pleasant." Surprisingly, they had never heard of Chapel Hill or the University of North Carolina, but Gertrude found it a nice town, with students "from everywhere in the world." Neighboring Duke University, UNC's biggest rival, "was made by tobacco," Gertrude observed. "Lucky Strikes and Camels, the better cigarette that we had met when the dough-boys first came over had made the Duke fortune and they built this university and now there was the depression and they did not have very much money and so Chapel Hill was the better. So they said and we believed them." Lifelong smoker Alice did not venture an opinion.[29]

En route to Charleston they stopped for the night at historic Cheraw, a small town with a large past on the Pee Dee River just below the state line. In its heyday Cheraw had been the largest cotton market in the region and the home of the largest bank in South Carolina outside of Charleston. The first public call for secession had taken place at the Chesterfield County Courthouse there, and the first postwar Confederate monument had been erected in Cheraw in 1867. Gertrude and Alice were taken on a tour of a ruined plantation. The African American houses in the region were raised on stilts, said Gertrude, "to keep them off the ground and let the chickens and things live under." Spanish moss was hanging from the trees, which struck her as "very pretty in the hand but dirty in the trees." She fretted that the invasive moss would spread all the way to California and bring with it the equally invasive mockingbird—"nothing can stop them." She was wrong about Spanish moss, which requires a more humid environment than California's to survive, but she was right about the quarrelsome and tenacious mockingbird, a subspecies of which now thrives there. Harper Lee, creator of the most famous literary mockingbird of them all, was an eight-year-old tomboy growing up in Monroeville, Alabama, at the time of Gertrude's American tour, but the closest Gertrude and Alice got to Monroeville was Birmingham, 120 miles northeast. It wouldn't have mattered anyway. Harper, called Nell, was busy just then playing with her flaxen-haired next-door neighbor, himself destined to become a gay literary icon: Truman Capote.[30]

In Charleston they met DuBose Heyward, author of the 1925 novel *Porgy*, which their recent acquaintances George and Ira Gershwin were busy adapting for their 1935 opera, *Porgy and Bess*. Heyward, doubly misidentified by Stein biographer James R. Mellow as "the Negro writer Du Bose Heyward," was actually a descendant of a signer of the Declaration of Independence and a member of one of Charleston's first families. His novel *Porgy*, about a crippled, Gullah-speaking beggar on the waterfront's Catfish Row, is credited with being the first sympathetic fictional portrayal of African Americans by a white Southern writer. No less a judge than Broadway legend Stephen Sondheim has called Heyward "the author of the finest set of lyrics in the history of the American musical theater. Most of the lyrics in *Porgy*—and all of the distinguished ones—are by Heyward. It's a pity he didn't write any others." Heyward had heard of Gertrude and her work.

"We liked you in Charleston, tremendously," he told her, "even if we did not always understand you." She liked him as well, saying he was "a gentle man like his Porgy."[31]

In Charleston, Gertrude appropriately delivered her lecture "Poetry and Grammar" to the Poetry Society of South Carolina at the South Carolina Hall. She was a bit under the weather, having caught a cold the previous day at Cheraw while being rowed through the swamp in the rain. Local poet-novelist Josephine Pinckney, founder and president of the society, hosted them afterward at her luxurious home at 21 Walk Street. Pinckney, like Heyward, was a member of the Charleston elite, with various governors and senators in her background. She was also a Radcliffe girl like Gertrude. Her Italianate home was known locally as "O'Donnell's Folly" after its builder, Joseph O'Donnell, who had spent so long building the mansion for his beloved that she left him for another man before it was completed. The mansion later sold for $7.2 million—at the time the largest sum ever paid for a single house in Charleston.[32]

They flew from Charleston to New Orleans by way of Atlanta. Near the Atlanta airport Gertrude saw a billboard that delighted her: "Buy Your Meat and Wheat in Georgia." She wasn't sure if it was prose or poetry, but either way it amused her. The Southern attachment to states' rights puzzled her. "What is the use of a country if you have a state," she wondered. "I was brought up to believe in the North." They continued on to New Orleans, skimming so low over the Mississippi delta that it frightened Alice but didn't faze Gertrude. Their hotel, the Roosevelt, struck Gertrude as "very political...it looked as if everybody in it had something to do with politics." Her instincts were correct. The hotel, named not for the current president but for his distant cousin Theodore, was the headquarters of another presidential contender—Louisiana senator and former governor Huey Long. The larger-than-life "Kingfish" was away at the moment on a nationwide tour of his own, drumming up support for his populist Share Our Wealth program and planning to run for president in 1936. Long kept a twelfth-floor suite at the Roosevelt, comped for him by his good friend Seymour Weiss, the hotel's owner. Gertrude struck up a conversation with Long's official photographer, who "told me all about his life photographing Huey Long." She later pronounced the briefest of elegies for Long: "He might have been there but he was not and now he is dead and that is all there is to him." Long was assassinated in Baton Rouge seven months later by a man also named Weiss—no relation to Seymour.[33]

Gertrude always enjoyed talking to photographers, she said, since, unlike reporters, they actually listened to her when she was speaking. Once she said to a photographer, "You do understand what I am talking about don't you. Of course I do he said you see I can listen to what you say because I don't have to remember what you are saying." This struck Gertrude as "interesting"—one of her favorite adjectives—since "nobody can listen if they have to remember what they are hearing and that is the trouble with newspapers and teaching with government and history." Despite her liking of photographers, Gertrude was sometimes a difficult subject herself. One photographer, she reported,

> said he was sent to do a layout of me. A layout I said yes he said what is that I said oh he said it is four or five pictures of you doing anything. All right I said what do you want me to do. Why he said there is your airplane bag suppose you unpack it, oh I said Miss Toklas always does that, well he said there is the telephone suppose you telephone well I said yet but I never do Miss Toklas always does that, well he said what can you do, well I said I can

put my hat on and take my hat off and I can put my coat on and I can take it off and I like water I can drink a glass of water all right he said do that.

Gertrude, as she wished to make clear, left the menial tasks to Alice.[34]

Sherwood Anderson called for them at the Roosevelt, carrying a large sack of fresh oranges as a gift. Anderson had lived in New Orleans for the past eleven years, and he gave Gertrude and Alice a lengthy driving tour of the city. With Alice sitting on Gertrude's lap in the front seat, he drove them around the French Quarter, the city market, and the old Creole homes of the city's first settlers. They lunched at the famed Antoine's Restaurant, where Gertrude and Alice had Oysters Rockefeller for the first time. Alice later included the recipe in her cookbook: "Place oysters on the half shell in preheated deep dishes filled with sand (silver sand glistens prettily). Cover the oysters thickly with ¼ chopped parsley, ¼ finely chopped raw spinach, ⅛ finely chopped tarragon, ⅛ finely chopped chervil, ⅛ finely chopped basil and ⅛ finely chopped chives. Salt and pepper some fresh breadcrumbs, cover the herbs completely, dot with melted butter and put for 4 or 5 minutes in a preheated 450" oven. Serve piping hot." She noted that the dish was "an enormous success with French gourmets. It makes more friends for the United States than anything I know." Each morning of their visit Alice walked to the downtown market, "realizing that I would have to live in the dream of it for the rest of my life. How with such perfection, variety and abundance of material could one not be inspired to creative cooking?"[35]

Anderson was playfully indignant when Gertrude refused to be impressed by the Mississippi River. "Can't you see that it is a mile deep as well as a mile wide?" he complained. Gertrude was unmoved: "I said that Mark Twain's Life on the Mississippi had made it so real to me when I was a little girl and there was a story of a flood and I had liked that and now well there was something the matter I could not quite get used to it not looking quite as enormous as I had always seen it when I read about it." Gertrude's complaint echoed that of fellow literary tourist Oscar Wilde, who had gotten his own first sight of the rain-swollen Mississippi during a visit to St. Louis in 1882. The river, turned yellow-brown by churned-up mud, was foaming and surging over its banks, sweeping all manner of debris along with it. "No well-behaved river ought to act this way," Wilde scoffed.[36]

Gertrude's schedule in New Orleans was crowded. She spoke at Tulane University on February 18 and at the Gallery of Arts and Crafts Societies the following day, and then she lunched on the 20th at Galatoire's Restaurant. At Tulane she and Alice were shown the college's prized Live Oak Society, a society consisting exclusively of trees that were at least one hundred years old. Alice, a true daughter of California, was sure that there were a lot of equally old oak trees in her home state. "Perhaps," said their guide, "but the oaks like any chosen one have to have their papers to prove their birth and age and everything has to be in order." Human sponsors paid the trees' annual dues and agreed to spread one hundred acorns each around town. The couple met playwright Marc Connelly, one of the original (and eventually last surviving) members of the Algonquin Round Table. Connelly's Pulitzer Prize–winning 1930 play *The Green Pastures*, a retelling of the Old Testament through the eyes and voice of a young African American girl, had preceded Gertrude's *Four Saints in Three Acts* in bringing the first all-black cast to Broadway. They also visited the site of the city's infamous Storyville red-light district, where they thumbed through "the social registry of the bawdy houses and a charming little blue book with the simple advertisements of the ladies by themselves." Having lived in Paris for three decades, they were unshocked.[37]

▼ ▼ ▼

GERTRUDE AND ALICE LEFT NEW ORLEANS AND THE DEEP South on February 22, bound for Chicago, where Gertrude was scheduled to begin teaching a seminar for Thornton Wilder's class at the university. Their flight was diverted to Memphis, but, seasoned travelers that they were, they didn't bother to ask why. "We now know that when they did not go on any further it really did not matter there was reason for it and why bother. We used to want to know the reason but now we just got out and went on some other way." Memphis when they arrived looked just like it should have looked, said Gertrude without explanation. There were a lot of men and women on the streets, "and they all seemed to be there as if there was no choice anywhere all the life they lived they lived there." From Memphis, Gertrude and Alice took the train north to St. Louis, with Gertrude avidly looking out the window at the Tennessee and Arkansas farms they were passing. The conductor told them that "foreigners who settled down there made a better living than those who came from there," an inexplicable statement that Gertrude let stand without comment.[38]

In St. Louis, Gertrude the Civil War buff wanted to see the sites Winston Churchill had written about in his best-selling study of the war, *The Crisis*. The locals were willing to oblige, but they were not as familiar with Churchill's book as Gertrude was, so she had to settle for visiting the rough wooden farmhouse that Ulysses S. Grant had built by hand before the Civil War. Grant had named the four-room cabin Hardscrabble, which was all too appropriate—the five years Grant spent in St. Louis as a farmer and bill collector were the nadir of his life. Gertrude found the site equally unimpressive. "It was a cabin and it had once been lived in," she wrote, "when you read Grant's memoirs it does not quite sound as if that was the sort of place that he lived in but there seems to be no doubt about it that was the house he did live in." Gertrude wondered aloud how so many St. Louis residents still managed to live in such large mansions, seventy years after Grant's victory in the Civil War had created a certain servant shortage in the South. Well, her guides shrugged, there were a lot of big families in St. Louis. Gertrude had no response. "We ate very well there," was all she said.[39]

SEVEN

No There There

O N MARCH 17, 1935, GERTRUDE AND ALICE FLEW TO Dallas to begin the western leg of their tour. They spent three enjoyable days at the exclusive Hockaday School for Girls, which had recently added a junior college to its ranks. Gertrude's talk would inaugurate the new College Building on campus. Texas native Ela Hockaday had founded the school in 1913 after a brief career as a farm owner in Falfurrias with her partner, Sarah Trent. (Disapproving neighbors called them "the farmerettes.") The girls at the school wore crisp forest-green and white uniforms and saddle oxfords and followed a strict regimen based on the four cornerstones of character, courtesy, scholarship, and athletics. They were known familiarly as Hockadaisies—the athletic teams were the Killer Daisies. Among the school's most prominent alumnae are movie actress Dorothy Malone, singer-songwriter Lisa Loeb, Democratic politician Frances "Sissy" Farenthold, the twin daughters of President George W. Bush, and Hollywood screenwriter Jay Presson Allen, whose best-known works included scripts for Alfred Hitchcock's *Marnie*, *Cabaret*, *Funny Lady*, *Travels with My Aunt*, and the British boarding school drama *The Prime of Miss Jean Brodie*, whose severe but nurturing heroine is reminiscent of Ela Hockaday.[1]

Gertrude found the girls at Miss Hockaday's school "very interesting, as we were staying there we got to know them. They did understand what I had written, and that was a pleasure to me." And, she added, it was "a very great pleasure" to them. As for Alice, she was more interested in the school kitchen, "the most beautiful one I have ever seen, all old coppers on the stove and on the walls, with a huge copper hood over the stove. Everything else was modern white enamel." Gertrude confessed that they ate "almost too well" at the school, and she ventured her opinion that since the school cook came from Louisiana, it logically followed that "Louisiana cooking in Texas is almost the best." Alice disagreed. "All good Texas food was Virginian," she said, quoting Miss Hockaday. She took away a recipe for the school's corn sticks, "not knowing in my ignorance that a special iron was required in which to bake them." When they boarded their ship to return to France, they found just such an iron waiting for them in their stateroom, compliments of Ela Hockaday. German soldiers later carried off the iron when they raided the couple's farmhouse at Culoz during World War II, causing a still-aggrieved Alice to wonder ten years later "what they expected to do with it, and what are they doing with it now?"[2]

While walking on campus one afternoon, Gertrude was hailed by a car full of students. The driver was a young car salesman, and when Gertrude mentioned that she and Alice were going to Austin, he volunteered to drive them. "It would be a pleasure to us," said Gertrude. They left on March 21. As always, she sat up front, while Alice, a student, and one of the teachers sat in the back. Gertrude was fascinated by the mechanics of the car, which had an automatic transmission—"nothing in front to be a bother as there is in every car"—and wondered if she should buy one of the young man's vehicles and ship it back to France. Later, she test-drove one of the cars in San Francisco, where she found the transmission a bit slow and tentative on the hills, of which there were plenty around Bilignin, so "I did not think it would do." It was perfect for the flat countryside of central Texas, however, and Gertrude enjoyed seeing the blue Texas wildflowers and the cattle pass by. Once in Austin, the student called up a friend and invited her to dinner, saying, "Come, I am here with Gertrude Stein." "Oh yeah," replied the girl, with what exact inflection Gertrude did not say.[3]

As yet more proof that Gertrude managed to meet virtually everyone of any importance on her tour, she sat down for an interview in Austin with an eighteen-year-old freshman reporter for the University of Texas school newspaper, the *Daily Texan*. His name was Walter Cronkite. Under the headline "Miss Stein Not Out for Show, but Knows What She Knows," Cronkite already displayed the deft hand for reporting that would carry him to the anchorman's chair at CBS Television. Gertrude, he wrote, was "genuine—the real thing in person. Her thinking is certainly straightforward; her speech is the same." Asked about her writing, she told the neophyte reporter, "A writer isn't anything but contemporary. The trouble is that the people are living Twentieth Century and thinking Nineteenth Century." As for the Depression, Gertrude considered it "more moral than actual." When the people no longer thought they were depressed, she said, the Depression would be over. Franklin Roosevelt must have wished it were that easy. Turning to foreign policy, Gertrude observed that her neighbors in France did not think there would be another war. "But then war is like anything else," she said. "When people get tired of peace they will have war and when they get tired of war they will have peace." She was more concerned, just then, that Cronkite be sure to note correctly that Alice's proper title was not "secretary." She did not say what the proper title was.[4]

That night Gertrude gave her lecture "Poetry and Grammar" at Hogg Memorial Auditorium. At lunch beforehand they were served "a stiff punch," but when Alice went to light a cigarette, she was asked not to; only men were allowed to smoke. Perhaps because of that, Gertrude said nothing at all about their two days in Austin or her interview with the school newspaper, and Cronkite never mentioned it either. The interview was subsequently unearthed after the newsman's death in 2009 and posted on the *Daily Texan*'s website—one of the few modern innovations that Gertrude failed to anticipate during her visit.[5]

En route to Houston she struck up a conversation with their African American driver. Having lived in France for three decades, Gertrude was not necessarily au courant with American race relations. Except when it came to the law, the man told her, jokingly or not, his race "had nothing at all to complain of." What did he mean? Gertrude wondered. They could go into a profession and earn an ordinary living, the man said, but "if by any chance he does something and the white man is against him and it comes up into court why then of course it is another thing then he does not get the same justice as a white man." Eventually her attention drifted—she was no civil rights pioneer—and Gertrude looked out the window at the blue wildflowers and the cattle, "not so many of them it had been a bad year for cattle as there had been too much cold weather and too much dry weather and as they do not in any way protect them they all died not all of them but a lot of them." She saw some cowboys (and one cowgirl) going to herd the cattle. It promised to be a lovely spring.[6]

In Houston, Gertrude delivered her "Narration" lecture to the ultraexclusive Houston Junior League. She was pleased and flattered when an eighty-year-old woman came up to her afterward and said that she had driven all the way from Galveston to hear Gertrude speak. She had been reading Gertrude's work for years, the woman said, adding, "You see, it is the middle-aged people that have no feeling, they are not young enough and not old enough to have any understanding." That encounter may have been the source for Gertrude's subsequent observation that "old people and young people understand me easily. It is only the ones in the middle who have trouble." Gertrude liked Texas women, she said, because "they were what the Middle West used to be and New England before them and what Virginia remembered having been." They were naturally active, a trait she could admire in others—starting with Alice—while not necessarily embodying it herself.[7]

After returning to Austin, they caught a plane to Oklahoma City. It was their first view of the western badlands, which Gertrude had read about in stories, but "I never did think that I would ever see them certainly not fly over them, and they were just as bad as they had been called with nothing growing and a very strange color and not hills or flat land either." The skyscrapers in Oklahoma City, "coming right up out of the flat oil country," reminded her somewhat of the ruins of Strasbourg Cathedral in Alsace after World War I. "Seeing the oil wells and the funny shapes they made the round things as well as the Eiffel Tower ones gave me a feeling like I have in going to Marseilles and seeing the chimneys come out of the earth and there are no houses or anything near them." Alice's father had once drilled for oil, Gertrude claimed, which seems unlikely since Ferdinand Toklas, at least on record, had spent most of his life as a sedate bookkeeper and store owner in New York, Seattle, and San Francisco. The oil wells resembled prehistoric animals, Gertrude said, "moving slowly very very slowly."[8]

Gertrude liked Oklahoma City, where the stores were nice and the men were big. The native-born Sooners would have been pleased to know that she considered them "very different from the Texans, not a bit at all like the Texans, not a bit." She gave her lecture "The Gradual Making of *The Making of Americans*" to the Town Club at Harding Hall, and then she and Alice departed Oklahoma City in an honest-to-god dust storm like something out of *The Wizard of Oz*. "The airplane went up through one and came out on top," Gertrude observed, "it was like when we were above the clouds only such dirty ones and the sunset on top." It was all a bit discouraging, she said, a mood that was not helped by the fact that their hotel in Fort Worth was "a bad one." There were no flowers waiting for them in their room, and the mutton chops they were served for dinner were inedible, even upon second try. Ela Hockaday handily arrived to rescue them for a farewell lunch with the Hockadaisies, a dozen of whom would later visit Bilignin during a school-sponsored European tour.[9]

Invited to attend an all-black performance of *Porgy and Bess* by the Houston Little Theater, Gertrude and Alice dined beforehand with the show's director, "a Princeton man," and his party. Gertrude fell into conversation with the big blond man sitting next to her. "My mother wrote to me that she had met you," he said. "Who is your mother?" Gertrude asked. "Mrs. Franklin Roosevelt," he replied. It was FDR's third son, Franklin Delano Roosevelt Jr. "Oh," said Gertrude. The younger Roosevelt wanted her advice on how to handle the pressure of being the president's son. Forget about it, said Gertrude. "You can do nothing about it so why worry about it?" He did worry, said Franklin, because in a year "my father is going to be the most unpopular man in America." "In that case forgetting it will be easier," said Gertrude. As it turned out, they were both wrong—FDR's popularity never waned.[10]

▼ ▼ ▼

THE NEXT MORNING, MARCH 28, GERTRUDE AND ALICE LEFT Texas for their home state of California and the last leg of their American journey. Landing in Los Angeles, they were met by a public relations flack from Warner Brothers who invited them to lunch and a personal tour of the studio. To his surprise, they declined. They did agree to attend a private screening at Pathé News of Gertrude's newsreel filmed the day of their arrival in New York. Gertrude found the experience of watching herself onscreen a bit disconcerting. "When I saw myself almost as large and moving around and talking I did not like it," she reported, "particularly the talking, it gave me a very funny feeling." Maybe if she saw it often enough, she thought, it would get better, since "you can get used to anything if it happens often." Alice had no reported reaction.[11]

But if Gertrude had slight interest in Hollywood, it was beginning to show interest in her. Two of the year's top-grossing films, *Top Hat* and *The Man on the Flying Trapeze*, referenced her directly or indirectly. In the first, star Ginger Rogers is read a puzzling telegram that says in part, "Come ahead stop stop being a sap stop…stop when do you start stop." "Sounds like Gertrude Stein," cracks Rogers. And in *The Man on the Flying Trapeze*, the eternally put-upon W. C. Fields glumly listens to his affected wife read aloud a *Tender Buttons*–like poem from the local newspaper. He gives a subtle start and then wordlessly resumes eating his toast. In a mock interview with Gertrude in *Vanity Fair*, movie and radio star Gracie Allen, known for her calculatedly ditsy malapropisms, advises, "Now Gertie, don't you start to make sense, or people will begin to understand you, and then you won't mean anything at all." The joke, of course, was that in real life both women were brilliant.[12]

At the Pasadena Community Playhouse on March 31 Gertrude lectured on English literature. On April Fools' Day she and Alice attended a party in their honor at the Beverly Hills home of Lillian Mae Ehrman, another society friend of Carl Van Vechten's whom they had met in New York City. It was a gala event. Among those attending were Charlie Chaplin and his actress wife Paulette Goddard—"an enfant terrible," in Alice's jaundiced view—*Dr. Jekyll and Mr. Hyde* director Rouben Mamoulian, writer Anita Loos, playwright Lillian Hellman, and Hellman's longtime lover, Dashiell Hammett. The author of *The Thin Man* was Gertrude's favorite mystery writer, and she had specifically asked that he be invited. "It is very nice being a celebrity," Gertrude observed, "a real celebrity who can decide who they want to meet and say so and they come or do not come as you want them." Hammett came, although it took Mrs. Erhman a good deal of phoning around before she got his address, and when she sent the reclusive writer a telegram inviting him to meet Gertrude Stein, he thought at first it was an April Fools' joke. In the end he showed up, and it was one of the highlights of Gertrude's trip. "I never was interested in crossword puzzles or any kind of puzzles," she confessed, "but I do like detective stories. I never try to guess who has done the crime and if I did I would be sure to guess wrong but I like somebody being dead and how it moves along and Dashiell Hammett was all that and more."[13]

Rather than talking mysteries with Hammett, Gertrude engaged him instead in a long discussion about serious literature. "I said to Hammett there is something that is puzzling. In the nineteenth century the men when they were writing did invent all kinds and a great number of men. The women on the other hand never could invent women they always made the women be themselves seen splendidly or sadly or heroically or beautifully or despairingly or gently, and they never could make any other kind of woman." But now, said Gertrude, it was the men who were writing about themselves, "as strong or weak or mysterious or passionate or drunk or controlled but always themselves as the women used to do in the nineteenth century." Why was that, she wondered. Hammett, whose partner Lillian Hellman was a notably self-confident woman herself, said it was because modern men had no confidence anymore, "and so they have to make themselves as you say more beautiful more intriguing more everything and they cannot make any other man because they have to hold on to themselves not having any confidence." "That's interesting," said Gertrude, without elaborating. Since all her books were more or less about herself, she was not overly concerned with the creation of other characters, fictional or not. Still, the discussion was a memorable one for her. Three years later she would begin her memoir of the American tour, *Everybody's Autobiography*, with an account of her talk with Dashiell Hammett. "Anything is an autobiography," she wrote, "but this was a conversation."[14]

The most famous person at the party, of course, was Charlie Chaplin. Gertrude said the actor reminded her of a Gypsy bullfighter she had known in Spain "who could not kill a bull but he could make him move better than anyone ever could." Chaplin was not a Gypsy, she said, "but he might have been." As usual, she was instinctively on the mark. The British comedian had suffered through a stark Dickensian childhood in which he was abandoned by his alcoholic father and sent to the Central London School for Paupers. Meanwhile, his actress mother served two terms in the poorhouse before being committed permanently to a mental hospital. Chaplin's rise to fame was literally rags to riches. Without his performing genius, the Little Tramp might well have been one in real life—a Gypsy without a caravan. He and Gertrude discussed the recent introduction of talkie movies, which Chaplin lamented, since "he wanted the sentiment of movement invented by himself." Gertrude told him she had attempted to do much the same thing in *Four Saints in Three Acts*. "I said that what was most exciting was when nothing was happening, I said that saints should naturally do nothing if you were a saint that was enough." Chaplin said politely that he understood. Alice blushingly told him that his were the only movies she had ever seen, which she later admitted was an exaggeration but which pleased the superstar nonetheless.[15]

After dinner Gertrude inadvertently offended the publicity-hungry crowd of Hollywood bigwigs by attributing her own popularity to small crowds. "I said if you have a big audience you have no publicity," she told the puzzled movie moguls, "this did seem to worry them and naturally it would worry them they wanted the publicity and the biggest audience." To director Rouben Mamoulian she asserted, "You people in the movies need publicity, but you have to pay for it. You get little waves of publicity and then it dies down and you have to pay for some more. The only publicity that matters comes from one person in a great many hundred saying—and meaning it—that they have read something of value." Alice, watchful as ever, noticed that the filmmakers quickly "shoved their chairs away from her, discouraged with what she had to advise." Literary scholar Karen Leick sees their reaction as evidence of widespread disapproval of Gertrude among the filmmaking community for her supposed anti-intellectualism and her failure to make "important and obvious distinctions between writers, artists and culture." But this ignores the overriding impetus of Hollywood filmmakers, then and now, to reach the broadest possible audience. Few critics ever accused such hard-bitten studio executives as Harry Cohn, Jack Warner, or Louis B. Mayer of being overly intellectual in their tastes.[16]

Before leaving Los Angeles, Gertrude rented a car to drive up the coast to San Francisco, a new Ford that was "a much better one than they had given me in Chicago." Unlike Illinois, the state of California required a valid driver's license, which was a pointless bother in Gertrude's opinion. "They asked some twenty questions and nothing had anything to do with how you drive or with machines," she complained, "it all had to do with your health and your mother's and father's health and with what you would do if anything happened and what the rules of the road are, well I answered them all and they were mostly right after all those things are just ordinary common sense and I said afterward but Alice Toklas who cannot drive at all could have answered just as well." They might as well have asked her how she made her legs work when she walked, Gertrude complained.[17]

The couple drove north through the San Joaquin Valley, savoring the sights and smells of fresh oranges, fig trees, olives, avocados, and artichokes. At Yosemite they paid a young man a dollar to drive them safely through the mud, the rain, and the occasional snow—it was a cold spring in California. "Although he was very young he could drive," said Gertrude. "Anybody anywhere in America can." They saw the huge Sequoia trees, which delighted Gertrude because, ironically, they had no roots. "Did anybody want anything to be more interesting than that the oldest and the solidest and the biggest trees that could be grown had no foundation, there it was sitting and the wind did not blow it over it sat so well." She resumed the driving and took them up the coast to Monterey, where teenaged Alice had spent many happy hours away from her family at Senorita Bonifacio's adobe inn. The inn had been rechristened Sherman's Rose for the local legend that the ruthless Civil War general, as a young soldier, had once planted a Gold of Ophir rosebush in the senorita's garden as proof of his enduring love. Alice had stabled a horse in Monterey and galloped it seventeen miles a day, an image completely at odds with the stiffly proper hostess of the rue de Fleurus. Not only that, but the usually serious, phlegmatic Alice sometimes had donned a fringed Spanish shawl and playfully posed for tourists' cameras as the senorita's supposed daughter. Maybe it was the rosebush.[18]

Both the adobe inn and Sherman's rose were missing when Gertrude and Alice drove into town on the evening of March 7. They were in the process of fruitlessly looking for them when a Monterey policeman pulled them over and wanted to know what they were doing. "I am trying to find Madame Bonifacio's adobe home, where I used to stay," Alice replied. "He said, They have moved it up into the hills. Moved an adobe house? I said. Oh, yes, he said, Eastern millionaires do that. And Sherman's rosebush? I said. Did that go up into the hills with the house?" The policeman didn't know anything about the rosebush, "but he wafted us on." In the cookbook she wrote twenty years later, Alice commemorated the sweet drink called dulce that Senorita Bonifacio made—or rather had Alice make while she went to mass: "In a huge copper pan put quantities of granulated sugar, moisten with cream, turn constantly with a copper spoon until it is done. Then pour into glasses." There were people who liked it a lot, Alice said, sounding a trifle unconvinced.[19]

They checked into the Del Monte Lodge, another local landmark from Alice's youth, where they had abalone for the first time—an odd dietary omission for two women who had grown up on either side of San Francisco Bay. Alice recorded the hotel's recipe for gooseberry jelly and its "ineffable" iced soufflé, "a particular favorite with men." It was a good enough lunch, Gertrude conceded, but the view from the hotel reminded her of a bad nineteenth-century painting of the Loire River valley in France. Alice, though, was in her element—"God's own country," she said nonironically. "California was unequalled. Sun and a fertile soil breed generosity and gentleness, amiability and appreciation. It was abundantly satisfying."[20]

Even more satisfying to Alice was the brief telephone conversation she had with Mabel Dodge Luhan, who called from her home in nearby Carmel, wanting to know when she was going to see Gertrude. "I don't think you are going to," Alice told her old rival from the Villa Curonia. But, Mabel spluttered, California's reigning poet, Robinson Jeffers, wanted to meet her. "Well," said Alice, "he will have to do without." Adding salt to the wound, Gertrude gave an interview to the local newspaper the next day in which she allowed that she had no use for artists' colonies in general. "I like ordinary people who don't bore me," she said. "Highbrows, you know, always do." The *San Francisco Examiner*, getting wind of the interview, ran a follow-up story beneath the headline, "A Snub, A Snub, A Snub: Gertrude Stein Gives Carmel's Highbrows the Go-By." One imagines Alice smiling in the background.[21]

They did find time to meet another Golden State writer who lived in Carmel, novelist Harry Leon Wilson, author of *Merton of the Movies*, which Gertrude somewhat perplexingly considered "the best book about twentieth century American youth that has yet been done." Wilson also wrote *Ruggles of Red Gap*, which had been turned into a movie starring British actor Charles Laughton that was just about to debut. (*Merton of the Movies*, with Red Skelton in the title role, would follow in 1947.) Although suffering from the lingering effects of a near-fatal car crash two years earlier, Wilson received Gertrude and Alice affably. He was, thought Gertrude, "just like the kind of man who should have written the best American story about a young American man, he is gentle and American and mysterious without a mystery and tired without fatigue." Why she thought so highly of *Merton of the Movies* was a mystery in its own right. Most critics considered the book, about a small-town doofus who goes to Hollywood to become a screenwriter and instead becomes a film star by mistake, fairly lightweight. That did not stop Gertrude from handing it out in Paris to any visitors who "could read English." There were a lot to choose from.[22]

▼ ▼ ▼

THE COUPLE PULLED INTO ALICE'S HOMETOWN OF SAN FRAN-
cisco on April 8, the same day that the first commuter airline
service was inaugurated between Honolulu and the mainland.
Settling into their panoramic rooms in the Mark Hopkins Hotel
atop Nob Hill, they happened to catch a glimpse of the Hawaii-
bound airplane, which moved Gertrude to remark, "I would
like to go around the world in an airplane. I never did want to
do anything and now I wanted to do that thing." Alice, eyeing
the ongoing construction of the Golden Gate Bridge, was more
concerned just then about the bridge destroying the landscape.
Nevertheless, Alice the native San Franciscan was a good deal
more comfortable in their surroundings than Gertrude. "It was
frightening quite frightening driving there and on top of Nob
Hill where we were to stay," Gertrude noted. "Alice Toklas found
it natural but for me it was a trouble yes it was, it did make me
feel uncomfortable." There were consolations: the food in San
Francisco was divine—a "gastronomic orgy," Alice said. During
their visit, they dined on sand dabs meuniere, rainbow trout in
aspic, grilled soft-shell crabs, roast fillet of pork, eggs Rossini,
and tarte Chambord, a local specialty predating the San Francisco fire. On touristy Fisherman's Wharf they waited for two
giant crabs to be cooked in a sidewalk cauldron; they ate the
crabs, still warm, on a picnic in the Napa Valley.[23]

Once again their rooms were filled with flowers, this time
courtesy of Alice's friend Clare de Grucy, the American Wom-
en's Club, and San Francisco's long-reigning literary queen,
Gertrude Atherton. During the twenties, Atherton had spent
time in Paris, where she met Gertrude and Alice at the rue de
Fleurus—she was just glad, she said, that she had been allowed

to sit by Gertrude's side and not relegated to the rear of the room with Alice. Atherton had scheduled an ambitious series of events for the couple, including lunch at her favorite seafood restaurant on Fisherman's Wharf, dinner at her club, and an intimate cocktail party for seventy-five of the city's most prominent citizens. First came dinner at the ultraexclusive Bohemian Club, the smoky refuge of San Francisco writers, journalists, and performers since 1872. Among the club's active or honorary members were Mark Twain, Bret Harte, Ambrose Bierce, Frank Norris, Ina Coolbrith, Oliver Wendell Holmes, Theodore Roosevelt, and even Oscar Wilde, who had visited the club during his 1882 tour and posed for a portrait that still adorned the wall. According to club legend, members had planned to drink Oscar under the table and make sport of him afterward, only to wind up under the table themselves while their guest continued happily drinking and nattering on. "I never saw so many well-dressed, well-fed, business-looking Bohemians in my life," Oscar quipped triumphantly.[24]

Atherton, like Alice a native San Franciscan, was another strong, self-made woman of the sort that Gertrude and Alice gravitated toward and attracted all their lives. A severely beautiful woman in her youth, the seventy-year-old Atherton still looked a good twenty years younger than her age, thanks to a controversial hormone treatment that she later fictionalized in her best seller *Black Oxen*, in which a drab postmenopausal woman is transformed overnight into a fiery femme fatale. Atherton herself was something of a literal femme fatale—her husband, George H. B. Atherton, died at sea and was shipped home in a barrel of rum; her journalist mentor Ambrose Bierce disappeared into the West during the Mexican Revolution; and her globe-trotting friend and adventurer Richard Halliburton would disappear four years hence while attempting to sail a Chinese junk from Hong Kong to San Francisco in time for the 1939 World's Fair. It was dangerous for men to get too close to Gertrude Atherton.[25]

The Bohemian Club hosted a dinner on April 9 for the San Francisco chapter of P.E.N., whose acronym stood for "poets, playwrights, essayists, editors, and novelists," although Atherton as president so dominated the club that many said it should simply have been called the Friends of Atherton. Gertrude was guest of honor at the dinner, but for once homegirl Alice found herself surrounded by a crowd of her own. "Coming back to my native town was exciting and disturbing," Alice wrote. "It was all so different, and still quite like it had been." During her stay, she reunited with old friends Harriet Levy and Sidney Joseph, the brother of Nellie Joseph, but not her own troubled brother Clarence, with whom she had argued over real estate holdings. Gertrude observed, a little dryly, that Alice had seen and been seen by a great many of her old schoolmates, "but then she had been to a private school. I had been to a public one in Oakland and if you have been to a public one you do not seem to have as a good a memory." Radcliffe, of course, was not exactly PS 101.[26]

Two days later, at Gertrude's address to the San Francisco Women's City Club, Alice "went in to the lecture hall alone, seeing an endless number of familiar faces who bowed and waved their hands at me. I settled down as quietly as I could, but found that there were too many people who wanted to speak to me." Her old friend May Coleman, whom she had not seen in almost thirty years, was there. Another unnamed guest offered to drive Gertrude and Alice back to their hotel, telling Alice, "You know we were tremendously fond of your father, your mother was an angel, and you are very dear to us." Alice duly noted "the descending order" of the compliment.[27]

The indefatigable Atherton took them on a rainy ferry ride to

San Rafael to meet her granddaughter, a Dominican nun teaching at the convent school there. Atherton confided, a bit conde-
scendingly, that she had spoken at the school a year earlier and
had been astonished by the students' request that she talk about
Gertrude Stein. The mother superior was equally nonplussed,
telling Gertrude frankly that she could not understand her work.
"What did that matter if the little ones could," asked Gertrude.
"She said but little ones always look as if they understand and I
said yes but if they look it it is as pleasant as if they do it besides
anyway if any one listens to it that is as much understanding as
understanding is." The whole business of understanding, thought
Gertrude, was "awfully worrying to any American." Mechanical devices were the only things every American could properly
understand—"a thing shoves something else." It was all just a
matter of opinion anyway—of which Gertrude had as many as
anyone.[28]

The next day they went to Oakland, where Gertrude spoke
to the English Club at Mills College. The college was near Gertrude's old neighborhood, but unlike Alice, she did not relish
revisiting her roots. "I think I must have had a feeling that I
had lost my roots or I should not have come back," she wrote.

> I went to California. I saw it and felt it and it had a tenderness
> and a horror too. Roots are so small and dry when you have them
> and they are opposed to you. Our roots can be anywhere and we
> can survive, because if you think about it we take our roots with
> us. I always knew that a little and now I know it wholly. I know
> because you can go back to where they are and they can be less
> real to you than they were three thousand, six thousand miles
> away. Don't worry about your roots so long as you worry about
> them. To think of only going back for them is to confess that the
> plant is dying.[29]

Gertrude had lived on the corner of Thirteenth Avenue and Twenty-Fifth Street, and later on Tenth Avenue in East Oakland. The Old Stratton House on Thirteenth Avenue, where she spent most of her childhood, sat on a rise among pepper shrubs, rosebushes, and peach, eucalyptus, and blue gum trees. In *The Making of Americans*, Gertrude had recalled the house with uncharacteristic lyricism reminiscent of Dylan Thomas's golden memories of Fern Hill in Wales:

> It was very wonderful there in the summer with the dry heat, and the sun burning, and the hot earth for sleeping; and then in the winter with the rain, and the north wind blowing that would bend the trees and often break them, and the owls in the wall scaring you with their tumbling. The sun was always shining for them, for years after. Sunday meant sunshine and pleasant lying on the grass with a gentle wind blowing and the grass and flowers smelling, it meant good eating, and pleasant walking, it meant freedom and the joy of mere existing.[30]

Now, revisiting the old neighborhood in the flesh, she saw it through different eyes. "Ah Thirteenth Avenue was the same," she said, "it was shabby and overgrown the houses were certainly some of them those that had been and there were not bigger buildings and they were neglected and lots of grass and bushes growing." The house itself was missing, as were the rosebushes and eucalyptus trees. "What was the use of my having come from Oakland it was not natural to have come from there," she fretted, adding famously, "There is no there there." As with Gertrude's rose, much tortured speculation has been devoted to explaining what she really meant by the third *there*. Defenders of Oakland have insisted that she merely meant her old neighborhood—not the entire city. But the context of the quote in *Everybody's Autobiography* seems fairly straightforward. It is Oakland itself that she is talking about; she mentions it by name. No amount of after-the-fact boosterism, including the postmodern stainless-steel letters defiantly spelling out the word "THERE" at the entrance to the city, can gainsay the conclusive name check in the original quotation. Unlike Alice, Gertrude was no proud daughter of the Golden State. When someone at one of her lectures asked where she had been born, Gertrude responded firmly, "Pittsburgh, Pennsylvania." The man was shocked. "Yes, it should have been California," Alice agreed, "but there was no persuading her to change her place of birth." And Alice knew her better than anyone.[31]

There was a minor controversy when Gertrude went to speak to the Phi Beta Kappa Honor Society at the University of California at Berkeley. School officials would not allow her to speak on campus at the then-conservative college, so they moved the venue to the nearby International House. After lunch, Gertrude took questions from the audience. "There were a lot of questions," she recalled. "They thought I answered them very well the only thing I remember is their asking why I do not write as a I talk and I said to them if they had invited Keats for lunch and they asked him an ordinary question would they expect him to answer with the Ode to the Nightingale." It was only natural that people thought she had answered well, Gertrude said, "because after all if I do not talk too much or too long...if I do talk too much or too long then it gets to be arguing and that is not interesting, because after all what is said is not meant and what is meant is not said." It was a novel philosophy for a college lecturer to hold—visiting or not.[32]

Gertrude wrapped up her California appearances with two lectures at Stanford University, which had been built with money from Central Pacific Railroad magnate Leland Stanford. She and Alice went to lunch with the son of one of Stanford's fellow "Big

Four" monopolists, William H. Crocker, whose father Charles had joined Stanford, Mark Hopkins, and Collis P. Huntington in cornering the West's transcontinental railroad service in the 1880s and 1890s. Crusading journalist Ambrose Bierce had mercilessly attacked the Big Four for years, calling them "Railrogues" and defining their business motto as "everything that is not nailed down is mine, and anything I can pry loose is not nailed down." When Crocker threatened to move to New York to escape Bierce's ceaseless calumny, Bierce expressed the hope that Crocker would devote to the task of leaving "the same energy and activity as two laborious decades of public and private sinning have left him." He wished Crocker Godspeed "from a state whose industries he has impoverished, whose legislation he has sophisticated and perverted, whose courts of justice he has corrupted, of whose servants he has made thieves, and in the debauchery of whose politics he has experienced a coarse delight irrelative to the selfish advantage that was its purpose."[33]

Crocker did leave the state and soon afterward was permanently injured in a carriage accident in New York, dying two years later after turning over his chief financial interests to his eldest son, William. It was at William's sumptuous estate in Hillsborough, seventeen miles north of San Francisco, that Gertrude and Alice lunched on April 16. The primary reason for their visit was to view the 1862 Jean-François Millet painting *The Man with the Hoe*, which Crocker and his art patron wife, Ethel, had recently acquired. It was one of the first paintings Gertrude had seen (in reproduction) while still a girl; her older brother Michael had taken one look at the glum painting of a French peasant bowed down by the weight of hard physical labor and a lifetime of systemic repression and observed, inarguably, "It is a hell of a hoe."[34]

Now, seeing the real thing, Gertrude did not dispute her

brother's opinion, but after lunch she and Alice disagreed over whether there had been a bridge at the famous Cliff House overlooking the Pacific. "I said that there had been a bridge a little weak bridge out to the seal rocks," Gertrude said, "and Alice Toklas said that there never had been. Well anyway." They picnicked in Napa Valley on the crabs they had bought at Fisherman's Wharf and met a man from St. Helena, a resort town at the north end of the valley from where Gertrude and her brother Leo often had hitchhiked to the mineral springs at Etna. "We had intended to walk but everyone gave us a lift from St. Helena to Etna," she said. Ambrose Bierce had lived in St. Helena for a time, and it is amusing, if unlikely, to imagine that he was one of those stopping to give a ride to young Gertrude and Leo Stein. Bierce probably did not pick up hitchhikers.[35]

Gertrude and Alice left San Francisco on April 19 on a night flight to Omaha, before heading on to Chicago and New York. Before they left, Mayor Angelo J. Rossi gave Gertrude a gold-plated wooden key to the city, "all very lovely and very grand," she said. Except for not getting a key of her own, it is safe to say that Alice had enjoyed the return to San Francisco more than Gertrude had. Despite experiencing the 1906 earthquake, Alice had lived a somewhat more sedate and upper-middle-class life than Gertrude, stuck as she was in Oakland. Seeing her old neighborhood had aroused uncomfortable family memories for Gertrude, who described her adolescent years as "medieval," when "nothing is clear and nothing is sure, and nothing is safe and nothing is coming." Years later, hearing Gertrude's account of those trying times, Alice was shocked: "I'd never heard of anything like that. I said, 'How horrible.' She said, 'Didn't you have that period too?' I said, "Not I' and she said, looking at me, 'Lucky you.'"[36]

On the flight to Omaha, Gertrude amused herself by passing

handwritten notes to a young Stanford student in the next seat who asked her about Will Rogers, literature, and the difference between writing and lecturing. And she looked out at the Great Salt Lake, which seemed to her "like going over the bottom of the ocean without any water in it." It was nice to know the difference, she said, "between the ocean with water and the ocean without water in it. After all it is a satisfaction to know that an ocean is interesting even if there is no water in it." All America, she thought, "is just as interesting with no water or too much water or no ocean or no grass there." She sought confirmation from the diminutive dark-haired woman sitting beside her. Harking back to *Blood on the Dining Room Floor*, she asked, "Lizzie, you do know Lizzie what I mean." Alice usually did.[37]

▼ ▼ ▼

AFTER A FINAL DINNER WITH BOBSY GOODSPEED AND THORNton Wilder in Chicago, the couple returned to New York on April 21. Once back in the city, they resumed their life as street-level celebrities. When they first arrived, observed Alice, everyone said, "There goes Gertrude Stein." Now they said, "There goes Miss Stein." Either way, said Gertrude, "it was still a pleasure." Someone asked Alice if Gertrude was annoyed by all the strangers coming up to talk to her. "No," she said, "to her it is exactly like the country neighbors at Bilignin." They shared meals with the Van Vechtens at the Algonquin and sat for a private "listening" of the recordings she had made at ERPI Studios for the National Council of Teachers of English. A last scheduled lecture to the American Arbitration Association at the French Institute of New York was canceled because the sponsors wanted to charge admission. It was a disappointment to all involved, since Virgil Thomson was to have conducted members of the original cast in selections from *Four Saints in Three Acts* after Gertrude's talk. A rule is a rule is a rule.[38]

On April 30, Bennett Cerf gave a farewell dinner party for Gertrude and Alice that lasted until 4 a.m. Among those attending were Carl Van Vechten, actress Miriam Hopkins, author Edna Ferber, and composer George Gershwin, who serenaded them with selections from *Porgy and Bess*. As a parting gift, Cerf reaffirmed his promise to publish one of Gertrude's books each year. The *New York Herald Tribune* finished publishing the last of six essays it had commissioned from Gertrude on topics ranging from American state capitals to newspapers, higher education, food, houses, and—a subject dear to Gertrude's heart—"American Crimes and How They Matter." There were two kinds of crimes that captured the imagination, Gertrude wrote, "the crime hero and the crime mystery, all the other crimes everybody forgets as soon as they find out who did them." John Dillinger, who had been gunned down by FBI agents in Chicago three months before she and Alice arrived in America, seemed to her the prototypical American hero, since he was the sort of all-American native son whose father could "say that he is a good boy that he has always been a good boy. If they could not say that of him he would not have been on the front page of the newspaper." The price of that fame was an FBI bullet to the back of the head, but the publicity-loving Dillinger might well have taken the trade-off.[39]

Journalist Joseph Alsop stopped by the Algonquin for a final interview a few days before they were scheduled to depart. The suite was filled with souvenirs from places they had visited, including a shell necklace, a pair of carnelian earrings, paintings of New England snow scenes, and even a "pink sugar woman donated by Carl Van Vechten." Alsop found Gertrude as bouncy as ever. "Her cheerful sanguine-complexioned face was ruddier, her sharp eye was brighter," he wrote. She looked "even healthier than ever." The trip had delighted her, Gertrude said, more than Christopher Columbus's had delighted him—not a stretch, since Columbus had lost his flagship, the *Santa Maria*, several Spanish sailors, and a dozen or so Indian hostages on his first visit to the New World, while failing utterly to discover an opening to the Orient. Gertrude had been more successful. "We've seen everything," she told Alsop. "We've seen it from the air, and we've seen it from the ground and in all kinds of ways, and in every way we've found it completely fascinating." She and Alice were hoping to return to America as soon as possible.[40]

Before she left, Gertrude sat down with Canadian reporter John Hyde Preston for one last interview for *Atlantic Monthly*. Preston thought of himself as a professional skeptic, but even he was won over by Gertrude's directness and honesty. Having confessed at the start that he could only guess what she meant in her writing, Preston observed that Gertrude "seems peacefully resigned to the attacks that have been made upon her all her life and she has that air, so rare in writers, of living outside of both fame and criticism." The interview began in their suite at the Algonquin while Alice was packing their steamer trunks to leave and concluded with a stroll down Madison Avenue through the noontime traffic.[41]

Gertrude began by defending herself against the charge that what she did was simply automatic writing. "Creation must take place between the pen and the paper, not before in a thought or afterwards in a recasting," she explained. "It will come if it is there and if you will let it come, and if you have anything you will get a sudden creative recognition. You won't know how it was, even what it is, but it will be a creation if it came out of the pen and out of you and not out of an architectural drawing of the thing you are doing." Still, it was not automatic. "You have a little more control over your writing, than that," she said. "You have to know what you want to get; but when you know that, let it take you and if it seems to take you off the track don't hold back, because that is perhaps where instinctively you want to be and if you hold back and try to be always where you have been before, you will go dry." She seldom went dry.[42]

Gertrude gave a quick, precise rundown of other American writers. Most of them, she said, "look gigantic at first. Then they get to be thirty-five or forty and the juices dry up and there they are. Something goes out of them and they begin to repeat according to formula. They become writers. They cease being creative men and soon they find that they are novelists or critics or poets or biographers, and they are encouraged to be one of those things because they have been very good in performance or two or three, but that is silly. When a man says, 'I am a novelist,' he is simply a literary shoemaker." Robert Frost was a good poet, she said, because he thought of himself as a farmer first—a fiction that Frost successfully managed to perpetrate on many more people than just Gertrude Stein. Sherwood Anderson had "achieved that perfect freshness of creation and passion, as simply as rain falling on a page, and rain that fell from him and was there miraculously and was all his." Hemingway, by comparison, was not really good after 1925. "Hemingway did not lose it," she said. "He threw it away. When I first met Hemingway he had a truly sensitive capacity for emotion, and that was the stuff of the first stories; but he was shy of himself and he began to develop, as a shield, a big Kansas City–boy brutality about him, and so he was 'tough' because he was really sensitive and ashamed that he was." William Faulkner and Erskine Caldwell were "good craftsmen and honest men," but they didn't have passion. There was no one else worth mentioning.[43]

The Preston interview was Gertrude's most direct and un-guarded assessment of her fellow American writers. Perhaps the fact that she had one foot out the door, so to speak, embold-ened her to speak frankly, although she generally did not need an excuse to say what was on her mind. Perhaps she was just tired. Whatever the case, by the time the other writers read her opinions of them, if they ever did, she would be safely out of the country. "Oh dear oh dear we do not want to go we love it so," said Gertrude. But go they did, on May 4, 1935, having spent just shy of seven months in their native country, visiting thirty-seven cities in twenty-three states, appearing before thousands of their fellow citizens, and making memories they would cherish for the rest of their lives. Never again would the name Gertrude Stein be known only to the intellectual few. Now every man and woman on the street, from New York City to Del Monte, California, knew who she was. Gertrude Stein, it was safe to say, had well and truly arrived.[44]

I Am Already Homesick for America

GERTRUDE AND ALICE ARRIVED BACK IN PARIS ON MAY 12 after an uneventful seven-day return voyage aboard the SS *Champlain*. Their adopted hometown seemed somehow smaller and shabbier than before. Gertrude explained her new perspective in an interview with the Associated Press. "Coming back to anything is always a bother," she said, "you have to get used to seeing it as it looks all over again until it looks as it did which it does at last." At any rate, she no longer considered herself a Parisian. "I am married to America," she declared, "it is so beautiful. I am already homesick for America. I never knew it was so beautiful. I was like a bachelor who goes along fine for twenty-five years and then decides to get married. That is the way I feel—I mean about America."[1]

Alice, as usual, kept her feelings to herself, but she would later describe the American trip as "an experience and adventure which nothing that might follow would ever equal." They were hoping to return in the near future, she told her old friend Harriet Levy. She was sorry she had insisted on the return of an umbrella she left behind in a San Francisco restaurant—it would have given them a reason, however nonurgent, to go back. The rediscovery of their American roots had been an unexpected bonus to Gertrude and Alice. It was a function both of the warm, unquestioning reception they had received during the tour and of their own willingness to open themselves up to new people and experiences along the way. Like a thrown-together party that comes off better than anyone has a reason to expect, the welcome they had received from Americans great and small had surprised and touched them both. They never forgot it.[2]

Content to be back at Bilignin, Alice planted her yearly crop of vegetables, though not without peril. One day, climbing atop a box to reach her string beans, the box collapsed and she fell heavily, pulling the string beans down on top of her. Gertrude made a rare horticultural suggestion. "Fewer vegetables," she said, "would leave us still with enough variety." Alice, shaken by the fall, conceded the point, although she continued pursuing her longtime ambition of matching their neighbor Baroness Pierlot's feat of growing fifty-seven varieties of plants "like the Heinz pickles." She finally gave up after realizing that "the more I grew, the more I cooked, so that by the end of the day I wasn't fit for much else." Gertrude didn't care about the baroness or her record, one way or the other.[3]

Armed with Bennett Cerf's promise to publish whatever she wrote, Gertrude began a new book on her favorite topic—human identity. "I am I because my little dog knows me," she was fond of saying, and in *The Geographical History of America*—an almost sublimely misleading title—she set out to prove "what the human mind is." As she explained it, "There is no knowing what the human mind is because as it is it is...you could only remember yourself you could not feel yourself and I therefore began to think that insofar as you were yourself to yourself there was no feeling of time inside you you only had the sense of time when you remembered yourself." Gertrude undercut her philosophical meditations with a number of puzzling injunctions: "Please remember the cuckoo," "Become because," "Beware of be," "Detective story number 1." Old friend Thornton Wilder, stopping at Bilignin en route to a session with Sigmund Freud in Vienna, read the book in manuscript. "Don't be mad at me if I say again there are stretches I don't understand," he told Gertrude. "This time it doesn't seem important I don't understand, because there's so much I do understand and love and laugh at and feed on." Bennett Cerf was less amused, ordering up a minimal number of one thousand copies of the book, bound in black, almost as though in mourning for Gertrude's lost lucidity.[4]

Her next book, *Everybody's Autobiography*, was a conscious attempt to duplicate the popular style and success of the first autobiography. Encouraged, Random House tripled the print run and switched to a jauntier tan cover, with several Carl Van Vechten photographs included in the body of the text. But Gertrude's relaxed, easygoing account of her American adventures did not strike the same strong chord with either the public or the critics. Sales were slow, and the *New York Times* rendered a stern verdict: "Easy to read and easy to forget, it is now obvious that Miss Stein's chief asset in writing is her colossal egotism and her chief inability to create character. Her mind is acute and lively, as intelligent a recording instrument as one could wish for, but it is extraordinarily limited and almost purely parasitical." The book's reception was notably cooler than the critical and popular acclaim *The Autobiography of Alice B. Toklas* had enjoyed three years earlier, and this time there was no lecture tour to support it. By then the world was moving on to more serious matters.[5]

▼ ▼ ▼

IN EUROPE ONCE AGAIN THERE WERE PORTENTS OF WAR. THAT summer twenty-five hundred French Army reservists began training at Bilignin, including twenty-five who took up residence in Gertrude's barn. Basket and Pepe, as might be expected, were beside themselves, but Gertrude was philosophical about the intrusion. "After all they were drunk a good deal," she recalled. "They cannot discipline reservists they can only keep them walking and however much they walk they must stop sometimes and naturally if they stop they must occupy the time and the only way to occupy the time is by drinking that is natural enough." One of the soldiers had brought along an accordion, which entertained Gertrude, if not the dogs.[6]

Never a deep thinker about political issues, Gertrude was blithely untroubled by the ominous undercurrents. She did not foresee another war breaking out in Europe. "Europe is like a dog and a child playing together and when they see somebody looking it spoils their game because when they see anybody looking, they cannot get the same solemnity and intensity," she reasoned rather reductively. "I mean it is more difficult to have a convincing war or be convinced the West world is its audience. In the old days, Europe was its own audience but now farthest North and South America are the audience. Europe cannot talk about the balance of power because European decisions are no longer world decisions." The German Army, currently on the march through Austria and the Sudetenland, might have begged to disagree.[7]

For Gertrude there was one last public triumph before war descended again on the continent. In the spring of 1937 she and Alice went to London for the premiere of a new ballet, *A Wedding Bouquet*, which reunited Gertrude, as librettist, with choreographer Frederick Ashton from *Four Saints in Three Acts*. The ballet, performed by the Sadler's Wells Company with a young Margot Fonteyn as one of the leads, had been adapted for the stage by noted British eccentric Lord Gerald H. T. W. Berners, who ranged freely through Gertrude's 1931 play, *They Must Be Wedded to Their Wife*, for source material. Gertrude and Alice had first met the madcap lord through mutual friends the year before and stayed at his enormous Berkshire estate, Faringdon, said to be the only stately home in England with adequate heating. Berners had risen to prominence as a boy when, having heard that one could teach a dog to swim by throwing it into the water, he attempted to teach his mother's dog to fly by throwing it out an upstairs window. (The dog survived.) Upon becoming lord of the manor, he dyed the estate's pigeons pink, purple, and blue; drove around the grounds in a ghost-white pig's-head mask to frighten the locals; bedecked his dogs with faux diamond necklaces; planted paper flowers in his garden; drew false mustaches on ancient family portraits; jogged through other people's dining rooms to "aid his digestion"; and once had Poet Laureate John Betjeman's horse in to tea.[8]

Besides composing music, including the score for the 1947 movie version of *Nicholas Nickelby*, and painting endless portraits of men, women, and horses, Berners also wrote novels. Among them were *The Camel*, in which a vicar's wife falls in love with the title character; *Count Omega*, in which a penniless composer pursues a slumming blonde trombonist guarded by a eunuch; *The Romance of a Nose*, in which Cleopatra has her famous profile bobbed in an unsuccessful attempt to look like Helen of Troy; and *The Girls of Radcliffe Hall*, a broad-gauged spoof that name-checked the well-known lesbian novelist while depicting Berners and his male friends as cross-dressing students at an all-girls school. His self-penned epitaph concluded, no doubt accurately, "Praise the Lord! / He seldom was bored."[9]

After the premiere, Gertrude joined Berners, Ashton, and the cast on stage for a curtain call. "We went out and on to the stage," Gertrude reported, "and there where I never had been with everything in front all dark and we bowing and all of them coming and going and bowing, and then again not bowing but coming again and then as if it was everything, it was all over and we went back to sit down." At the opening-night party she was treated like an A-list celebrity. "We met everyone and I always do like to be a lion," she confessed. "I like it again and again, and it is a peaceful thing to be one succeeding." London was still reeling from the abdication of King Edward VIII for "the woman I love," American divorcee Wallis Warfield Spencer Simpson. Gertrude had lived across the street from the infant Simpson forty years earlier on East Biddle Street in Baltimore, proving yet again that she seemed to know every famous person in the world. Her novel *Ida*, loosely based on Mrs. Simpson's alleged romantic escapades in the United States, concluded with the heroine "resting but not resting enough." (The English people might have thought the same thing.) Gertrude sent a complimentary copy to her former neighbor, who graciously thanked her for the book and expressed the modest hope that one day she might be able to understand it.[10]

As always, Gertrude and Alice entertained steadily at Bilignin. Bennett Cerf came over, as did Pablo Picasso, Thornton Wilder, Jo Davidson, Francis Rose, Lord Berners, William Rogers, and his wife, Mildred. *Time* and *Life* publisher Henry Luce and his wife, Clare, also came to call following a tour of jittery European capitals. Mrs. Luce, an experienced journalist herself, worried that war would soon come again to the continent, since Europeans had "too many guns, and now nobody can think what to do with them but shoot them off." Gertrude remained unworried. Hitler, she said, "will never really go to war. He is not the dangerous one. He wants the illusion of victory and power, the glory and glamour of it, but he could not stand the blood and fighting involved in getting it." As a measure of precaution, however, she had Alice retype all her unpublished manuscripts and send them to America for safekeeping. Against the advice of her brother Michael, who already had returned to America, Gertrude left her collected paintings at her new apartment at 5 rue Christine, where she and Alice had moved after their landlord unceremoniously threw them out of 27 rue de Fleurus in January 1938 to make room for his soon-to-be-married son.[11]

Gertrude and Alice took the loss of their legendary apartment with surprising equanimity. The new apartment was on a short, narrow street between the rue Dauphine and the rue des Grands Augustins. The view was disappointing, but the apartment itself was bright and open, with wainscoted walls and wooden parquet floors. Alice, ever practical, had the floors carpeted to cut down on noise and provide more insulation in the cold winter months. Far more painful than the loss of their old apartment was the death of Basket, their much-loved, much-publicized poodle, who passed away unexpectedly at the age of ten. "It did us all up," Gertrude wrote to Rogers, "and we are just now able to smile and tell you about it." Picasso offered them his Afghan hound as a replacement, but they opted to follow the advice of other friends and get another poodle immediately. They found him at a dog show in Bordeaux and brought him back to Paris with them. Basket II, as he was inevitably named, moved effortlessly into his new role, his only notable flaws being a propensity to eat Alice's handkerchiefs, chew the buttons off Gertrude's slippers, and drag his greasy dog bones into bed with them at night. Like all good dogs, which is to say all dogs, he would stand by them loyally in the dark days to come.[12]

▼ ▼ ▼

GERTRUDE AND ALICE WERE STILL AT BILIGNIN WHEN THE Germans invaded Poland on September 1, 1939. They viewed the event less gloomily—and less presciently—than English poet W. H. Auden, who famously sat in a bar on 52nd Street in New York City, "Uncertain and afraid / As the clever hopes expire / Of a low dishonest decade." They took a more parochial view. Their most recent houseguest, fashion photographer Cecil Beaton, had thrown everyone into a panic by managing to get lost while going for a walk in the drenching rain. When a neighbor stopped by to ask if Gertrude had heard the news that war had broken out, she shrugged it off. "War?" she said. "Who cares about war? We've lost Cecil Beaton!" They found him two hours later, trudging unharmed down the hillside in the dark. Meanwhile, back in New York, Wystan Auden got good and drunk.[13]

Despite Gertrude's airy indifference and the well-considered warnings of various observers, including the American consul at Lyon, that they leave France at once, the couple stayed on. "Here we are and here we stay," Gertrude announced. When Gabriel Putz, the French captain who had leased them the farmhouse at Bilignin, retired from duty and wanted his old property back, they moved to Culoz, a railroad town ten miles northeast of Belley in the shadow of the French Alps. It proved to be a fortuitous move, since the mayor of Culoz, Justin Rey, at some risk to himself, intentionally left their names off the required list of resident aliens. Townspeople, too, kept their secret, even though many locals, suspected of cooperating with the French resistance, were shot by German occupiers during the war.[14]

Remarkably, despite being well-known Jewish American lesbian intellectuals—ordinarily a whole series of red flags to murderous Nazi bureaucrats—she and Alice managed to remain in France and survive, thanks in part to their old friend Bernard Faÿ. As a high-ranking member of the collaborationist Vichy government, Faÿ claimed after the war to have secured a promise from acting prime minister Philippe Petain to protect Gertrude and Alice from harm. The women's ability to survive, at a time and place where so many of their fellow Jews did not, has remained a controversial subject for modern biographers. Charges and countercharges have swirled around the issue of their supposed collaboration with the Nazis, based on mistaken readings—or willful misreadings—of the facts. Gertrude's puckish 1934 suggestion that Adolf Hitler be given the Nobel Peace Prize (for bringing peace to Germany by driving out all Jews, democrats, and leftist activists who might actually have protested his rule) has been offered as proof of her protofascist leanings. And her translation of a few of Petain's speeches in late 1941 and early 1942, at a time when the United States was not yet at war with Vichy France, has also come in for attack by critics who fail to note either the ongoing diplomatic relationship between the two countries or Gertrude's long-standing gratitude for the savior of France during World War I. Besides, she was doing it as a favor for Bernard Faÿ.[15]

Stein's defenders have argued more persuasively that Gertrude and Alice's survival during the war depended less on their supposed collaboration with the Nazis than on the goodwill, courage, and kindness of their French neighbors, among whom they had been living congenially for the better part of two decades. The two women did not enjoy pampered, protected lives during the occupation, as some of their more extreme critics have charged, but had to sell their last remaining painting (a Cezanne) to pay for food and sometimes had to walk for miles to obtain one egg or cup of flour. A special treat was a bag of two hundred crawfish that a sympathetic butcher smuggled in to them. Their food situation, said Alice, "was a protracted, indeed, a perpetual, Lent." The fact that French Resistance fighters offered to help them escape to Switzerland—not an offer they would have made to despised collaborators—is proof in itself that the people most familiar with the couple's actions on the ground had no complaint against them, either then or later. Short of actively working with the Nazis, betraying their neighbors, or making (as did Ezra Pound) treasonous radio broadcasts to America, Gertrude and

Alice would seem to have done nothing wrong. They had simply kept their heads down and done their best to survive from one day to the next—the fundamental goal of anyone trapped under the jackboot and the swastika.[16]

Still, it was a narrow escape. During the occupation, Gertrude and Alice managed to survive two separate Nazi visitations. The first involved a couple of German officers and their orderlies, who requisitioned the kitchen at Culoz for their private use but otherwise ignored the two frumpy women who were careful to speak French in their presence. The intruders left after two weeks. The second intrusion was much more dangerous. A squad of one hundred German soldiers in full retreat from the Allied landings on D-Day took over the house. They butchered one of Alice's cows on the patio, roasted it on a spit, and tromped through the premises for a long day and night, ransacking the house before continuing their retreat. Alice and the servants dragged out mattresses for the intruders to sleep on, while Gertrude and Basket II hid in an upstairs bedroom until they were gone.

A few weeks later, American soldiers liberated the region. "Lead me to them," Gertrude cried when she heard the news. At a hotel in Belley she marched into a room filled with hard-bitten French Resistance fighters, the vaunted Maquis, and called out, "Are there any Americans here?" Three men stood up—Lieutenant Walker E. Oleson and Privates Edward Landry and Walter Hartze of the 120th Engineers. "We held each other's hands and patted each other and we sat down together and I told them who we were and they knew," Gertrude remembered. "I always take it for granted that people will know who I am and at the same time at the last moment I kind of doubt, but they knew of course they knew."[17]

She invited two other GIs, Lt. Col. William O. Perry of the 47th Infantry Division and his driver, Private John Schmaltz, back to her house for a celebratory dinner prepared by Alice. They feasted on trout in aspic, chicken in tarragon, tomato and lettuce salad, chocolate soufflé, wild strawberries, coffee, and white cake filled with frangipani cream and decorated with little French and American flags. A few days later Alice baked a twelve-pound "liberation fruit cake" with an inch-thick frosting of almond paste and hazelnuts and sent it along with her compliments to Lt. Gen. Alexander "Sandy" Patch, commander of the US Seventh Army. Patch was still in mourning for his son, Alexander Patch Jr., a captain in the hard-fighting 79th Infantry Division who had died during the last advance, but he graciously returned his thanks.[18]

CBS Radio correspondent Eric Sevareid, who had met Gertrude and Alice in Paris before the war, tracked them down in Culoz following the liberation. They shared lunch with him, and he shared gossip with them: Thornton Wilder was working for Army Intelligence, Alexander Woollcott had died, Francis Rose had gotten married, and Ernest Hemingway was about to trade in his third wife, Martha Gellhorn, for his fourth, Minnesota-born magazine writer Mary Welsh. "Tsk, tsk, tsk," said Alice. Sevareid arranged for Gertrude to appear on a radio broadcast two days later at American headquarters in Voiron. Calling upon her past experience from the many interviews she had given during her tour of the United States a decade earlier, Gertrude leaned into the microphone and spoke in her clear, cultivated voice to her countrymen back home:

> What a day is today that is what a day it was the day before yesterday, what a day. I can tell everybody that none of you know what this native land business is until you have been cut off from that same native land completely for years. This native land business gets you all right. Day before yesterday was a wonderful day.

Everybody in the village cried out the Americans have come the Americans have come and indeed the Americans have come, they have come, they are here God bless them. And now thanks to the land of my birth and the land of my adoption we are free, long live France, long live America, long live the United Nations and above all long live liberty.[19]

The war gave Gertrude the raw material for her last two books, *Wars I Have Seen* and *Brewsie and Willie*. The first, begun in 1943 when the conflict was still undecided, was a journal of the occupation years in France, leading up to the liberation. As a precaution, Alice did not type out the manuscript, in case it fell into German hands. (She knew they would never be able to decipher Gertrude's handwriting.) The book itself was simultaneously revealing and concealing. Gertrude avoided identifying herself or Alice as Jews—surely the most salient point at a time when the Final Solution was being implemented pitilessly throughout Europe—but she duly reported on the various arrests, deportations, interrogations, denunciations, and random killings occurring all around them. Neighbors' sons and husbands were taken away; two young boys, a female schoolteacher, and an old man were shot down by the Germans; and the French Resistance sent admonitory miniature coffins to suspected collaborators (never Gertrude or Alice). Even the weather turned vicious: a *lune rouge*, or red moon, froze Alice's grapes and ruined her potatoes.

At the end of the book the Americans arrived, and *Wars I Have Seen* became an extended victory march. Gertrude explained the US Army's tactical recipe for success. "There is no use just in going forward or back and using yourself up," she wrote, "it is just the difference between old fashioned dancing and American dancing, in old fashioned dancing you were always sashaying forward and back waltz or polka or anything but in dancing as Americans invited it you stay put you do it all on one spot. Well that is the American idea, don't have your armies running all over the place but stay in one spot, bombard and bombard until all the enemy's material is destroyed and then the war is over." It was not quite that simple, as my own father, a combat infantryman in the same 79th Infantry Division as General Patch's late son, would have been quick to point out.[20]

Published by Random House in the spring of 1945, *Wars I Have Seen* was well received by readers and reviewers. Bennett Cerf reported that the book was doing "perfectly wonderful" and had sold more than ten thousand copies. *Brewsie and Willie*, written immediately after the war, did equally well. In it, Gertrude recorded the conversations, seemingly verbatim, of dozens of American soldiers and nurses she and Alice had met on occupation duty in Paris and the surrounding countryside. It was, in a way, the literary equivalent of cartoonist Bill Mauldin's beloved Willie and Joe, war-weary GIs "more solid, more scared, more articulate" than the doughboys Gertrude had known in World War I, but just as determined and in the end just as victorious.[21]

She concluded the book with an uncharacteristically emotional paean to her fellow countrymen. "G.I.s and G.I.s and G.I.s and they have made me come all over patriotic," Gertrude declared. "I was always patriotic, I was always in my way a Civil War veteran, but in between, there were other things, but now there are no other things. And I am sure that this particular moment in our history is more important than anything since the Civil War." It was up to them all in the aftermath of victory, she said, "to find a new way, you have to find out how you can go ahead without running away with yourselves, you have to learn to produce without exhausting your country's wealth, you have to learn to be individual and not just mass job workers, you have to get courage enough to know what you feel and not just be all yes or no men." Finally, she advised, "Look facts in the face, not just what they all say, the leaders, but every darn one of you so that a government by the people for the people shall not perish from the face of the earth." She knew it would not perish, for one simple reason, something she had learned—or relearned— during her memorable speaking tour of the United States. "We are Americans," she wrote. It was the last sentence of the last paragraph of her last book.[22]

In the end, despite her best intentions, Gertrude never made it back to America. She died in Paris following a failed operation for stomach cancer on July 27, 1946, a little less than two years after the liberation of France. Her final words, like so much else she said or wrote during her eminently quotable life, instantly entered into legend. "What is the answer?" she murmured under anesthesia. Getting no reply, she asked, a bit louder, "In that case, what is the question?" Alice, sitting alone at her bedside, made no response. Gertrude, as always, got the last say.[23]

Introduction

1. Gertrude Stein, *Everybody's Autobiography* (Cambridge: Exact Change, 1993), 9. Hereafter cited as *EA*.

2. Donald Gallup, ed., *The Flowers of Friendship: Letters Written to Gertrude Stein* (New York: Alfred A. Knopf, 1953), 266–67; Howard Mumford Jones and Walter B. Rideout, eds., *The Letters of Sherwood Anderson* (Boston: Little, Brown, 1953), 295.

3. *EA*, 115, 93–94.

4. *EA*, 173; John Malcolm Brinnin, *The Third Rose: Gertrude Stein and Her World* (Boston: Little, Brown, 1959), 308.

5. *EA*, 51; Brinnin, *Third Rose*, 334.

6. *EA*, 298.

7. *EA*, 219; William R. Rogers, *When This You See Remember Me: Gertrude Stein in Person* (New York: Avon Books, 1948), 108; Edward Burns, ed., *The Letters of Gertrude Stein and Carl Van Vechten, 1935–1946*, 2 vols. (New York: Columbia University Press, 1986), 1:374.

8. *New York Herald Tribune*, May 13, 1935.

Chapter One. A Bell within Me Rang

1. Alice B. Toklas, *The Alice B. Toklas Cook Book* (New York: Harper & Row, 1954), 266. Hereafter cited as *CB*.

2. *EA*, 72.

3. Gertrude Stein, *The Autobiography of Alice B. Toklas*, in *Writings 1903–1932* (New York: Library of America, 1998), 910, 913. Hereafter cited as *ABT*.

4. *ABT*, 850.

5. *ABT*, 913.

6. *ABT*, 730, 736.

7. Brinnin, *Third Rose*, 23–24.

8. Brenda Wineapple, *Sister Brother: Gertrude and Leo Stein* (New York: G. P. Putnam's Sons, 1996), 113, 124.

9. *EA*, 272; Wineapple, *Sister Brother*, 124.

10. Wineapple, *Sister Brother*, 146.

11. Gertrude Stein, *Q.E.D.*, in *Writings 1903–1932*, 4; Wineapple, *Sister Brother*, 143; *ABT*, 743.

12. *ABT*, 660; Alice B. Toklas, *What Is Remembered* (San Francisco: North Point, 1985). Hereafter cited as *WIR*.

13. Linda Simon, *The Biography of Alice B. Toklas* (New York: Doubleday, 1977), 31.

14. *WIR*, 23; *ABT*, 660–61.

15. *ABT*, 685–93; Leo Stein, *Appreciation: Painting, Poetry and Prose* (New York: Crown, 1947), 158.

16. *ABT*, 705, 700.

17. *ABT*, 714; Fernande Olivier, *Picasso and His Friends* (New York: Appleton-Century, 1965).

18. *WIR*, 23–24; Simon, *Biography*, 53.

19. Gertrude Stein, *Picasso*, in *Writings 1932–1946* (New York: Library of America, 1998), 502; James R. Mellow, *Charmed Circle: Gertrude Stein and Company* (New York: Praeger, 1974), 93.

20. *ABT*, 666–68.

21. *ABT*, 665–69.

22. *ABT*, 669–72.

23. *ABT*, 748.

24. Leo Stein, *Appreciation*, 187.

25. Mabel Dodge Luhan, *Intimate Experiences*, 4 vols. (New York: Harcourt, Brace, 1936), 2:327.

26. *WIR*, 54.

27. Edmund Fuller, ed., *Journey into the Self: Being the Letters, Papers and Journals of Leo Stein* (New York: Crown, 1950), 48–51.

28. *EA*, 70–79.

29. *ABT*, 790; Luhan, *Intimate Experiences*, 2:324, 326.

30. Luhan, *Intimate Experiences*, 2:332–33.

31. Gallup, *Flowers*, 71; Mabel Dodge, "Speculations, or Post-Impressionism in Prose," *Arts and Decoration*, March 1913, 172–74; Mellow, *Charmed Circle*, 173.

32. Gallup, *Flowers*, 96.

33. Gertrude Stein, *Tender Buttons*, in *Writings 1903–1932*, 322–23, 326; H. L. Mencken, "A Review of Reviewers," *Smart Set*, Oct. 1914, 159.

34. *ABT*, 802, 806.

35. *ABT*, 808.

36. *ABT*, 816.

37. *ABT*, 823.

38. *ABT*, 826.

39. *ABT*, 829.

40. *ABT*, 837.

41. Gertrude Stein, "The Work," quoted in Brinnin, *Third Rose*, 222; *ABT*, 842; Renate Stendahl, *Gertrude Stein in Words and Pictures* (Chapel Hill: Algonquin Books, 1994), 103; Rogers, *When This You See*, 13.

42. *ABT*, 848.

43. *WIR*, 104.

44. Janet Hobhouse, *Everybody Who Was Anybody: A Biography of Gertrude Stein* (New York: G. P. Putnam's Sons, 1975), 116; Mellow, *Charmed Circle*, 247.

Chapter Two. Many Saints Seen

1. Gertrude Stein, *Lectures in America*, in *Writings 1932–1946*, 24.

2. Sylvia Beach, *Shakespeare and Company* (New York: Harcourt, Brace, 1959), 12–13.

3. *ABT*, 852.

4. Sherwood Anderson, *A Story Teller's Story* (New York: B. W. Heubsch, 1924), 362.

5. Gallup, *Flowers*, 138; *ABT*, 853.

6. Sherwood Anderson, "Four American Impressions," in *Sherwood Anderson's Notebooks* (New York: Boni & Liveright, 1926), 48–49.

7. Gallup, *Flowers*, 143; *ABT*, 869.

8. *ABT*, 748.

9. Alice Hunt Sokolov, *Hadley: The First Mrs. Hemingway* (New York: Dodd, Mead, 1973), 50; Ernest Hemingway, *A Moveable Feast* (New York: Bantam Books, 1965), 14.

10. *ABT*, 869; Hemingway, *Moveable Feast*, 15.

11. *ABT*, 870; Charles Fenton, *The Apprenticeship of Ernest Hemingway* (New York: Farrar, Straus & Cudahy, 1954), 262.

12. Simon, *Biography*, 118.

13. Gertrude Stein, "The Gradual Making of *The Making of Americans*," in *Writings 1932–1946*, 275; *ABT*, 872.

14. Ezra Pound, "A Few Don't's by an Imagiste," *Poetry* 1, no. 6 (March 1913): 200.

15. *ABT*, 856, 858; Ernest Hemingway to Sherwood Anderson,

March 9, 1922, in *Ernest Hemingway: Selected Letters 1917–1961*, ed. Carlos Baker (New York: Scribner Classics, 1981), 62.

16. *ABT*, 856–57.

17. *ABT*, 857.

18. William Carlos Williams, *The Autobiography of William Carlos Williams* (New York: Random House, 1951), 254; Mellow, *Charmed Circle*, 292.

19. *ABT*, 856, 875.

20. Hemingway, *Moveable Feast*, 28.

21. *WIR*, 117; Hemingway, *Moveable Feast*, 145.

22. Andrew Turnbull, ed., *The Letters of F. Scott Fitzgerald* (New York: Charles Scribner's Sons, 1963), 167; Carlos Baker, *Ernest Hemingway: A Life Story* (New York: Charles Scribner's Sons, 1969), 206; Ernest Hemingway, *The Torrents of Spring* (New York: Charles Scribner's Sons, 1972), 71–74.

23. *ABT*, 872.

24. *ABT*, 872–73; Ernest Hemingway, "The Farm," *Cahiers d'Art* 9 (1934): 28–29; "Steiniana," *New Yorker*, March 11, 1974, 11.

25. *CB*, 92.

26. *EA*, 53.

27. *CB*, 93.

28. Diana Souhami, *Gertrude and Alice* (London: Pandora, 1991), 169; *ABT*, 879.

29. Gertrude Stein, *Lucy Church Amiably* (New York: Something Else, 1969), 197; Donald Sutherland, *Gertrude Stein: A Biography of Her Work* (New Haven, CT: Yale University Press, 1951), 138.

30. *WIR*, 123.

31. *WIR*, 124; *EA*, 70.

32. Souhami, *Gertrude and Alice*, 181, 259; *EA*, 58–59.

33. Paul Bowles, *Without Stopping* (New York: Putnam, 1972), 5; *WIR*, 138; Souhami, *Gertrude and Alice*, 177.

34. Virgil Thomson, *Virgil Thomson* (New York: Alfred A. Knopf, 1966), 89.

35. Thomson, *Virgil Thomson*, 91.

36. Gertrude Stein, *Four Saints in Three Acts*, in *Writings 1903–1932*, 608–52.

37. Thomson, *Virgil Thomson*, 104, 196.

38. *ABT*, 900.

39. Simon, *Biography*, 149.

40. Gallup, *Flowers*, 259, 261.

41. Djuna Barnes, "Book News and Reviews," *New York Tribune*, November 2, 1923.

42. *EA*, 45, 93–94.

43. *EA*, 45, 66, 94; Mellow, *Charmed Circle*, 358.

44. *EA*, 42, 45.

45. Mellow, *Charmed Circle*, 358; *EA*, 51.

46. *EA*, 15.

47. *EA*, 16–19.

Chapter Three. You'd Better Come Over

1. Brinnin, *Third Rose*, 270; Simon, *Biography*, 144–45; Carl Van Vechten, ed., *Selected Writings of Gertrude Stein* (New York: Random House, 1946), 205.

2. Burns, *Letters of Gertrude Stein and Carl Van Vechten*, 1:277.

3. James Agee, "Stein's Way," *Time*, September 11, 1933, 57–60; Hemingway, *Moveable Feast*, 117.

4. Lucy Daniel, *Gertrude Stein* (London: Reaktion Books, 2009), 148; *ABT*, 875.

5. Edmund Wilson, "27 Rue de Fleurus," *New Republic*, October 11, 1933, 246–47; William Troy, "A Note on Gertrude Stein," *Nation*, September 6, 1933, 274–75.

6. Clifton Fadiman, "Books: I Like Being All Alone with English and Myself," *New Yorker*, September 2, 1933, 50–51; Isabel Patterson, "Turns with a Bookworm," *New York Herald Tribune Books*, October 1, 1933, 19; Eugene Jolas, ed., *Testimony against Gertrude Stein* (The Hague: Servire, 1935), 13.

7. Jolas, *Testimony*, 11–12.

8. Jolas, *Testimony*, 2, 11–12.

9. Fuller, *Journey*, 134–35.

10. Thomson, *Virgil Thomson*, 231.

11. *New York World-Telegram*, December 16, 1933.

12. Gallup, *Flowers*, 275; Karen Leick, *Gertrude Stein and the Making of an American Celebrity* (New York: Routledge, 2009), 157–58.

13. Gallup, *Flowers*, 273; Brinnin, *Third Rose*, 322.

14. Souhami, *Gertrude and Alice*, 198–99.

15. Brinnin, *Third Rose*, 326.

16. Gallup, *Flowers*, 276–77; Olin Downes, "Broadway Greets a New Kind of Musical," *New York Times*, February 21, 1934, 22; Brinnin, *Third Rose*, 327–28.

17. Leick, *Gertrude Stein*, 158; *Chicago Tribune*, November 25, 1934.

18. *EA*, 101; Lansing Warren, "Gertrude Stein Views Life and Politics," *New York Times*, May 6, 1934, 9.

19. *CB*, 265, 273.

20. *EA*, 56, 63–64.

21. *CB*, 169–99.

22. *EA*, 67–68.

23. For Willie Seabrook, see Marjorie Worthington, *The Strange World of Willie Seabrook* (New York: Harcourt, Brace & World, 1966).

24. *EA*, 55.

25. *EA*, 85.

26. *EA*, 103–4, 132–33.

27. *EA*, 51; Gallup, *Flowers*, 266–67; Jones and Rideout, *Letters of Sherwood Anderson*, 295.

28. *EA*, 89, 104.

29. *New York Times*, January 3, 1934.

30. *New York Times*, January 3, 1934.

31. Brinnin, *Third Rose*, 330.

32. Rogers, *When This You See*, 90.

33. *EA*, 164, 168; Gallup, *Flowers*, 285.

34. Rogers, *When This You See*, 93; Gertrude Stein, *Four in America* (New Haven, CT: Yale University Press, 1947), 166; Ulla E. Dydo with William Rice, *Gertrude Stein: The Language That Rises, 1923–1934* (Evanston, IL: Northwestern University Press, 2003), 619.

35. Gertrude Stein, "What Is English Literature," in *Writings 1932–1946*, 222–23.

36. *WIR*, 139; *EA*, 169.

37. Gertrude Stein, "Meditations on Being about to Visit My Native Land," in Brinnin, *Third Rose*, 331–32.

38. *CB*, 186; *WIR*, 139.

Chapter Four. Gertrude Stein Has Arrived

1. *WIR*, 142; *EA*, 173; Ernest Dimnet, *The Art of Thinking* (New York: Simon & Schuster, 1929), 169.

2. Simon, *Biography*, 157.

3. *EA*, 175; *WIR*, 143.

4. *WIR*, 143; *EA*, 175.

5. Rogers, *When This You See*, 95; *Nation*, November 7, 1934; *New York Times*, October 25, 1934; Brinnin, *Third Rose*, 335.

6. *New York Herald Tribune*, October 25, 1934.

7. Rogers, *When This You See*, 98; *New York Times*, October 25, 1934.

8. Rogers, *When This You See*, 100; Evelyn Seeley, "Alice Toklas Hides in Shadows of Stein," *New York World-Telegram*, October 25, 1934; *Publisher's Weekly*, August 5, 1933, 340.

9. Arthur Ransome, *Oscar Wilde: A Critical Study* (New York: Mitchell Kennerley, 1912), 64. For Wilde's American tour, see Roy Morris Jr., *Declaring His Genius: Oscar Wilde in North America* (Cambridge, MA: Harvard University Press, 2013).

10. *New York Times*, October 25, 1934.

11. Bennett Cerf, *At Random: Reminiscences* (New York: Random House, 1971), 103.

12. *WIR*, 144.

13. *New York Herald Tribune*, October 25, 1934.

14. Rogers, *When This You See*, 96–97.

15. *WIR*, 144; *EA*, 279–80.

16. *EA*, 177; *CB*, 123–24.

17. *EA*, 174, 182–83.

18. Gertrude Stein, "Pictures," in *Writings 1932–1946*, 224–43.

19. *New York Times*, November 2, 1934; Joseph W. Alsop Jr., "Gertrude Stein Likes to Look at Paintings," *New York Herald Tribune*, November 2, 1934, 1.

20. *WIR*, 145; Simon, *Biography*, 160.

21. *New York American*, November 3, 1934; Stein, "Gradual Making," 270–86.

22. Gertrude Stein, "Poetry and Grammar," in *Writings 1932–1946*, 313–36; *New York Times*, November 19, 1934.

23. Simon, *Biography*, 159–60.

24. Rogers, *When This You See*, 106–7.

25. Leick, *Gertrude Stein*, 176–77.

26. *WIR*, 145.

27. *New York Herald Tribune*, November 25, 1923.

28. *EA*, 203–4.

29. *EA*, 187, 210.

30. *EA*, 189–91; Simon, *Biography*, 146–47; *Bryn Mawr College News*, November 21, 1934.

31. *Poughkeepsie Courier*, November 11, 1934; *WIR*, 150; *CB*, 126.

32. *Boston Sunday Post*, October 21, 1934; Simon, *Biography*, 162–63.

33. *Boston Evening Transcript*, November 20, 1934; Daniel, *Gertrude Stein*, 166; *EA*, 193.

34. *EA*, 193–94.

35. *EA*, 206.

36. *EA*, 5–6.

37. Brinnin, *Third Rose*, 314; Mellow, *Charmed Circle*, 389.

38. *New Yorker*, October 13, 1934, 22–23; *EA*, 89.

39. Simon, *Biography*, 162; Edward M. Burns and Ulla E. Dydo, eds., with William Rice, *The Letters of Gertrude Stein and Thornton Wilder* (New Haven, CT: Yale University Press, 1996), 340.

40. *EA*, 183.

41. *New Yorker*, November 24, 1934, 12–13; *Philadelphia Inquirer*, November 16, 1934, 5.

42. Stephen Meyer, "Gertrude Stein: A Radio Interview," *Paris Review* 116 (Fall 1990): 88.

43. Meyer, "Gertrude Stein," 89, 93, 95, 97; *New York World-Telegram*, October 31, 1934.

44. Rogers, *When This You See*, 101–2.

45. Burns and Dydo, *Letters of Gertrude Stein and Thornton Wilder*, 351.

46. *New York Times*, November 8, 1934; James Thurber, "There's an Owl in My Room," *New Yorker*, November 17, 1934, 19; Daniel, *Gertrude Stein*, 166.

47. *New Yorker*, October 13, 1934, December 1, 1934; George S. Kaufman and Moss Hart, *The Man Who Came to Dinner* (New York: Random House, 1939), 94–95.

48. Gallup, *Flowers*, 292.

49. *New York American*, March 22, 1934.

Chapter Five. Yes Chicago Too

1. *EA*, 196–97; Souhami, *Gertrude and Alice*, 210.

2. Fanny Butcher, *Many Lives, One Love* (New York: Harper & Row, 1972), 418; Andrea Walker, "In Praise of Wanton Women," *New Yorker*, August 12, 2008.

3. *EA*, 200–201; *Chicago Tribune*, November 8, 1934.

4. *Chicago News*, November 8, 1934; June Provines, "Front Views and Profiles," *Chicago Tribune*, November 29, 1934, 2.

5. *New York Evening Post*, March 4, 1935; *New York Herald Tribune*, March 5, 1935; Fanny Butcher, "Paris Aroused over Reply to Gertrude Stein: Six Declare 'Autobiography Is Inaccutrate,' " *Chicago Tribune*, March 9, 1935, 15; Rogers, *When This You See*, 110.

6. Geoffrey Johnson, "Portrait of a Lady," *Chicago Magazine*, October 23, 2008, 3.

7. *EA*, 212–13; Johnson, "Portrait of a Lady," 3; *WIR*, 148.

8. Johnson, "Portrait of a Lady," 4.

9. *WIR*, 149; *EA*, 213–15.

10. *EA*, 214.

11. Sonny Watson, "Dance Marathons: Pageants of Fatigue," www.streetswing.com/histmain/d5marthn.htm; see also Paula Becker, "Dance Marathons of the 1920s and 1930s," www.historylink.org/File/5534.

12. *EA*, 216.

13. *EA*, 194, 207–8.

14. *EA*, 213, 219–20.

15. *EA*, 222; Mellow, *Charmed Circle*, 41.

16. Rogers, *When This You See*, 104; Mellow, *Charmed Circle*, 396.

17. *CB*, 126, 128.

18. *EA*, 229.

19. *EA*, 223–24.

20. *EA*, 229–30.

21. *EA*, 230.

22. Souhami, *Gertrude Stein*, 214; Stendahl, *Gertrude Stein in Words and Pictures*, 141; *EA*, 231.

23. *EA*, 230.

24. *WIR*, 126.

25. Simon, *Biography*, 168; *EA*, 232–33.

26. Rogers, *When This You See*, 112.

27. *EA*, 226–27.

28. *EA*, 234–35.

29. Samuel M. Steward, *Dear Sammy: Letters from Gertrude Stein and Alice B. Toklas* (Boston: Houghton Mifflin, 1977), 129.

30. For Samuel Steward, see Justin Spring, *Secret Historian: The Life and Times of Samuel Steward, Professor, Tattoo Artist, and Sexual Renegade* (New York: Farrar, Straus & Giroux, 2011); Gertrude Stein, *Alphabets and Birthdays* (New Haven, CT: Yale University Press, 1957), 50.

31. *EA*, 188.

32. *EA*, 189.

33. *CB*, 131.

34. Thornton Wilder, *Heaven's My Destination* (New York: Harper & Brothers, 1935), x; Penelope Niven, *Thornton Wilder: A Life* (New York: HarperCollins, 2012), 135; *EA*, 137.

35. Gertrude Stein, *Narration: Four Lectures by Gertrude Stein* (Chicago: University of Chicago Press, 1935), 7, 10.

36. *EA*, 275.

37. Stein, *Four in America*, vi.

38. *London Guardian*, June 29, 1974; Liesl Olson, "An Invincible Force Meets an Immovable Object: Gertrude Stein Comes to Chicago," *Modernism/modernity* 17, no. 2 (2010): 346; Gertrude Stein, *Stanzas in Meditation* (Los Angeles: Sun & Moon, 1994), 217.

39. *EA*, 277–78.

40. *EA*, 278; Gallup, *Flowers*, 322; Bruce Kellner, ed., *A Gertrude Stein Companion* (Westport, CT: Greenwood, 1988), 217.

41. Mellow, *Charmed Circle*, 405; *EA*, 269–70; Burns and Dydo, *Letters of Gertrude Stein and Thornton Wilder*, 24.

Chapter Six. Naturally the Northern Girls Came South

1. Mellow, *Charmed Circle*, 393.

2. *EA*, 236–38.

3. Barbara Pollack, *The Collectors: Dr. Claribel and Miss Etta Cone* (New York: Bobbs-Merrill, 1962), 231.

4. David S. Brown, *Paradise Lost: A Life of F. Scott Fitzgerald* (Cambridge, MA: Harvard University Press, 2017), 227.

5. Simon, *Biography*, 169.

6. Turnbull, *Letters of F. Scott Fitzgerald*, 518.

7. *EA*, 237; Brinnin, *Third Rose*, 314.

8. *WIR*, 150; *EA*, 241–42.

9. *WIR*, 150.

10. *EA*, 244, 247–49; Rogers, *When This You See*, 110.

11. Rogers, *When This You See*, 108–9; *EA*, 246–47; Burns, *Letters of Gertrude Stein and Carl Van Vechten*, 1:374.

12. *EA*, 249; Burns, *Letters of Gertrude Stein and Carl Van Vechten*, 2:728.

13. *EA*, 244.

14. *EA*, 245; William Carlos Williams, "To Elise," in *Spring and All* (Paris: Contact Editions, 1923), 67.

15. Theodore Hall, "Quips and Quiddities, or How Gertrude Stein Has Mark Twain Backed Off the Map," *Washington Post*, November 15, 1934; Rogers, *When This You See*, 116; *EA*, 187.

16. For Katharine Cornell, see Tad Mosel with Gertrude De Macy, *Leading Lady: The World and Theatre of Katharine Cornell* (Boston: Little, Brown, 1978).

17. T. S. Matthews, "Gertrude Stein Comes Home," *New Republic*, December 5, 1934, 100–101; *Daily Oklahoman*, March 26, 1935; *Los Angeles Illustrated Daily News*, March 30, 1935; Gertrude Stein, "How She Bowed to Her Brother," in *Portraits and Prayers* (New York: Random House, 1934), 238–40.

18. *EA*, 252, 255.

19. Shelby Foote, *The Civil War: A Narrative*, 3 vols. (New York: Random House, 1958–74), 3:3.

20. *EA*, 243.

21. Carl Van Vechten, "Some 'Literary Ladies' I Have Known," *Yale University Library Gazette* 26, no. 3 (January 1952): 101.

22. Aleister Crowley, *The Confessions of Aleister Crowley* (London: Routledge, 1979), 78; *WIR*, 150.

23. Rogers, *When This You See*, 103; *EA*, 253–54.

24. *EA*, 255.

25. *EA*, 255–56.

26. *EA*, 256–57.

27. Will Grunewald, "How the Strange Story of Sweet Briar College's Founding Could End Up Saving the School," *Washingtonian*, May 15, 2015, www.washingtonian.com/2015/05/15/how-the-strange -story-of-sweet-briar-colleges-founding-could-end-up-saving-the -school/.

28. *EA*, 258; *Sweet Briar News*, February 14, 1935.

29. *EA*, 258–59.

30. *EA*, 260–61.

31. Mark C. Carnes, ed., *Invisible Giants: Fifty Americans Who Shaped the Nation but Missed the History Books* (New York: Oxford University Press, 2002), 150; *EA*, 261.

32. For Josephine Pinckney, see Barbara Bellows, *A Talent for Living: Josephine Pinckney and the Charleston Literary Tradition* (Baton Rouge: Louisiana State University Press, 2006).

33. *WIR*, 151; *EA*, 262.

34. *EA*, 224–25.

35. *CB*, 130–31.

36. *EA*, 265; Morris, *Declaring His Genius*, 118.

37. *EA*, 264–65; Elizabeth Sprigge, *Gertrude Stein: Her Life and Work* (New York: Harper & Brothers, 1957), 194.

38. *EA*, 266.

39. *EA*, 267–68.

Chapter Seven. No There There

1. Joan Jenkins Perez, "Hockday, Ela," Texas State Historical Association, https://tshaonline.org/handbook/online/articles/fh006.

2. *EA*, 280; *CB*, 131–32.

3. *EA*, 281–82.

4. Walter Cronkite, "Miss Stein Not Out for Show, but Knows What She Knows," *Daily Texan*, March 22, 1935.

5. *CB*, 132.

6. *EA*, 282–84.

7. *EA*, 284.

8. *EA*, 284–85.

9. *EA*, 285–86.

10. *EA*, 286–87.

11. *EA*, 288.

12. Leick, *Gertrude Stein*, 191–92; *Vanity Fair*, January 1935, 25.

13. *EA*, 2; *WIR*, 151–52.

14. *EA*, 3–4.

15. *EA*, 291–92; *WIR*, 152.

16. *EA*, 292; *WIR*, 152; Leick, *Gertrude Stein*, 182.

17. *EA*, 256, 289.

18. *EA*, 294–95.

19. *WIR*, 153; *CB*, 133.

20. *CB*, 133–34.

21. *WIR*, 153; *New York Herald Tribune*, April 7, 1935; *San Francisco Examiner*, April 8, 1935.

22. *EA*, 296.

23. *EA*, 297; *CB*, 134.

24. Morris, *Declaring His Genius*, 139–40.

25. For Gertrude Atherton, see Emily Wortis Leider, *California's Daughter: Gertrude Atherton and Her Times* (Redwood City, CA: Stanford University Press, 1991).

26. *WIR*, 153–54; *EA*, 298.

27. *WIR*, 154.

28. *EA*, 298–99.

29. Linda Simon, *Gertrude Stein Remembered* (Lincoln: University of Nebraska Press, 1994), 157.

30. Gertrude Stein, *The Making of Americans* (New York: Something Else, 1966), 40.

31. *EA*, 298, 300; *WIR*, 155.

32. *EA*, 301–2.

33. Roy Morris Jr., *Ambrose Bierce: Alone in Bad Company* (New York: Crown, 1996), 176.

34. *EA*, 302.

35. *EA*, 302–3.

36. *EA*, 303; Souhami, *Gertrude and Alice*, 32.

37. *EA*, 303–4.

38. *EA*, 304; *WIR*, 155.

39. Gertrude Stein, "American Crimes and How They Matter," *New York Herald Tribune*, March 30, 1935, 13.

40. *New York Herald Tribune*, April 30, 1935.

41. Simon, *Gertrude Stein Remembered*, 154.

42. Simon, *Gertrude Stein Remembered*, 154–55.

43. Simon, *Gertrude Stein Remembered*, 158–61.

44. Souhami, *Gertrude and Alice*, 219.

Epilogue. I Am Already Homesick for America

1. *EA*, 306; Rogers, *When This You See*, 118.

2. *CB*, 135.

3. *WIR*, 157–58.

4. *EA*, 88; Gertrude Stein, *The Geographical History of America*, in *Writings 1932–1946*, 411, 421, 424, 455; Burns and Dydo, *Letters of Gertrude Stein and Thornton Wilder*, 61.

5. *New York Times*, December 5, 1937.

6. *EA*, 308.

7. *New York Herald Tribune*, May 19, 1935.

8. For Berners, see Sofka Zinovieff, *The Mad Boy, Lord Berners, My Grandmother and Me* (London: Jonathan Cape, 2014).

9. Kellner, *Gertrude Stein Companion*, 157–58.

10. *EA*, 327–328; Gertrude Stein, *Ida*, in *Writings 1932–1946*, 704.

11. Brinnin, *Third Rose*, 364–65.

12. Rogers, *When This You See*, 78.

13. W. H. Auden, "September 1, 1939," in *Another Time* (New York: Random House, 1940); Cecil Beaton, *The Wandering Years: Diaries, 1922–1939* (Boston: Little, Brown, 1961), 381.

14. Gertrude Stein, *Wars I Have Seen* (New York: Random House, 1945), 50.

15. For a good overview of the controversy, see Renate Stendahl, "Why the Witch-Hunt against Gertrude Stein?," *Tikkun*, June 4, 2012, www.tikkun.org/nextgen/why-the-witch-hunt-against-gertrude-stein. Related articles are listed in the bibliography.

16. *CB*, 203, 214; Rogers, *When This You See*, 171.

17. Stein, *Wars I Have Seen*, 244–45.

18. *CB*, 219–23.

19. Eric Sevareid, *Not So Wild a Dream* (New York: Alfred A. Knopf, 1946), 457–62.

20. Stein, *Wars I Have Seen*, 93. My father, PFC Roy Morris, survived the war and proudly carried his shoulder patch from the 79th Infantry in his billfold for the rest of his life.

21. Stein, *Brewsie and Willie*, in *Writings 1932–1946*, 68.

22. Stein, *Brewsie and Willie*, 778.

23. *WIR*, 173.

Anderson, Sherwood. *Sherwood Anderson's Notebooks*. New York: Boni & Liveright, 1926.

———. *A Story Teller's Story*. New York: B. W. Heubsch, 1924.

Baker, Carlos. *Ernest Hemingway: A Life Story*. New York: Charles Scribner's Sons, 1969.

———, ed. *Ernest Hemingway: Selected Letters, 1917–1961*. New York: Scribner Classics, 1981.

Beach, Sylvia. *Shakespeare and Company*. New York: Harcourt, Brace, 1959.

Beaton, Cecil. *The Wandering Years: Diaries, 1922–1939*. Boston: Little, Brown, 1961.

Becker, Paula. "Dance Marathons of the 1920s and 1930s." www .historylink.org/File/5534.

Bellows, Barbara L. *A Talent for Living: Josephine Pinckney and the Charleston Literary Tradition*. Baton Rouge: Louisiana State University Press, 2006.

Bergin, Thomas. *The Game: The Harvard-Yale Football Rivalry, 1875–1983*. New Haven, CT: Yale University Press, 1984.

Bowles, Paul. *Without Stopping*. New York: Putnam, 1972.

Bridgman, Richard. *Gertrude Stein in Pieces*. New York: Oxford University Press, 1970.

Brinnin, John Malcolm. *The Third Rose: Gertrude Stein and Her World*. Boston: Little, Brown, 1959.

Brown, David S. *Paradise Lost: A Life of F. Scott Fitzgerald*. Cambridge, MA: Harvard University Press, 2017.

Burns, Edward. "Gertrude Stein: A Complex Itinerary, 1940–1944." https://jacket2.org/article/gertrude-stein-complex-itinerary -1940–1944.

———, ed. *The Letters of Gertrude Stein and Carl Van Vechten, 1935–1946*. 2 vols. New York: Columbia University Press, 1986.

Burns, Edward M., and Ulla E. Dydo, eds., with William Rice. *The*

Letters of Gertrude Stein and Thornton Wilder. New Haven, CT: Yale University Press, 1996.

Butcher, Fanny. *Many Lives, One Love*. New York: Harper & Row, 1972.

Carnes, Mark C., ed. *Invisible Giants: Fifty Americans Who Shaped the Nation but Missed the History Books*. New York: Oxford University Press, 2002.

Cerf, Bennett. *At Random: Reminiscences*. New York: Random House, 1971.

Conrad, Bryce. "Gertrude Stein in the American Marketplace." *Journalism of Modern Literature* 19, no. 2 (Autumn 1995): 215–33.

Cronkite, Walter. "Miss Stein Not Out for Show, but Knows What She Knows." *Daily Texan*, March 22, 1935.

Crowley, Aleister. *The Confessions of Aleister Crowley*. London: Routledge, 1979.

Daniel, Lucy. *Gertrude Stein*. London: Reaktion Books, 2009.

Dimnet, Ernest. *The Art of Thinking*. New York: Simon & Schuster, 1929.

Dodge, Mabel. "Speculations, or Post-impressionism in Prose." *Arts and Decoration*, March 1913, 172–74.

Dydo, Ulla E., with William Rice. *Gertrude Stein: The Language That Rises, 1923–1934*. Evanston, IL: Northwestern University Press, 2003.

Fenton, Charles. *The Apprenticeship of Ernest Hemingway*. New York: Farrar, Straus & Cudahy, 1954.

Foote, Foote. *The Civil War: A Narrative*. 3 vols. New York: Random House, 1958–74.

Fuller, Edmund, ed. *Journey into the Self: Being the Letters, Papers and Journals of Leo Stein*. New York: Crown, 1950.

Gallup, Donald, ed. *The Flowers of Friendship: Letters Written to Gertrude Stein*. New York: Alfred A. Knopf, 1953.

Gambino, Megan. "When Gertrude Stein Toured America." Smithsonian.com, October 13, 2011, www.smithsonianmag.com/arts-culture/when-gertrude-stein-toured-america-105320781/.

Gopnik, Adam. "Understanding Steinese." *New Yorker*, June 24, 2013.

Greenhouse, Emily. "Gertrude Stein and Vichy: The Overlooked History." *New Yorker*, May 4, 2012.

Grunewald, Will. "How the Strange Story of Sweet Briar College's Founding Could End Up Saving the School." *Washingtonian*, May

Bibliography

15, 2015, www.washingtonian.com/2015/05/15/how-the-strange
-story-of-sweet-briar-colleges-founding-could-end-up-saving-the
-school/.

Hemingway, Ernest. "The Farm." *Cahiers d'Art* 9 (1934): 28–29.

———. *A Moveable Feast*. New York: Bantam Books, 1965.

———. *The Torrents of Spring*. New York: Charles Scribner's Sons, 1972.

Hobhouse, Janet. *Everybody Who Was Anybody: A Biography of Gertrude Stein*. New York: G. P. Putnam's Sons, 1975.

Johnson, Geoffrey. "Portrait of a Lady." *Chicago Magazine*, October 23, 2008, 1–5.

Jolas, Eugene, ed. *Testimony against Gertrude Stein*. The Hague: Servire, 1935.

Jones, Howard Mumford, and Walter B. Rideout, eds. *The Letters of Sherwood Anderson*. Boston: Little, Brown, 1953.

Karlin, Mark. "Gertrude Stein's 'Missing' Vichy Years." Truthout, October 2, 2011. https://truthout.org/articles/gertrude-steins-miss ing-vichy-years/.

Kaufman, George S., and Moss Hart. *The Man Who Came to Dinner*. New York: Random House, 1939.

Kellner, Bruce, ed. *A Gertrude Stein Companion*. Westport, CT: Greenwood, 1988.

Leick, Karen. *Gertrude Stein and the Making of an American Celebrity*. New York: Routledge, 2009.

Leider, Emily Wortis. *California's Daughter: Gertrude Atherton and Her Times*. Redwood City, CA: Stanford University Press, 1991.

Linzie, Anna. *The True Story of Alice B. Toklas: A Study of Three Autobiographies*. Iowa City: University of Iowa Press, 2006.

Luhan, Mabel Dodge. *Intimate Experiences*. 4 vols. New York: Harcourt, Brace, 1936.

Malcolm, Janet. *Two Lives: Gertrude and Alice*. New Haven, CT: Yale University Press, 2007.

Mellow, James R. *Charmed Circle: Gertrude Stein and Company*. New York: Praeger, 1974.

———. *Hemingway: A Life without Consequences*. Boston: Houghton Mifflin, 1992.

Meyer, Stephen. "Gertrude Stein: A Radio Interview." *Paris Review* 116 (Fall 1990): 85–97.

Morris, Roy, Jr. *Ambrose Bierce: Alone in Bad Company*. New York: Crown, 1996.

———. *Declaring His Genius: Oscar Wilde in North America*. Cambridge, MA: Harvard University Press, 2013.

Mosel, Tad, with Gertrude De Macy. *Leading Lady: The World and Theatre of Katharine Cornell*. Boston: Little, Brown, 1978.

Neuman, Shirley, and Ira B. Nagel, eds. *Gertrude Stein and the Making of Literature*. Boston: Northeastern University Press, 1988.

Niven, Penelope. *Thornton Wilder: A Life*. New York: HarperCollins, 2012.

Olivier, Fernande. *Picasso and His Friends*. New York: Appleton-Century, 1965.

Olson, Liesl. "An Invincible Force Meets an Immovable Object: Gertrude Stein Comes to Chicago." *Modernism/modernity* 17, no. 2 (2010): 331–61.

Perez, Joan Jenkins. "Hockaday, Ela." Texas State Historical Association. https://tshaonline.org/handbook/online/articles/fho06.

Pollack, Barbara. *The Collectors: Dr. Claribel and Miss Etta Cone*. New York: Bobbs-Merrill, 1962.

Pound, Ezra. "A Few Don'ts by an Imagiste." *Poetry* 1, no. 6 (March 1913): 200–206.

Ransome, Arthur. *Oscar Wilde: A Critical Study*. New York: Mitchell Kennerley, 1912.

Rogers, William R. *When This You See Remember Me: Gertrude Stein in Person*. New York: Avon Books, 1948.

Sevareid, Eric. *Not So Wild a Dream*. New York: Alfred A. Knopf, 1946.

Simon, Linda. *The Biography of Alice B. Toklas*. New York: Doubleday, 1977.

———. *Gertrude Stein Remembered*. Lincoln: University of Nebraska Press, 1994.

Sokolov, Alice Hunt. *Hadley: The First Mrs. Hemingway*. New York: Dodd, Mead, 1973.

Solomon, Jeff. *So Famous and So Gay: The Fabulous Potency of Truman Capote and Gertrude Stein*. Minneapolis: University of Minnesota Press, 2017.

Souhami, Diana. *Gertrude and Alice*. London: Pandora, 1991.

Sprigge, Elizabeth. *Gertrude Stein: Her Life and Work*. New York: Harper & Brothers, 1957.

Spring, Justin. *Secret Historian: The Life and Times of Samuel Steward, Professor, Tattoo Artist, and Sexual Renegade*. New York: Farrar, Straus & Giroux, 2011.

Bibliography

Stein, Gertrude. *Alphabets and Birthdays*. New Haven, CT: Yale University Press, 1957.

——. *Blood on the Dining Room Floor*. With an introduction by John Herbert Gill. Berkeley: Creative Arts Books, 1982.

——. *Everybody's Autobiography*. Cambridge, MA: Exact Change, 1993.

——. *Fernurst, Q.E.D., and Other Early Writings*. New York: Liveright, 1971.

——. *Four in America*. New Haven, CT: Yale University Press, 1947.

——. *Look at Me Now and Here I Am: Selected Works 1911–1945*. London: Peter Owen, 2004.

——. *Lucy Church Amiably*. New York: Something Else, 1969.

——. *The Making of Americans*. New York: Something Else, 1966.

——. *Narration: Four Lectures by Gertrude Stein*. Chicago: University of Chicago Press, 1935.

——. *Portraits and Prayers*. New York: Random House, 1934.

——. "A Stitch in Time." *Ex Libris* 2, no. 6 (March 1925): 177.

——. *Wars I Have Seen*. New York: Random House, 1945.

——. *Writings 1903–1932*. New York: Library of America, 1998.

——. *Writings 1932–1946*. New York: Library of America, 1998.

Stein, Leo. *Appreciation: Painting, Poetry and Prose*. New York: Crown, 1947.

Stendahl, Renate, ed. *Gertrude Stein in Words and Pictures*. Chapel Hill, NC: Algonquin Books, 1994.

——. "Why the Witch-Hunt against Gertrude Stein?" *Tikkun*, June 4, 2012. www.tikkun.org/nextgen/why-the-witch-hunt-against -gertrude-stein.

Steward, Samuel M. *Dear Sammy: Letters from Gertrude Stein and Alice B. Toklas*. Boston: Houghton Mifflin, 1977.

Stewart, Allegra. *Gertrude Stein and the Present*. Cambridge, MA: Harvard University Press, 1967.

Sutherland, Donald. *Gertrude Stein: A Biography of Her Work*. New Haven, CT: Yale University Press, 1951.

Thomson, Virgil. *Virgil Thomson*. New York: Alfred A. Knopf, 1966.

Tillman, Lynne. "Reconsidering the Genius of Gertrude Stein." *New York Times*, January 27, 2012.

Toklas, Alice B. *The Alice B. Toklas Cook Book*. New York: Harper & Row, 1954.

——. *What Is Remembered*. San Francisco: North Point, 1985.

Turnbull, Andrew, ed. *The Letters of F. Scott Fitzgerald*. New York: Charles Scribner's Sons, 1963.

Van Vechten, Carl, ed. *Selected Writings of Gertrude Stein*. New York: Random House, 1946.

———. "Some 'Literary Ladies' I Have Known." *Yale University Library Gazette* 26, no. 3 (January 1952): 97–116.

Walker, Andrea. "In Praise of Wanton Women." *New Yorker*, August 12, 2008.

Watson, Sonny. "Dance Marathons: Pageants of Fatigue." Sonny Waterson's StreetSwing.com. www.streetswing.com/histmain/d5m arthn.htm.

Wilder, Thornton. *Heaven's My Destination*. New York: Harper & Brothers, 1935.

Williams, William Carlos. *The Autobiography of William Carlos Williams*. New York: Random House, 1951.

———. *Spring and All*. Paris: Contact Editions, 1923.

Wilson, Edmund. *Axel's Castle: A Study in the Imaginative Literature of 1870–1930*. New York: Charles Scribner's Sons, 1931.

Wineapple, Brenda. *Sister Brother: Gertrude and Leo Stein*. New York: G. P. Putnam's Sons, 1996.

Winnett, Susan. *Writing Back: American Expatriates' Narratives of Return*. Baltimore: John Hopkins University Press, 2012.

Worthington, Marjorie. *The Strange World of Willie Seabrook*. New York: Harcourt, Brace & World, 1966.

Zinovieff, Sofka. *The Mad Boy, Lord Berners, My Grandmother and Me*. London: Jonathan Cape, 2014.

INDEX

Page numbers in *italics* indicate illustrations.

Index

Dillinger, John, 103, 133, 205
Dimnet, Ernest, 97–98
Dionne quintuplets, 140–41
Dodge, Mabel, 28, 29–32. *See also* Luhan, Mabel Dodge
Douglas, Alfred, 146
Douglas, Mahala Dutton, 138
Downes, Olin, 81
Drake Hotel, Chicago, 129–30
drugstores, GS on, 117
Duchamp, Marcel, 38
Dutch Treat Club, New York City, lecture at, 120

echolalia, 81, 119
Edward VIII, 216
Ehrman, Lillian Mae, 189
Eliot, T. S., 13, 47, 48–49. *See also Making of Americans, The*
Evans, Donald, 32
Evans, Walker, 73
Everybody's Autobiography (Stein), 164–65, 191, 200–201, 213

Fadiman, Clifton, 74–75
Farragut, David S., 151
Faulkner, William, 207
fauvist movement, 22, 23
Faÿ, Bernard, 71, 89, 92, 94, 125, 218, 219
Federal Bureau of Investigation, 103
Ferber, Edna, 205
Fernhurst (Stein), 114
Fields, W. C., 189
"Fifteenth of November, The" (Stein), 49
Fitzgerald, F. Scott, 7, 13, 51–52, 157–59
Fitzgerald, Scottie, 158
Fitzgerald, Zelda, 7, 52, 157–58
Flint, Edith Foster, 150
Fonteyn, Margot, 214
Ford, Ford Madox, 47
Fort Worth, Texas, visit to, 188
Foster, Stephen, 143–44
Four in America (Stein), 82–83, 151
Four Saints in Three Acts (Stein): Ashton and, 214; auction of copy of, 120; cast of, 117; in Chicago, 127, 128–29; at 44th Street Theatre, 70; in Hartford, 77–79, 111; Lundell on, 121–22; in New York City, 80–82; publica-

tion of, 76; reviews of, 105; writing of, 60–62
France: Belley, 55, 57, 220; Culoz, 218, 219–20, 221; German occupation of, 220; liberation of, 220–23; Nimes, 36; Perpignan, 35–36. *See also* Bilignin, France; Paris
Frost, Robert, 207
Fuller, Buckminster, 78

Gable, Clark, 103
Garfield, James A., 102
Garrett, Mary Elizabeth, 16
genius/geniuses: AT on, 44, 56; Dimnet on, 98; GS on, 12, 22, 29, 89–90
Geographical History of America, The (Stein), 212–13
Geography and Plays (Stein), 43
Gershwin, George, 80, 174–75, 205
Gershwin, Ira, 80, 174–75
Gertrude Stein (Sutherland), 114
Gillis, Lester Joseph (Baby Face Nelson), 133
Gilman, Lawrence, 81
Glasgow, Ellen, 168–69, 172
Goddard, Paulette, 189–90
Goodspeed, Charles (Barney), 126, 128
Goodspeed, Elizabeth (Bobsy), 126, 127–28, 129, 130, 131–32, 204
Gouel, Eva, 34
"Gradual Making of *The Making of Americans*, The" (Stein), 91, 109, 113–14, 143–44, 187
Grant, Ulysses S., 82–83, 151, 167, 179–80
Greet, W. Cabell, 166
Gris, Juan, 13, 37

Hale, Dorothy, 79
Halliburton, Richard, 197–98
Hammett, Dashiell, 190–91
Harcourt, Alfred, 81, 112
Harcourt, Brace, 3, 63, 101
Hart, Moss, 125
Hartford, Connecticut: *Four Saints in Three Acts* in, 77–79, 111; lecture in, 164
Hartze, Walter, 220
Haynes, Mabel, 18, 19
Heaven's My Destination (Wilder), 148
Hellman, Lillian, 190
Hemingway, Ernest: Anderson and,